AMERICAN THEATER

grove new

AMERICAN THEATER

EDITED AND WITH AN INTRODUCTION BY

michael feingold

GROVE PRESS · NEW YORK

Published by Grove Press
A division of Grove Press, Inc.
841 Broadway
New York, NY 10003-4793

Published in Canada by General Publishing Company, Ltd.

Library of Congress Cataloging-in-Publication Data

Grove new American theater / edited by Michael Feingold.—1st ed.
    p.   cm.
  ISBN 0-8021-3278-2 (alk. paper)
   1. American drama—20th century. I. Feingold, Michael.
PS634.G76   1991
812'.5409—dc20   91-38276
                                                   CIP

Manufactured in the United States of America

Printed on acid-free paper

Designed by Kathy Kikkert

First Evergreen Edition 1993

10 9 8 7 6 5 4 3 2 1

PERMISSIONS

The Mysteries and What's So Funny? copyright © 1991 by David Gordon. All rights reserved. Reprinted with permission. For inquiries please contact the author care of The Pick Up Co., 104 Franklin Street, New York, NY 10013.

Sincerity Forever copyright © 1990 by Mac Wellman. All rights reserved. Reprinted by permission of author's agent: Wiley Hausam, International Creative Management, 40 West 57th Street, New York, NY 10019.

The American Plan copyright © 1990 by Richard Greenberg.
   CAUTION: Professionals and amateurs are hereby warned that *The American Plan* is subject to a royalty. It is fully protected under the copyright laws of the United States of America, and of all countries covered by the International Copyright Union (including the Dominion of Canada and the rest of the British Commonwealth), and of all countries covered by the Pan-American Copyright Convention and the Universal Copyright Convention, and of all countries with which the United States has reciprocal copyright relations. All rights, including professional, amateur, motion picture, recitation, lecturing, public reading, radio broadcasting, television, video or sound taping, all other forms of mechanical or electronic reproduction, such as information storage and retrieval systems and photocopying, and the rights of translation into foreign languages, are strictly reserved. Particular emphasis is laid upon the question of readings, permission for which must be secured from the author's agent in writing. The stage performance rights in *The American Plan* (other than first class rights) are controlled exclusively by the Dramatists Play Services, Inc., 440 Park Avenue South, New York, NY 10016. No professional or non-professional performance of the play (excluding first class professional performance) may be given without obtaining in advance the written permission of the Dramatists Play Service, Inc., and paying the requisite fee. Inquiries concerning all other rights should be addressed to Helen Merrill, Ltd., 435 West 23rd Street, Suite 1-A, New York, NY 10011. Special note on songs and recordings: For permission of such songs and recordings mentioned in this play as are in copyright, the permission of the

v

CONTENTS

I'm going on the theory that the United States, instead of being the most successful country in the world, is the greatest failure . . . because it was given everything, more than any other country. Through moving as rapidly as it has, it hasn't acquired any real roots. Its main idea is that everlasting game of trying to possess your own soul by the possession of something outside it too . . .

—Eugene O'Neill,
interviewed for
Time magazine
cover story,
October 21, 1946

Every twenty years or so, America remembers it has a theater. There's a surge of interest and youthful talent to the form, like a rush of blood to the head. Then there's a battle royal: The new talents struggle to overthrow the old conventions, and old figureheads, that have made the theater boring; the old ways fight back. The noise of the fracas attracts wide attention. The younger generation, always turned on by a fight, comes in droves. The older generation, horrified by breaches of "taste" and "morality," try to suppress the whole thing. After about ten more years of this to-and-fro, there's a parting of the ways: Some of the newbloods become established popular successes, some shrink into embittered obscurity. A sinister breed of middle-of-the-roaders arrives to take over the wild new institutions, turning them mild and corporatized. The theater starts to get boring again. A few of the aging newbloods survive, on the fringes, keeping up the old battle, trying to stay fresh. Eventually, after about ten more years, some youngsters notice and begin to take risks of their own. America remembers it has a theater, and the whole thing starts all over again.

What this cyclical pattern means, essentially, is that the American theater, as an institution, never grows up, never evolves a native tradition, never accrues the sense of perspective that comes with maturity. And if the theater doesn't grow up, the American public doesn't grow up either. Instead, it gets hotted up, every twenty years or so, over the same issues: sex, politics, and religion—the three matters that art, according to some strangely permanent lunatic fringe of American opinion, must never be allowed to deal with, at least not in any open manner. Art that doesn't deal with such matters, of course, can't be said to offer much to an adult mind. The commitment to staying immature—overgrown babies awash in a comforting sea of consumer goods—seems oddly built into our national character.

Most Americans don't agree with the lunatic fringe that our individual rights should be suppressed on behalf of some totalitarian notion of God (porn video of choice has become one of those comforting consumer essentials), but the idea of dealing with the three touchy subjects publicly, as a community, gets them itchy: The right to masturbate in the home, to your own private degradation fantasy, is one thing; the right to watch Karen Finley use her body as an arena for dramatizing a prevalent pattern of abuse is apparently something quite different. Different, of course, because a Finley performance speaks with an emotional force the porn video doesn't have. Instead of allowing you to wrap yourself in hypnotic fantasy, it de-hypnotizes, making you think of all the disturbing emotions and tragic consequences an abusive act can cause. The power of metaphor to evoke was never more graphically confirmed than in the spectacle of a Senate committee debating, with infinite solemnity and outrage, the validity of Finley's right to cover her body with bean sprouts "symbolizing sperm." Really, one would think, if a woman wants to cover her body with bean sprouts onstage, that's *her* problem; any offense a senator sees in bean sprouts—that harmless and healthful legume—is purely a matter of his imagination.

Imagination, naturally, is just what the anti-arters wish to remove from American life. Imagination is unpleasant and frightening; it puts you in touch with parts of yourself you may be trying to conceal; it shows you how things might be, in dramatic contrast to the way they actually are. The educated heart can look on all this with unfrightened calm; people with something to fear, either in themselves or in their actions, cover their fear with blustering rage. It's no coincidence that the leader of the Cincinnati antismut crusade which culminated in the attempt to ban the Mapplethorpe exhibit was also the biggest criminal in the savings and loan scandal from which our economy is still reeling. Maybe his followers feared that the whip whose handle is shoved up Mapplethorpe's butthole in one of the more controversial photographs was going to be applied to him. Or secretly thought it ought to be. (Advice to local communities: When people attack an artist, ask them what they're hiding.)

For the sophisticated, the public statements of our smuthounds offer an unending source of bitterly ironic amusement. With the aid of a few judicious guidelines from Freud, one might deduce that the Reverend Donald Wildmon, for instance, appears to have a rather intense problem about male homosexuality, while Senator Jesse Helms seems deeply preoccupied with the sexuality of preadolescent girls. (Better advice to local communities: When people attack an artist, read their speeches and figure out for yourself what they're hiding. Then tell *them*.) I don't imply, of course, that what Reverend Wildmon really wanted all along was a date with David Wojnarowicz, or that Senator Helms's favorite novel is *Lolita*. But they both might be happier if those statements were true. The liberating thought that art is a system of expressive choices, in which you pick your preference, has never occurred to them, as it doesn't occur to middle Americans generally, who've been conditioned to view reality as a vast blank monolith of materialistic sameness: If we can eat under the golden arches anywhere from Fiji to Frankfurt, why can't there be only one kind of art, which everybody likes and which doesn't offend anybody?

We have created that one kind of art, of course: It's called television. The technological alternative to reality has shrunk, as movies and radio never did, the number of people the theater reaches; to most Americans, today, a live stage performance is a marginal and exotic phenomenon. But television has failed, significantly, to take over either the theater's scope or its intensity. Even at its best, it's a cold, two-dimensional form. At its corporate mass-produced worst (which is always what it's at in America), it's an addictive, meaningless pablum—an opiate of the people much more dangerous than anything Marx ever anticipated. It's not the content of television that breeds the blankness, but the repeated act of watching it. Good things, mostly from other modes of art, have appeared on television, but there has never been any such thing as good television. Television corrupts; absolute television corrupts absolutely.

The result, as every teacher in America knows, is a generation of passive, uninquiring children who stare at you in class, expecting to have entertainment and knowledge poured into their brains and wishing they could change the channel; "Stepford students" an academic colleague of mine calls them. No doubt, from the point of view of Jesse Helms and his corporate sponsors, these dead-eyed little creatures, brought up to believe that everything in the universe *has* a corporate sponsor, are a consummation devoutly to be wished. If sex is the one thing they aren't passive about (and a good many of them are passive-aggressive about it), politics, which requires activity in order to function, puts them in a deep state of apathy: Most Americas don't vote, have no understanding of any political issue beyond the margin of their tax returns, and are interested in political scandals—of which our politics often seems to consist entirely—only as an excuse to reinforce their condition of denial. With the exception of Jimmy Carter, and, more dubiously, Gerald Ford, every president we've had since Lyndon Johnson should be in jail; the full truth about the Iran-Contra and Iraqgate scandals, if it ever came out (which it won't), would probably justify George Bush and his predecessor being shot for treason. But the number of people who care, and remember, is undoubtedly too few to achieve this admirable goal.

Falling asleep with the TV on is one of the central images of our culture; falling asleep in the theater implies criticism of the performance. That crucial difference underscores what makes the theater, enfeebled, starved, and confused as it is, so important: It's a waking place, where human senses, feelings, and brains come alive. If it isn't that it's nothing. The sleepwalkers who keep our system working still have some residual perceptions left: They notice crime, drugs, graffiti; they notice, in cities and even in some suburbs, crowds of homeless people drifting through the public spaces; they notice (sometimes) the ways their kids choose to tune out, so dramatically different from their own ways. And for every hundred sleepwalkers, there's one or two awakened souls, who've managed to avoid the hypnotic media net in which America wraps itself. When the wide-awake ones go into a theater, as makers or as watchers, there's often noise: a shout of surprise, a shriek of wild laughter, sometimes even applause. The noise wakes up others. And so it begins.

For the artists, the provokers of noise, this is a great opportunity. The present moment is the most propitious time we've had for theater in years, possibly in decades. Today the theater can offend people who run scared through life and want to force the rest of us to run with them. Every time they take offense, more interest is aroused. The theater can dramatize the issues in the air around us, and what a lot of issues there are—including the air around us itself, which is dangerously diminished and poisoned as a result of our corporate procedures. I'm not proposing that the theater ought to lecture Americans on politics; oh, how dreary that would be, and the history of European drama has plenty of episodes to prove it, including the four or five worst plays of Bertolt Brecht (good thing he was a great poet who wrote twenty-five others!). With the opportunity, for American artists, comes the responsibility to be great, to rise to the opportunity in an artistic way.

A nation that will not listen, that willfully destroys itself, is tragic, and a theater artist first of all has to have a sense of that tragedy. Artists who hector their societies on the right way to live are forgotten, the way the world has forgotten Brieux, Richard Steele, the tearful dramas of Voltaire. Artists who confront their society with a vision of itself, however scandalous in the moment, live on, as Euripides and Ibsen live on. I often tell theater students the famous anecdote about Ibsen, at a banquet given in his honor by the King of Sweden: When the monarch averred that *Ghosts* was a nasty play, Ibsen pounded the table and shouted, "Your Majesty, I HAD to write *Ghosts!*" That's a useful guideline for artists: If it's not something you *have* to do, don't do it. Many of the means contemporary playwrights and theatermakers use might startle Ibsen, but he would recognize the tragic necessity behind them just as, when *Ghosts* was first published, the only reviewer in Norway to recognize its tragic stature was a professor of Greek.

To study the theater of Ibsen's time and after is to discover an endless parade of writers who, like him, didn't particularly want to become *causes célèbres,* but were driven to it by a society too busy wallowing in imperial pride and consumer complacency to listen. The scenes that flash by look all too distinctly like more recent American events: Abuse from the press over the London premiere of *Ghosts* ("a loathsome sore, a dirty act done publicly"—Clement Scott, *Times*). Wedekind banned and threatened with jail for writing *Spring's Awakening* and the *Lulu* plays. A riot at the Odéon, in Paris, over the expletive first word of Jarry's *Ubu Roi* ("After us the savage god"—W.B. Yeats). Oskar Panizza slammed into a mental hospital for writing *The Council of Love*. Arnold Daly and his troupe arrested and dragged to a police court in New Haven for producing Shaw's *Mrs. Warren's Profession*. A riot at the Abbey Theater in Dublin, because an actress playing a young girl in Synge's *Playboy of the Western World* is obliged to use the word "shift" in the sense of "a female undergarment." Spontaneous cheering at the Moscow Art Theater when Stanislavsky, as Dr. Stockmann in Ibsen's *Enemy of the People,* speaks a line that the audience takes as alluding to a recent police massacre of protestors; the next night there are armed guards in the house and a state censor onstage to ensure that no newly forbidden words are slipped back into the performance.

The armed guards and the onstage censor aren't with us yet, but the rest is uncomfortably close, including the banning of *Spring's Awakening,* a production of which was shut down at an Idaho theater in 1991, when its board of directors got jumpy over a nude scene. Free speech may be all right for anti-abortionists, screaming abuse at terrified adolescent girls on their way to see a doctor, or training small children to run out into the middle of the street and block traffic, but it's apparently not all right for artists, even if they wrote their plays in Germany a hundred years ago. In its endlessly sticky and hysterical debate over the National Endowment for the Arts, the Senate keeps trying to establish some magic limit to the permissibility of free speech when it's funded by federal tax dollars. But there can't be any such limit: What's the point of accepting the tax dollars if you have to waive your equal rights to do so? It makes the artist a second-class citizen. And it doesn't protect the NEA from complaint: The eight people in every hundred thousand who take offense at Mapplethorpe's photograph of a nude boy on the back of a chair are going to find Dürer's famous engraving of a similar boy in an identical pose equally offensive.

Art exists to expand the imagination; to do that, sooner or later, it has to provoke. And every provocation, by definition, is bound to offend somebody. In addition, art, no matter how transcendent, exists in this world, which means it always carries a sensual component. Puritans, who object to all sensual stimulation, find the work of artists a prolonged assault on their inhibitions. As Tom Lehrer once put it, concisely, in a witty song about censorship and obscenity, "Properly construed / everything is lewd." And so it can be: The eye of the beholder is a magic circle of sorts, summoning up every kind of image and thought, whether the maker of what is beheld intended it to do so or not. Genuine artists go into their work knowing this for a fact, accepting the risk involved, possibly even trembling with excitement over the creative ways in which they will be misunderstood. The one thing they never expect—and always get from the puritan—is to be loathed, despised, treated like outcasts.

In other countries, art has a role and the artist a social position. Not in the U.S. Here art is understood, if at all, only as a commodity—conceptual art was probably created, in part, as an attempt to wriggle out of this particular trap—and artists don't exist until they become something else: celebrities. After which, they can do anything they please, with the understanding that any art they create is irrelevant to their status. Thanks to Andy Warhol, we know that celebrities can exist, like the lilies of the field, without actually doing anything at all; in fact they're not people but creations, produced by the collaborative art of many unseen hands. The license extended them goes far beyond what any artist can reasonably expect: Nancy Reagan, the most uptight First Lady of the century, was willing to be photographed sitting on Mr. T's lap; try to name five American poets, painters, playwrights, or composers on whose laps she would have scheduled a similar photo opportunity.

Not that (to choose names randomly) Elliott Carter, John Ashbery, Edward Albee, or even the politically misguided Helen Frankenthaler would *want* to be photographed with our lady of the donated china sitting on their respective knees. The peculiar character of American life, its distinctive meld of crassness and sanctimony, repels artistic temperaments as much as it fascinates them. It's the fuel that gives our art a mania for large, sprawling structures full of screwy juxtapositions; at the same time, it's the quality that makes every American artist, from the Maine watercolorist to the rapper on the L.A. ghetto streets, an outcast. To be an artist in America means being an oddball, but to be American *without* being an artist is just too fucking weird: you have to be partially dead, in heart or brain, to manage it. Which may be why movies about the walking dead have become another key part of our culture. Granted, they're made for crowds of giggly teenagers in search of a gross-out, but teenagers, even when giggling, *know* what their parents have systematically forgotten: that something's wrong. If they move as a crowd, randomly, in search of random thrills, it's because they're rarely exposed to the possibility of something better—another joyous result of having replaced our educational system with television. As time goes on, the need for thrills wears off, the teens grow up dull, their kids discover new thrills, and their own become nostalgia: Get ready now for the *Friday the 13th* retrospectives and Freddy Kruger memorabilia auctions of the year 2010.

That's assuming the country lasts another twenty years. Which, of course, it won't in its present form: Life is change. ("Dear life, life is strife."—Gertrude Stein.) The only question's whether the change will be a tumultuous collapse, brought about by those at the top refusing to deal with the anger, the misery, the crumbling infrastructure underneath, or more peaceably, by everyone's facing and tackling the problems endemic to our national life in a sane and democratic way. No rational person would want the first, and the second is probably too much to hope for; instead we're likely to get a random evolutionary muddle, with some good and some bad in it, until either our resources or the ozone layer reach the breaking point. After which, presumably, there won't be time for us to worry about how we might have solved our problems as a nation.

Our theater, such as it is, will of course have run out of resources —financial support, audiences, performance space, etc.—much earlier: It's already starting to do so. But the beauty of theater is that it doesn't need much resource beyond the imagination, the strength of which, well exercised, outdoes anything the makers of those huge mechanized spectacles we now miscall Broadway musicals can do. "Two boards and a passion"—the old recipe—is all the theater needs. The passion's already in place: Young artists, in their drifty and TV-taught way, are angrier and more worried than they've been in years. I'm writing this the day after a faculty meeting in the Dramatic Writing Program at New York University, where I try haplessly to teach would-be playwrights how Western drama evolved, from Aeschylus to Beckett. It seems that my colleagues who teach them about their own writing are worried: More and more, the students turn out reams of pages full of affectless violence, anger seeking a home, incessant rage without resolution. "I'm as angry as they are," I said. "Aren't you?" Once the young learn to locate the deeper sources of their anger, and crystallize it in an image, all that matters is making sure they have a place to express it, along with its attendant and contrasting emotions. When the feelings are that strong, audiences wanting to share them will appear.

Just now the number of places where the theater has free expression is in a crunch: After twenty-five years of polite and pro forma subsidy, art is embattled on the economic front as well as the political. Established theaters are collapsing. Risk, a kind of ambition, is being curtailed along with every other ambition. Like every movement, this shrinkage automatically stirs up a countermovement. Theaters may be going out of business, but a surprisingly large number of new ones are starting. A serious play can't sustain itself financially on Broadway, where nobody wants to be serious. (John Guare's *Six Degrees of Separation,* its seriousness cloaked in chic comedy of manners, is the recent exception that proves the rule.) This merely means that New York gets its tastes of the serious more fleetingly than other cities, and has to be quicker in pursuing them. But networks spring up, just as new theaters do when a real estate downturn leaves rows of empty storefronts, and these days a theater piece of substance from Denver or Atlanta can find its way to Pittsburgh, Portland, or St. Paul with surprising speed.

GNAT, as we call this volume, is meant among other things to abet that kind of networking. The plays in it are representative in one simple respect: They're all recent works that a single critic (me) has thoroughly enjoyed, onstage and/or in script form. I don't offer them as a complete definition of my taste, or as a ponderous, prototypical exhibit of "American Playwriting Today." And I haven't tried to make up one of those one-from-column-A, one-from-column-B anthologies in which the genders and ethnic groups represented are more varied than the writing. These are simply plays, pieces, texts, that struck me forcibly as being in tune with the currents of the time. Some are angry, some questioning; one—the most traditional in form—is more elegiac than anything else. Two are by writers who have suffered personal attack from the lunatics of the right for disturbing its sanctimony of mind, and in one of these cases the comic progress of the attack is chronicled in the documents prefacing the play. In a sense, it now strikes me, all six of the plays are about art, and how you create it in a time and country where the life of the imagination, the artist's substance, is under constant attack by people whose lack of principle constitutes a definite, and frightening, program.

I've tried to say something specific about this, and other relevant matters, in the prefatory note that precedes each play. The playwrights are not responsible for these notes, and haven't seen them; I hope they will forgive me for any misunderstandings. What's most important, after all, is that the plays are here, in your hands, and that together they make up a picture (not a definition) of our time. An angry time; a time of loss and despair; a time of confusion, searching, and change; a time of starvation, of homeless and jobless agonies, in which the upper 5 percent of the population has a 25 percent increase in real income, while the rest of us have a loss; a time of oppression, violence, and the shrinkage of civil rights. An angry time—which is also a time of unique opportunity, of empty storefronts and empty hearts waiting to be filled by a living spirit. The kind of unhappy time, every twenty years or so, when America remembers it has a theater. . . .

grove new

AMERICAN
THEATER

david gordon

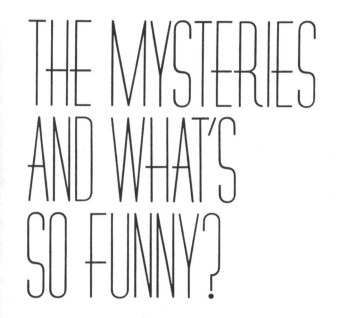

THE MYSTERIES AND WHAT'S SO FUNNY?

MARCEL DUCHAMP (Valda Setterfield) descends the staircase as his life whirls about him. *Left to right,* Ben Bodé, Dean Moss, Karen Graham, Ralph Williams, Lola Pashalinski, Scott Cunningham, Norma Fire.

Interviewing David Gordon before *The Mysteries* opened in New York, I asked him, "Is it a dance or a play?" His answer, appropriately, was, "I'm not sure." Modern dance has employed spoken text intermittently since Martha Graham paved the way with *Letter to the World* (1941); many contemporary choreographers—especially those, like Gordon, who emerged from the Judson Dance Theater movement of the 1960s—have used words even more aggressively, as a means of questioning and dissecting the elements of dance and the whole process of making it. A whole new set of dramatic possibilities has come out of the tension between the act of moving on a stage and the words that comment on it, directly or by contrast.

But *The Mysteries and What's So Funny?* is the first work to come out of this movement that strikes me as having literary as well as theatrical substance. It exists to wed its pairs of modes, writing and performance, the verbal and the physical, acting and dance, just as it welds together its two dramas: the struggle of a married couple to sustain their relationship and the struggle of an artist to maintain integrity of spirit in the face of an innately exploitative world. Gordon always builds his works out of personal elements: The first drama is based on his vision of his parents and their family history, the second on the career and thinking of Marcel Duchamp, an artist whose questioning of the whole nature of art has been a central influence on Gordon's approach.

The juxtaposition of the two dramas, in alternating scenes, is like a surreal, nonlinear version of the double-plotted Elizabethan play structure. The fact that both stories are partly "documentary" in nature (many of Duchamp's lines are in fact quoted from him verbatim) gives Gordon's surrealism some of its wry, matter-of-fact charm. Finally the two become one: We see that love, like creativity, is an act of tremendous risk, calling for huge efforts of concentration, and always prone to the destructive pressures of society.

The connection was underscored, in production, by Gordon's casting his wife and longtime partner, Valda Setterfield, in the role of Duchamp, in which she was obliged to assert, repeatedly, that marriage and family commitments were unhealthy for an artist, compromising his independence and possibly damaging his work; her existence was in effect a continuing denial of the lines she spoke, making the ironies dance in the air—as everything in Gordon's production danced, including the highly mobile elements of Red Grooms's design, to Philip Glass's subtle, airy music. The melancholy underpinnings of the intertwined stories didn't keep the event from having the playful appeal of an old-fashioned musical revue, as sophisticated as it was innocent, as rueful and somber as it was whimsical. In that sense, Gordon's greatest achievement was to have brought off the wedding every theater artist strives for: that of pure art, at its most free-flowing and complex, with pure popular entertainment.

Dedicated to:
  Rose Gordon (September 15, 1912–October 19, 1992)
  Samuel Gordon (July 1, 1913–October 31, 1991)
  Marcel Duchamp (July 28, 1887–October 2, 1968)

I am grateful to:
  Jedediah Wheeler
  Nigel Redden
  and Alyce Dissette

PRODUCTION NOTES

The Mysteries and What's So Funny? was developed over an eighteen-month period at workshop/residencies with the Guthrie Theater Lab, Minneapolis, Minnesota; Playwrights Horizons Theatre School, New York, New York, and the American Repertory Theatre's Institute for Advanced Theatre Training, Cambridge, Massachusetts.

The first performances were presented in May 1991, at the Spoleto Festival U.S.A. in Charleston, South Carolina, with additional performances following at the Bardavon Opera House, Poughkeepsie, New York; Serious Fun! at Lincoln Center, New York, New York, and the American Repertory Theatre, Cambridge, Massachusetts.

Music by Philip Glass
Visual Design by Red Grooms
Directed by David Gordon

Music Director: Alan Johnson
Lighting Designer: Dan Kotlowitz
Sound Designer: David Meschter
Casting: Vince Liebhart and Judy Dennis
Assistant Directors: Mary Ann Kellogg and Chuck Finlon
Producer: Jedediah Wheeler

ORIGINAL CAST

MARCEL DUCHAMP: Valda Setterfield
YOUNG ARTIST: Dean Moss
OLD ROSE: Lola Pashalinski
OLD SAM: Ralph Williams
YOUNG ROSE: Karen Graham
YOUNG SAM: Ben Bodé
DETECTIVE; ONLY, OLDEST CHILD: Norma Fire
FANNY: Jane Hoffman
MRS. HIM: Gayle Tufts
MR. HIM: Jonathan Walker
ANGER I: Scott Cunningham
ANGER II: Karen Evans-Kandel
ACTOR (GRANDFATHER, FATHER, ETC.): Alice Playten
PIANIST: Alan Johnson

Produced in association with David Gordon/Pick Up Company, Inc.

Commissioned by Spoleto Festival U.S.A. and Serious Fun! at Lincoln Center.

The principal sponsor of this project was the Lila Wallace-Reader's Digest Fund. The development of this project was made possible by a grant from the Ford Foundation. The commission fees for this composer/choreographer collaboration were made possible by a grant from Meet the Composers Composer/Choreographer Project, a national program funded by the Ford Foundation and the Pew Charitable Trusts.

Additional project support was provided by the Jerome Foundation, John and Sage Cowles, AT&T Foundation, Foundation for Contemporary Performance Arts, Greenwall Foundation, and the Harkness Foundations for Dance.

CHARACTERS

MARCEL DUCHAMP

YOUNG ARTIST

OLD ROSE

OLD SAM

YOUNG ROSE

YOUNG SAM

DETECTIVE

FANNY

MRS. HIM

MR. HIM

ANGER I

ANGER II

ACTOR (GRANDFATHER, FATHER, CRITIC, BROTHER I, BROTHER II, MOTHER, VENDOR, MAILMAN, PAULINE, STRANGER, WAITER, *baby sound*, DOCTOR, SALESPERSON)

During the overture, which lasts approximately two minutes, the entire company enters or is revealed in ways that suggest their subsequent characters and the physical-cyclical nature of the event, its links to the cycle of the seasons, and of human life. The figures rotate through the space. The focal figures are DU-CHAMP, OLD ROSE, and OLD SAM, framed (literally by a large Red Grooms–designed picture frame) in various ways by the action. A swinging door, in a doorframe mounted on wheels, moves through the action, revealing characters as they enter through it. OLD ROSE and OLD SAM end up in chairs where they will remain for most of the performance, facing upstage, watching a TV set. (They will return to this position at play's end.) Here, as throughout the piece, YOUNG ARTIST is instrumental in setting up and transforming scenes, facilitating the action.

Time passes. Music stops.

DUCHAMP: I am Henri Robert Marcel Duchamp.

(Music starts.)

GROUP: Duchamp.

DUCHAMP: Born in France.

GROUP: A Frenchman.

DUCHAMP: On July 28th

GROUP: 1887

ACTOR (GRANDFATHER): I am his grandfather. I was an artist.

ANGER I: His father

ANGERS: however

ANGER II: said no to an art career

ANGERS: for his three sons.

ACTOR (FATHER): Listen to your father. No Art!

DUCHAMP: So, my brothers and I all became artists.

ACTOR (FATHER): These kids never listen.

YOUNG ARTIST: Time passes.

DUCHAMP: I'm drawing, painting.

GROUP: Drawing, painting.

ACTOR (CRITIC): In 1911, his work begins relating to Cubism.

DETECTIVE: What exactly is Cubism?

ACTOR (CRITIC): A geometrical reduction of natural forms.

ANGER I: To what end?

ANGER II: To end what?

DUCHAMP: I became interested in successive images of a single body in motion.

DETECTIVE (to CRITIC): How did you know?

ACTOR (CRITIC): I'm a critic. Why do you ask?

DETECTIVE: I'm a detective.

ACTOR (CRITIC): He also makes drawings and paintings—

DUCHAMP: I told you so—drawing, painting.

GROUP: Drawing, painting.

ACTOR (CRITIC): Of pairs of chess players.

DUCHAMP: Those were my brothers.

ACTOR (BROTHER I): I am Gaston. I call myself Jacques Villon.

ACTOR (BROTHER II): I am Raymond. I call myself Duchamp—Villon.

DUCHAMP AND ACTOR (BROTHERS DUCHAMP): We all loved chess.

GROUP: 1912

ACTOR (CRITIC): is the year of his most important Oil on Canvas works.

DUCHAMP: If you'd only told me I could have stopped (*music stops*) right then.

ACTOR (CRITIC): He painted *Nude Descending a Staircase.*

(*Music plays as* DUCHAMP *descends staircase, then stops.*)

ANGERS: It caused a furor.

(*Music starts.*)

GROUP: Mon Dieu!

DUCHAMP: I became a little famous.

ANGERS: Notorious.

DUCHAMP: Hilarious.

GROUP: In 1913

ACTOR (CRITIC): he abandons all conventional forms of painting and drawing.

DUCHAMP: I got a job as a librarian.

YOUNG ARTIST: Excuse me, where are the art books?

DUCHAMP: I don't know, I just started working here.

ACTOR (CRITIC): He mounts a bicycle wheel upside down

ANGERS: on a kitchen stool.

ACTOR (MOTHER): Marcel—Marcel, where is my kitchen stool?

DUCHAMP: And—

GROUP: in 1914

DUCHAMP: I bought a bottle rack at a Paris bazaar. (*Music stops.*) Combien Madame?

ACTOR (VENDOR): Twenty francs.

DUCHAMP: Ten francs.

ACTOR (VENDOR): Eighteen francs.

DUCHAMP: Twelve francs.

ACTOR (VENDOR): Fifteen francs.

DUCHAMP: I'll take it, and I signed it.

(*Music starts.*)

ACTOR (CRITIC): He calls these

GROUP: the *Readymades.*

DUCHAMP: Not yet. I wasn't ready.

GROUP: In 1915

DETECTIVE: he visits New York for the first time. Why did you go?

DUCHAMP: Why not?

ANGERS: He publishes a manifesto.

DUCHAMP: *A Complete Reversal of Art Opinions*

ACTOR (CRITIC): *by Marcel Duchamp, Iconoclast.*

DETECTIVE: What exactly is an iconoclast?

ACTOR (CRITIC): An attacker of popular ideas

ANGERS: and institutions.

DUCHAMP: I began work on the *Large Glass.*

DETECTIVE: What exactly is the *Large Glass*?

DUCHAMP: I'll tell you later.

GROUP: In 1916

ACTOR (CRITIC): he is a founding member of the Society of Independent Artists.

DUCHAMP: But in 1917 I resigned.

DETECTIVE: Why exactly does he resign?

ACTOR (CRITIC): They reject his *Readymade*

DUCHAMP: called *Fountain*

ACTOR (CRITIC): which he submits under the pseudonym

DUCHAMP: R. Mutt.

ANGERS: It's a toilet.

DUCHAMP: It was a urinal.

ANGERS: A urinal, a toilet, it's the same thing.

DUCHAMP: Not where I come from.

YOUNG ARTIST: Time passes.

DUCHAMP: I played chess more and more.

GROUP: More and more.

DUCHAMP: I designed a set of rubber stamps so I could play chess by mail.

ACTOR (MAILMAN): Madame Duchamp, here's a letter from Marcel.

GROUP: In 1919

ACTOR (CRITIC): he uses the *Mona Lisa* as a *Readymade*.

DUCHAMP: I gave her a mustache

ANGERS: and a beard.

DUCHAMP: A goatee.

ANGERS: A beard, a goatee, it's the same thing.

DUCHAMP: Not where I come from.

GROUP: In 1920

DETECTIVE: You invent a feminine alter ego. You call yourself *Rrose Sélavy.* Why exactly do you do that?

(*Music stops.*)

DUCHAMP: C'est la vie. Don't you get it? C'est la vie.

YOUNG ARTIST: Time passes.

(*Music starts.*)

ACTOR (CRITIC): He moves back to Paris. His first puns are published.

DUCHAMP: I love punning better than painting.

DETECTIVE: What exactly is a pun?

DUCHAMP: A play on words. A kind of game.

ACTOR (CRITIC): As Rrose Sélavy he signs another artist's work.

ANGERS: Another game.

GROUP: 1923

DUCHAMP: I brought the *Large Glass* to a state of incompletion—and I signed it.

DETECTIVE: What exactly is—

DUCHAMP: I'll tell you later. I perfected a roulette system in which one neither won nor lost. I trained seriously for chess competition. I shaved a star in the back of my hair. I gave French lessons to Americans to earn a little money. I lived my life. I had serious fun.

ANGERS: More games.

(*Music stops.*)

ACTOR (CRITIC): The *idea* reaches the public that Duchamp has ceased to produce art.

DUCHAMP: What a good idea.

YOUNG ARTIST: Time passes.

GROUP: 1925, 26, 28, 31, 35, 40.

(Music starts.)

ACTOR (CRITIC): He works.

GROUP: He thinks.

ACTOR (CRITIC): He plays chess

GROUP: more and more.

DUCHAMP: I played in chess tournaments.

GROUP: Real ones.

DUCHAMP: I wrote a chess column every Thursday

GROUP: for a while

DUCHAMP: for the Paris paper *Ce Soir.*

ACTOR (CRITIC): He arranges exhibits of the work of other artists and allows his own work to be shown.

DUCHAMP: Sometimes.

ANGER I: He gets married.

ANGER II: Gets divorced.

ACTOR (CRITIC): Continues an interest in optical phenomena.

DETECTIVE: What exactly is op—

DUCHAMP: Now you see it, now you don't.

ACTOR (CRITIC): And film, and puns, and *Readymades.*

GROUP: In 1942

DETECTIVE: you returned to the United States where you lived for the rest of your life. Why did you come back?

GROUP: Go back.

DUCHAMP: Exactly?

DETECTIVE: Oh yes. Why *exactly* did you go back?

GROUP: Come back.

DUCHAMP: A second wind.

YOUNG ARTIST: Time passes.

GROUP: In 1946

ACTOR (CRITIC): Duchamp begins to execute . . .

DUCHAMP (*aside*): Execute is an odd word.

ACTOR (CRITIC): his last major work.

DUCHAMP: "Marcel, do you want to go to the movies?" No, I think I'll just stay here and execute my last major work.

ACTOR (CRITIC): In complete secrecy. For twenty years he works on this composition.

GROUP: One.

ACTOR (CRITIC): For twenty years this assemblage.

GROUP: Two.

ACTOR (CRITIC): For twenty years this final chord.

GROUP: Three.

DETECTIVE: Did you do anything else?

DUCHAMP: Yes, I gave speeches, I gave interviews, I—organized exhibits.

GROUP: Four, five.

DUCHAMP: I remarried, I became an American citizen, I changed apartments.

DETECTIVE (*aside*): For the last time.

GROUP: Six, seven.

ACTOR (CRITIC): To see this last work you go through a low doorway into a small, empty, windowless room.

GROUP: Eight, nine.

DUCHAMP: And don't forget—I hand-colored nine hundred and ninety-nine foam-rubber falsies.

GROUP: Ten.

ACTOR (CRITIC): In the far wall, in an arched brick portal, there is an old wooden door.

GROUP: Eleven, twelve.

ACTOR (CRITIC): There are two small holes at eye level through which you can see a brick wall with a slit in it.

GROUP: Thirteen.

DETECTIVE: On October 2, 1968, during a customary visit to France . . .

GROUP: Fourteen.

ACTOR (CRITIC): Through the slit you see a naked girl on a bed of leaves and branches in a wide open space.

GROUP: Fifteen.

DETECTIVE: you died peacefully in your studio.

GROUP: Sixteen.

DUCHAMP: I was lucky right to the end.

GROUP: Seventeen.

ACTOR (CRITIC): Her face is almost covered by her blonde hair. Her legs are open and slightly bent. Her left arm is raised—the hand holding a small gas lamp.

GROUP: Eighteen.

(*Music stops.*)

DETECTIVE: Why—exactly—do you think you were so—

ANGERS: lucky.

ACTOR (CRITIC): A blue sky, two or three white clouds, wooded hills, mist, a small lake, some rocks, a waterfall.

GROUP: Nineteen.

ACTOR (CRITIC): Duchamp maintained an absolute silence on this subject until his death.

GROUP: Twenty.

DETECTIVE: Why, exactly?

DUCHAMP: It's a mystery to me.

PART I

Music starts.

Young Sam: Something about the mystery of knowing what you want.

Young Artist: Or the art of it . . . the art of knowing what you want.

Young Sam: Or the mystery of it.

Young Artist: Something about the mystery of how one person makes something . . . makes something to be interested in . . . makes something to *stay* interested in.

Young Sam: And the mystery of how somebody else is also interested. The mystery of two people getting interested in each other . . . staying interested . . . making something of being together.

Young Artist: The art of making something of being together.

Young Sam: The mystery of staying together . . . Or the art of it.

Young Artist: The art of staying together or the mystery of it.

Angers: Rose and Sam are well into their seventies

Group: No, that's not true.

Angers: Rose and Sam are *unwell* into their seventies.

Anger I: Something about his insides, his operations,

Anger II: her neck, her back, the sugar in her blood, his needing oxygen to breathe, his panic.

GROUP: His fury at not being able to breathe.

ANGER I: Her choking cough.

ANGER II: His toothlessness.

GROUP: His fury at not being able to chew.

ANGER II: Her headaches, her defensive sleeping.

GROUP: His fury at her sleeping.

ANGER I: His repeating.

GROUP: Repeating, repeating, repeating, repeating . . .

(*Music stops.*)

ANGER II: Her forgetting.

(*Pause. Music begins.*)

GROUP: His fury at her forgetting.

ANGER II: His deafness.

ANGER I: Her deafness.

GROUP: His fury at her deafness.

OLD ROSE (*speaking*):

> I'm Rose.
> I am Rose.
> I am old, I was young.
> I was thin, I am fat.
> It's true I'm growing deaf, I once could hear.
> I had no fear.
> Oh Sammie, do you remember?
> Remember me.
> I'm Rose.
> I am Rose

(*Singing.*)

> My hair was brown, now it's gray.
> Now I can't see, but my eyes were clear.
> I showed my legs, I wore high heels.

(*Speaking.*)

> Now I wear flat shoes, but I had no fear.
> Do you remember? Oh Sammie,
> Remember me.
> I'm Rose.
> I am Rose.

(*Singing.*)

> I forget the time, I forget the day.
> I forget the food burning on the stove.
> I lose my watch, I lose my thought.
> But I was strong,

(*Speaking.*)

> I bore a child.
> I was the one.
> I had no fear, more than fifty years.
> Nothing in this life prepared me for this life.

(*Singing.*)

> I was a daughter, I was a mother, I was a wife—

(*Speaking.*)

> I didn't realize I would end alone.
> My mother gone, my children grown,
> My husband sick and married to TV.

(*Singing.*)

> He don't want me, he don't know me.
> Oh Sammie, remember me, we had a child.

We made love, we were in love, we have a child.
Oh my dear, remember me—

(*Speaking.*) I'm Rose. (*Sits down. Music stops.*)

DETECTIVE: Rose and Sam live together, alone with his anger and her growing anger *at* his anger

GROUP: their only pleasure

DETECTIVE: their only child.

GROUP: The mystery

DETECTIVE: Of the only

ANGER II: The oldest

YOUNG ROSE: Child—the only

YOUNG SAM: The oldest child.

(*Music starts.*)

DETECTIVE: The one who

ANGER II: No matter

YOUNG ROSE: No matter how

YOUNG SAM: Independent

DETECTIVE: Independent, no matter how

ANGER II: Independent

YOUNG ROSE: Or far away

YOUNG SAM: Or far

DETECTIVE: Away

ANGER II: Away, the oldest

YOUNG ROSE: Child, the only

YOUNG SAM: Child

DETECTIVE: Goes, oh no

ANGER II: No, no matter

YOUNG ROSE: No, no matter how far

YOUNG SAM: There is

DETECTIVE: Always

ANGER II: A tie

YOUNG ROSE: Always a tie

YOUNG SAM: The one they had first

DETECTIVE: The only one

ANGER II: They had

YOUNG ROSE: First

YOUNG SAM: The only one who got

DETECTIVE: Who gives

ANGER II: The most—who got

YOUNG ROSE: Who gives

YOUNG SAM: The most

DETECTIVE: The only one—the only

DETECTIVE AND ANGER II: Only

ANGER II: One—the oldest

YOUNG ROSE: One. The one they dreamed

YOUNG SAM: They dreamed

DETECTIVE: Imagined

ANGER II: Imagined, invented

YOUNG ROSE: Protected

YOUNG SAM: Protected

DETECTIVE: Protected—over

ANGER II: Overprotected

ALL: And over
And over
The mystery
Of it,

ANGER II: Of being

YOUNG ROSE: The only

YOUNG SAM: The oldest, of being

DETECTIVE: Everything to them

ANGER II: Everything

YOUNG ROSE: To them, everything

YOUNG SAM: Everything

DETECTIVE: Somehow

ANGER II: Somehow more

YOUNG ROSE: Than each other

YOUNG SAM: More than each other

DETECTIVE: *To* each other

ANGER II: Is this child,

YOUNG ROSE: This only

YOUNG SAM: This oldest, first

DETECTIVE: First

ANGER II: Child, this child this never

YOUNG ROSE: Never, never

YOUNG SAM: Grown up

DETECTIVE: Child.

ANGER II: Child.

DETECTIVE: Did you eat

YOUNG ROSE: Did you eat something

DETECTIVE: Mom, I'm twenty-one years old

ANGER II: Old, Mom I'm thirty-one years

DETECTIVE: Old Mom, I'm forty-one

YOUNG SAM: Years—No matter

YOUNG ROSE: No matter how old

ANGER II: You get

YOUNG ROSE: You are, you're still

YOUNG SAM: My baby

DETECTIVE: Baby

SAM: Only

ANGER II: First

YOUNG ROSE: Baby

YOUNG SAM: Child

DETECTIVE: Baby

YOUNG SAM: Baby, do you need

DETECTIVE: Money?

YOUNG SAM: Do you

ANGER II: Need money?

YOUNG SAM: Do you need money?

DETECTIVE: Dad, I'm twenty-one years old

ANGER II: Old, Dad, I'm thirty-one years

DETECTIVE: Old Dad, I'm forty-one

YOUNG SAM: Years—No matter

YOUNG ROSE: No matter how old

YOUNG SAM: You get, no matter how

DETECTIVE: Old, The mystery of being

ANGER II: The old mystery

YOUNG ROSE: Of being the only

YOUNG SAM: Child, the oldest

DETECTIVE: Child, the first

ANGER II: Born, first

YOUNG ROSE: Born, only

YOUNG SAM: Born

ANGER II: First

DETECTIVE: First

ANGER II: First.

(*Music stops.*)

The characters carry scripts and periodically refer to them. Detective's lines are echoed softly by YOUNG ARTIST, *Mr. Him's and Actor's by the* ANGERS.

DETECTIVE: *First* is my name. My second name. When I was a child—

MR. HIM: You were a child detective. I'm guessing.

DETECTIVE: I began to be a sort of detective.

ACTOR: I knew she was a detective. I knew you were a detective.

MR. HIM: Maybe that means *you're* a detective.

DETECTIVE: My mother always lost things.

ACTOR: *My* mother always lost things.

MR. HIM: You're an actor. You only pretended your mother always lost things.

ACTOR: I thought I meant that.

MR. HIM: You're a great pretender.

DETECTIVE: Her glasses. Her keys. Her voice. Her temper. Once she lost a funny amount of something really funny.

ACTOR: Hey me! My mother once lost me.

MR. HIM: That's really funny. My mother got lost when I was six, along with our neighbor's husband, my father's new Chevrolet, and two German shepherds.

DETECTIVE: She paid a quarter for a found lost object.

MR. HIM: You knew my mother?

DETECTIVE: No. My mother paid me twenty-five cents to find things.

ACTOR: My mother said a German shepherd was too big to keep in the house.

MR. HIM: My father told my mother to get lost once too often. "Bob, let's take the kids out." "Get lost Jean!"

DETECTIVE: Fifty cents if I found it in under ten minutes.

ACTOR: So we had pet snails.

MR. HIM: For a while I used to try and get lost. I thought I might see my mother. I thought lost was a place. Like Paradise. Like Paradise Lost.

DETECTIVE: So I began to lose her things for her. I began to make a living losing her things. I began to charge more. In fact my mail-order criminal detection lessons were paid for by a series of lost pieces of my mother's dinette set. My mother paid me two hundred and fifty dollars for finding the table which cost me twenty dollars to hide in a warehouse in downtown Brooklyn.

ACTOR: A snail is a really hard pet to have. I mean winning the affection of a snail is really hard.

MR. HIM: I began to try and get the attention of older women. All older women, all women, all girls more grown up than me became a kind of world, a kind of universal mother whose attention I wanted.

DETECTIVE: My mother became frantic. Things were disappearing right and left. Whole rooms of furniture. All her shoes. Everything in the refrigerator. I was making a fortune by the time I was fourteen.

ACTOR: That's how old I was. I was just that old

MR. HIM: I grabbed the elbows of elderly women and forced them to cross the street.

ACTOR: when my mother served the snails for dinner.

DETECTIVE: Then I privately persuaded my brother to take a two-day hike; convinced my mother that she had misplaced my brother and that I needed several thousand dollars to find him. Opened an office downtown under the trade name "Finders/Keepers" with the motto "Your mystery is our meat."

MR. HIM: When I was twenty my mother walked back in. No man. No car. No dogs. No money and no mystery. Just an ordinary woman looking for a place to stay. And she stayed—and I went.

DETECTIVE: Why? Why did you go when you finally got her back?

MR. HIM: She was a nuisance.

ACTOR: That's what she said.

MR. HIM: Who?

ACTOR: My mother about the snails.

MR. HIM: The snails?

ACTOR: She said snails could not be trained. She said I didn't deal with reality. She said I was a mystery to her. She said snails were good with garlic. She made me eat them and I acted like it didn't matter.

MR. HIM: And you've been acting ever since.

ACTOR: Ever since.

DETECTIVE: Ever since then I ask questions and find answers. It's my living. (*Turning to* DUCHAMP:) Marcel Duchamp, it is now 1966. In a few months you will be eighty years old. Looking back over your whole life, what satisfies you most?

DUCHAMP: My whole life, well, that's quite a question. My luck—I suppose my luck. I think I've been lucky. I've done the things I wanted to do. (*Music starts.*) Deep down I'm enormously lazy. I've never had a pressing need to express myself. I've never had that kind of need—to draw, for instance, morning, noon, and night. Usually a man's brain interests me more than what he makes, you know. Because, I've noticed that most artists only repeat themselves. My life has been my art; my art, my life,

YOUNG ARTIST: His life, his art. His art, his life.

DUCHAMP: Each second, each breath, a work neither visual nor cerebral, inscribed nowhere. A sort of constant euphoria. That sounds rather poetic, doesn't it, but I just like—just breathing. I like breathing better than working.

DETECTIVE: Well, that's quite an answer. Yet, you are responsible for art objects, for art concepts, that continue to affect the world.

DUCHAMP: No, no, not the world. Perhaps a small portion of the art world—which is a very small portion of the whole world. Anyway, I avoid that word—responsible. Responsibility clouds direction. It's a false purpose. (*To* YOUNG ARTIST:) Don't you think so?

YOUNG ARTIST: Excuse me, I want to study with you.

DUCHAMP: That's very kind, but I have nothing to teach.

YOUNG ARTIST: I want to be an artist.

DUCHAMP: Yes. Well, stop wanting.

YOUNG SAM: But what about money? What about earning a living?

DUCHAMP: Well, the truth is—I had a little. Family money. No great amount. But then my needs weren't great. I made sure my needs were not great.

YOUNG ROSE: What about a wife? What about children?

DUCHAMP: For me, my dear, you see all of that was a budgetary question as much as anything. I believed I had to choose to be a man of art or to marry and have children.

DETECTIVE: But you did marry.

DUCHAMP: Yes. I was still young and she was a very nice girl. We were properly introduced and we were married the way one is usually married, but it didn't work.

YOUNG ROSE: Weren't you happy together? Why didn't it work?

DUCHAMP: Because (*smiling at* YOUNG ROSE) no offense, because I saw that marriage is as boring as anything.

YOUNG SAM: Oh, I don't think that. I love knowing who I'm coming home to, who I'm waking up with. I love it when nothing changes.

DUCHAMP: Well, I guess I was really much more of a bachelor than I thought. I was just not interested in the woman-wife, the mother, the children, etcetera. I carefully avoided all that until . . . I was . . . about . . . sixty-seven. Then I married a woman who, because of her age, couldn't have children.

DETECTIVE: But there were other women in your life?

DUCHAMP: Yes, of course. One is not, you know, obliged to marry every woman one is with.

YOUNG ARTIST: You protected yourself against "The Family."

DUCHAMP: Yes, I did. It's often the family, I think, that forces you to abandon your real ideas, to swap them for things *it* believes in. Society, you know, and all that paraphernalia.

YOUNG ARTIST: Excuse me—

DETECTIVE: Then you consider yourself—

DUCHAMP: I consider myself very happy.

YOUNG ARTIST: And probably tired of answering questions.

DUCHAMP (*smiling at* YOUNG ARTIST): Yes, a little. Anyway, I am happy. I've never had a serious illness, or melancholy. I've had even more luck at the end of my life than at the beginning. I've missed nothing. I can't tell you any more.

YOUNG ARTIST: Excuse me.

DUCHAMP: Yes?

YOUNG ARTIST: What about regrets?

(*Music stops.*)

DUCHAMP: I have no regrets.

(*Music starts.*)

YOUNG ARTIST: Meaning that everything you ever did was good.

DUCHAMP: No, meaning that everything you ever did or never did was okay with you.

DETECTIVE: Meaning that the memory of something, the memory of something

ANGERS: didn't make your stomach ache.

MR. HIM: Meaning that a stomach ache was okay with you.

ACTOR: Meaning that you had always said the thing you'd wished you'd said.

DUCHAMP: Meaning that what you did say,

YOUNG ARTIST: what you did say,

DUCHAMP: meaning that what you did manage to say was okay with you.

MRS. HIM: Meaning that who you met and married,

DUCHAMP: that who you met and didn't marry,

ANGER I: meaning that all the bodies in all the beds

ACTOR: that who you saw and never met,

ANGER II: that who you never met

FANNY: meaning that who you met and married and couldn't manage to stay with

MRS. HIM: meaning that who you met and married and couldn't manage to leave was all, was all okay with you.

ANGER I: Meaning that when you changed, and he changed,

ANGER II: when she changed and it changed

DUCHAMP: meaning that what it changed from and what it changed to was all,

YOUNG ARTIST: was all okay with you.

OLD ROSE: Meaning that having only one child,

DETECTIVE: that having had only one child

OLD ROSE: that having any child at all and then having had only one child was the right decision, was all right, was all all okay with you, meaning that the mystery of no regret

(*Music stops.*)

ANGER I: is not somehow

ANGERS: connected to

GROUP: the mystery of anger!

(*Music starts.*)

ANGERS: You know me. You've known me all your life.

ANGER I: We met the day you were born.

ANGER II: We met while you were half in

ANGERS: and half out.

ANGER II: I was there

ANGER I: when they pulled you from the

ANGERS: womb.

ANGER II: From the

ANGERS: womb.

ANGER I: I was there

ANGER II: when they hung you up

ANGER I: side

ANGER II: down.

ANGER I: Up

ANGER II: side

ANGER I: down.

ANGER II: I was there when they whacked you on the back

ANGER I: What a smack! I was there,

ANGERS: I'm anger,

ANGER I: your best

ANGERS: friend.

ANGER II: Your best

ANGERS: friend.

ANGER II: I was with you in that

ANGERS: crib! In that

ANGER II: high

ANGER I: chair!

ANGERS: In that

ANGER II: play

ANGER I: pen! Remember that damn playpen.

ANGER II: Remember the bars.

ANGER I: Remember that

ANGER II: damn

ANGER I: mesh

ANGER II: cage kept catching your toes

ANGER I: and your toys.

ANGERS: Remember screaming to be the hell out of there?

ANGER II: I was there.

ANGER I: I was there when she took away her

ANGERS: breast. (*Singing.*) That lovely breast.

ANGER II (*speaking*)**:** I was there when your teeth tore through your gums.

ANGERS: Through your gums. I was there, I am anger,

ANGER I: your best friend.

ANGER II: Your best friend. Remember doo doo?

ANGER I: Ka ka?

ANGER II: Wee

ANGER I: wee?

ANGER II: poo

ANGER I: poo?

ANGERS: poo.

ANGER I: For shit's sake, I couldn't get any time off.

ANGER II: How could I leave when they talked to you like that?

ANGER I: Remember when you had to sit on the toilet?

ANGER II: Remember how long you had to sit on the toilet.

ANGERS: Anger! I was there.

ANGER I: Remember that day one

ANGERS: September,

ANGER II: when they dressed you up,

ANGER I: took you for a walk,

ANGER II: and left you in a room

ANGERS: with thirty other screaming kids?

ANGER II: I was there when they left you in that room

ANGER I: In that damned room

ANGER II: They left you!

ANGER I: Not me! I stayed!

ANGER II: I stayed there,

ANGERS: I am anger,

ANGER I: your

ANGER II: best

ANGER I: friend.

ANGER II: Your

ANGER I: best

ANGER II: friend. I was there all through

ANGERS: school.

ANGER I: I was there when your

ANGER II: best girl

ANGERS: went to the prom. Oh, oh, oh—the prom

ANGER II: with somebody else.

ANGER I: It was my idea that you ask that

ANGER II: girl

ANGERS: from another school.

ANGER II: I made that up. We got

ANGERS: even didn't we!

ANGER II: I was there that

ANGERS: summer

ANGER II: at the

ANGERS: beach

ANGER II: when you almost

ANGERS: drowned. You almost drowned

ANGER II: It was my energy that saved you.

ANGER I: It was me who got you through the war.

ANGER II: It was me who

ANGERS: killed that guy with your bayonet.

ANGER I: You would have

ANGERS: died.

ANGER II: I saved your

ANGERS: life. Now it's true sometimes I take a rest—a vacation. I go away for your health. You expect me and I don't show.

ANGER I: It's not that I don't care—

ANGERS: I'm busy!

ANGER II: I do have other friends

ANGERS: you know.

ANGER I: But sometimes I just drop in—

ANGER II: Unexpected

ANGER I: uninvited.

ANGER II. I might appear at breakfast—

ANGERS: in fact—maybe tomorrow morning—

ANGER I: you might

ANGERS: roll over in bed

ANGER I: and find me lying there between

ANGERS: you and your lover

ANGER I: first thing—

ANGER II: first thing—

ANGERS (*singing*): first thing in the morning.

(*Music stops.* MR. and MRS. HIM *are in bed, covered by a sheet.* MR. HIM *stirs.*)

MR. HIM: Morning, hon.

(*An* ANGER *hits Mrs. Him's head. She wakes up. Note: Throughout the scene,* MR. *and* MRS. HIM *are physically besieged by the* ANGERS *in ways that escalate their argument, turning the scene into a quartet.*)

MRS. HIM (*in a muffled voice, turning away*): Morning.

MR. HIM: What's for breakfast, hon?

MRS. HIM (*pausing*): You know, you say that every morning.

MR. HIM: What?

MRS. HIM: Every damn morning. You say that every damn morning—as if I stayed awake all the damn night dreaming up your breakfast.

MR. HIM: Hon? What's wrong, hon? Wake up on the wrong side of the bed?

MRS. HIM: What does that mean? Wrong side of the bed? Did your mother used to say that to you? Wrong side of the—I went to sleep on this side, didn't I? I always sleep on this side, don't I?

MR. HIM: All I did was ask about breakfast, hon.

MRS. HIM: And my name's not hon. That's another thing—my name's not hon. Maybe your secretary is hon or your receptionist or that damn lady barber you go to—maybe she's hon. But I'm not hon.

MR. HIM: Look, now I'm getting angry. All I asked was a simple question. What's for breakf—all I asked was what's for—damn, now I'm angry.

MRS. HIM: What's for breakfast? Okay. Let's guess. Let's say orange juice to start.

MR. HIM: Damn, I hate orange juice.

MRS. HIM: What a surprise! Well how about tomato juice?

MR. HIM: Yeah, I like tomato juice.

(ANGER *climbs into bed between them.*)

MRS. HIM: Is that so? That must be why you have tomato juice every morning. That must be why the only juice in this house is tomato damn juice because it's the only damn juice you like. Because you drink it for breakfast every damn morning before you have your damn coffee—not just any damn coffee. Maxwell House, Maxwell damn House coffee because your mother made Maxwell House coffee which you have every morning before your (MRS. HIM *gets out of bed.* ANGER II, *behind her back, slaps her.*) Cheerios which is the only damn cereal you ever eat—not Rice Krispies, or Wheaties or Rice Chex or Cream of Wheat or Farina or Granola or . . .

ANGER II: Raisin Bran.

(*The bed is moved off as* MR. HIM *exits in the opposite direction, leaving* MRS. HIM *and* ANGER II *alone onstage.*)

MRS. HIM: Raisin Bran or Corn Flakes or Frosted Flakes or Oatmeal or Total . . .

My mother and father
both
call me
"Baby."
They always called me "Baby"
And they call me
"Baby"
now.
My sister is one year younger than me
and they call her
"Baby Baby."
My sister
"Baby Baby"
calls me

"Sissy"
And she calls her only son
"Only."
She calls him
"Only."
And she makes
"Only"
call me "Auntie."
"Auntie Baby."
My boyfriend in high school called me "Mama."
His "Mama."
Try to hold on to these facts.
My mama called me "Baby."
And my boyfriend called me "Mama."
At the same time.
My own son calls me "Mom."
Or on bad days
"Muh-thurr."
His teachers call me
"Ma'am"
And they always say
"Well"
Like a little song
"We— — —ll."
So you're
his
mother.
My husband
calls me "Hon."
"Hon."
Like Attila the —.
On MasterCard and Visa I'm
"Mrs. Him."
The butcher
and even my damned gynecologist

call me
"Mrs.
Him."
The kid who delivers from the supermarket
and the super
both just call me
"Mrs."
Just
"Mrs."
Just
plain
"Mrs."
Kids in the street who used to call me "Miss"
now call me "Lady."
I know
what that means.
Soon I'll be
"Granny"
"Granny Baby."
On my tombstone.
Here lies
Mrs.
Baby
Honey
Mommy
Granny

HIM!

(*Music starts. As* OLD ROSE *and* OLD SAM *tell their stories, the group, including one* ANGER, *does a top-speed, literal reenactment of it, supervised by* YOUNG ARTIST.)

OLD ROSE: Sam's mother and father emigrated to America. They didn't know each other. They met here. How did they meet? I don't know. She was much younger than him. Sam says she was a kid. Did they fall in love? Did "falling" or "love" mean the same thing then? I don't know. Anyway—she married him and before she was eighteen she had three kids.

OLD SAM: Rose's mother's brother Sam came from Russia and when he had the money he sent for his mother Rachel and his sisters Fannie and Ida. Rose was Fannie's daughter. Nobody talks about Rachel's husband, Fannie's father. Don't ask me,

GROUP: I don't know.

OLD ROSE: First comes

ACTOR: Adelaide called Mickey

GROUP: I don't know why,

OLD ROSE: then

ACTOR: Morris, then Molly or Eva

GROUP: who died

YOUNG SAM (*entering*): Then Sam.

ACTOR: Then Eva or Molly

GROUP: Who died.

OLD ROSE: Then what happened? Did she fall out of love? Did she suddenly realize she was a kid with three kids. I don't know. But she walked out. Sam says she couldn't take the kids.

YOUNG SAM AND OLD SAM: She couldn't take the kids.

OLD ROSE: All I know is she didn't—take the kids. Now Sam's father had three kids. No wife. And no second wife—yet. So he kept the girl to take care of the house and put the two boys in an orphanage. Sam says this was ordinary—in those days.

OLD SAM: This was ordinary in those days.

OLD ROSE: I don't know. My mother had six children, no husband, and kept us all home. Also, if you're counting, the girl who's keeping house is about five years old. Don't ask me.

GROUP: I don't know.

OLD SAM: Fannie grew up and met and married Morris—

OLD ROSE: Not Sam's brother Morris.

GROUP: Another Morris.

OLD SAM: Fannie grew up and met and married Morris—who was handsome and a bolter. Rose was born.

GROUP: Rose

OLD SAM: and Morris bolted. He came back. Fannie loved him. Pauline was born.

GROUP: Pauline

OLD SAM: and Morris bolted. He came back. Fannie loved him. Don't ask me. I don't know. Yetta was born.

GROUP: Yetta

OLD SAM: and Morris bolted. Irene was born.

GROUP: Irene

OLD SAM: and Morris bolted, Ruth was born.

GROUP: Ruth

OLD SAM: and Morris—you know, don't ask me, I don't know. At last Alfred the son was born,

GROUP: Alfred the son.

OLD SAM: Morris bolted and Fannie finally bolted the barn door.

OLD ROSE: Now Sam and his brother get bounced in and out of foster homes. Sam's mother marries another guy and can't tell his family that she already has three kids—

GROUP: I don't know why

OLD ROSE: —and has two kids with him. Sam's father marries a woman with three or four grown children of her own. Sam comes home from the orphanage.

OLD SAM: Fannie took in a boarder named Hymie, began making wigs for women in the kitchen, and raised her five daughters and her son alone. She sent her oldest girl Rose to college. Don't ask me how.

GROUP: I don't know.

OLD SAM: Rose was invited to a party in Brooklyn. Fannie didn't want her to go.

ALL WOMEN: Don't go.

OLD SAM: Rose who usually obeyed borrowed a black dress with beads on the sleeves from Pauline

YOUNG ROSE: Pauline, could I borrow your black dress

ACTOR (PAULINE): With beads on the sleeves?

OLD SAM: and went to the party . . .

ACTOR (PAULINE): Rosie,

ALL WOMEN: Rosie, take off your glasses.

(*Music stops.* ROSE *removes glasses.*)

OLD SAM: where she met me.

GROUP: Sam.

OLD ROSE: Not my mother's brother Sam.

GROUP: Another Sam.

(*Music starts.*)

OLD ROSE: He starts smoking at the age of nine (*all cough*), quits school at thirteen to get a job.

YOUNG SAM: I have to get a job.

OLD ROSE: joins the Marines at seventeen by asking a stranger in the street to pretend to be his father and sign for him.

YOUNG SAM: Will you pretend to be my father and sign for me?

ACTOR (STRANGER): Yes, I will.

OLD ROSE: Has teeth pulled, gets malaria, learns to speak Spanish

YOUNG SAM: Sí.

OLD ROSE: and is in an earthquake in Managua, Nicaragua, by the time he's twenty-one.

OLD SAM: I was in Marine uniform. I didn't own a suit.

GROUP: No suit.

OLD SAM: Later she bought that dress from Pauline—

OLD ROSE: I did buy that dress from Pauline.

OLD SAM: —and kept it for forty years.

GROUP: Forty years

(*Music stops.*)

OLD ROSE: Then on leave, at a party in Brooklyn, Sam meets me. Is this the exact truth?

(*Music starts.*)

OLD SAM: Don't ask me.

ALL: I don't know.

(*Music stops.*)

DUCHAMP: Let's talk about the mysterious act of making art. Can there be a mysterious act—a mysterious action? What do I mean by action? Do I mean doing? Isn't action doing? But by the time I'm doing, by the time I'm doing, by that time there is no question.

DETECTIVE: I thought mystery implied question. (*To audience:*) I thought mystery implied question.

ANGER I: Who says you know what you're doing?

DETECTIVE: And when.

YOUNG ARTIST (*accompanied by* DUCHAMP): Exactly. One mystery in making art is when will you know what you're doing.

DETECTIVE: Do we know what we're doing now?

ANGER I: I sure as hell don't.

DETECTIVE: Then are you making art?

ACTOR (CRITIC): Okay, not knowing what you're doing is not necessarily making art.

DUCHAMP: Unless, perhaps, if you're an artist.

ACTOR (CRITIC): You mean anytime an artist doesn't know what he's doing he's making art?

ANGER II: You mean anytime an artist knows what he's doing he's not making art?

ANGER I: Is knowing that something is or isn't art itself

ANGERS: a mystery?

DETECTIVE: To the viewer?

ANGERS: To the artist?

DUCHAMP: I made this thing the other day. (*Points to chair.*) I think it's art.

ACTOR (CRITIC): Looks like a chair to me.

YOUNG ARTIST: How about now? (*Frames chair.*)

ACTOR (CRITIC): Looks more like art. Wait a minute. Wait one damn minute.

(YOUNG ARTIST *knocks on door.*)

MR. HIM (*offstage*): Hon, can you get that? I'm on the toilet.

YOUNG ARTIST (*as* ANGER *opens door*): Right. The old "art has no function" routine.

ACTOR (CRITIC): Or is it doing

GROUP: something to something?

ACTOR (CRITIC): He did do something.

DETECTIVE: To the chair. Doing something to the chair.

ACTOR (CRITIC): What about *not* doing?

ANGERS: What *about* not doing?

ACTOR (CRITIC): What about him? What about the toilet bowl? What about not doing something to an ordinary toilet bowl?

YOUNG ARTIST: Duchamp did do something to that damn bowl. He took it out of the toilet.

DETECTIVE: But that's a different mystery.

ANGERS: You mean about plumbing?

DETECTIVE: No, the mystery of how he thought to do it.

ANGERS: To me it's plumbing.

ACTOR (CRITIC): Can the artist—

DETECTIVE: an artist—

ACTOR (CRITIC): because he's—

DETECTIVE: an artist

ANGERS: Or maybe it's water pressure.

ACTOR (CRITIC): point a finger

DETECTIVE: at some damn thing

ACTOR (CRITIC): While you and your upstairs neighbor

DETECTIVE: can't simultaneously flush

ACTOR (CRITIC): and call it art?

ANGERS: You can take a simultaneous shit

ACTOR (CRITIC) AND DETECTIVE: but you can't simultaneously flush.

ANGERS: I call that a mystery.

DETECTIVE: Well, he can call any damn thing any damn thing he wants. (*To* DUCHAMP:) What strikes me is your need for freedom, your taste for distance, for distance not only from movements, styles, and ideas, but also from artists themselves. Nevertheless, you were always acquainted with these movements, and didn't hesitate to borrow. What exactly prompted you?

DUCHAMP: An extraordinary curiosity. (*Exits.*)

(*Music starts.* YOUNG ROSE *and* YOUNG SAM *move through the scene in silence, framing their old selves as they speak.*)

OLD SAM: My name's Sam. I don't know too many people here.

OLD ROSE: I only know that girl, near the window, I came with her.

OLD SAM: You work together?

OLD ROSE: No, we go to school. We're in the same English class. She's my best friend.

OLD SAM: In high school?

OLD ROSE: No, in college. We go to college.

OLD SAM: Oh—no kidding. You don't look like—

OLD ROSE: I took off—I'm not wearing my glasses.

OLD SAM: You wear glasses.

OLD ROSE: Men don't make passes—my sister told me

OLD SAM: at girls who wear

OLD ROSE: glasses—that's what my sister said.

OLD SAM: Is your sister older? She gives advice—

OLD ROSE: No, I'm the oldest—sister. She's the one after me.

OLD SAM: Are there more? Sisters?

OLD ROSE: Yeah. I have four sisters. You? Do you have—

OLD SAM: I have one sister—and a brother.

OLD ROSE: I have a brother too. He's the youngest.

OLD SAM: I'm on leave. I only have about a week.

OLD ROSE: From the army?

OLD SAM: The army? Uh uh! This is Marine blues. I'm a Marine.

OLD ROSE: Oh, I'm sorry. I don't know about—uniforms.

OLD SAM: Say—you didn't tell me your name.

OLD ROSE: Oh, I'm sorry. Rose, I'm—Rose.

OLD SAM: I bet you forgot—

OLD ROSE: No I didn't. You're Sam.

(YOUNG ROSE *and* YOUNG SAM *go to Fanny's house.*)

YOUNG ROSE (*coming through the door*)**:** Mama, Mama.

(*Music stops.*)

I met somebody. I met a man, Mama.

FANNY: You see, what did I tell you? I told her. I told her not to go. I told her not to go to that party. I said "Rosie, don't go." But does she listen? No.

YOUNG ROSE: Mama—

FANNY: Does she listen? Ohhhh no. Not her. Not her. And now what? Now she meets a man.

YOUNG ROSE: Mama, he's coming over. He wants to meet you.

FANNY: Pooh pooh pooh. He's coming over. Do you hear this? He wants to meet me. He's coming over to meet me. Who says I want to meet him? Who wants to meet a man from a party? What kind of a prize can you meet at a party? What decent girl meets a man at a—

YOUNG ROSE: Mama, be nice. Please. His name is Sam. I—

FANNY: Sam.

YOUNG ROSE: I like him Mama.

FANNY: She likes him. Pooh pooh pooh. How does she know what she likes? What does a young girl know? One minute she likes some bum—the next minute she's raising six children all alone.

YOUNG ROSE: Mama, he's here. Please be nice, Mama, please. Come on in Sam. Mama this is Sam.

YOUNG SAM: How do you d—

FANNY: Oh my God. Oh my God. A uniform. It's a uniform. What is that uniform? He's a sailor. She brings me home a sailor.

YOUNG SAM: No Mama, I'm a Marine. These are Marine blu—

FANNY: He's a Marine. Pooh pooh pooh. Do you hear this? A big shot. A Marine. A Marine, a sailor—it's the same. It's the same thing. It's a uniform. He looks like Western Union.

YOUNG ROSE: Mama. Isn't it funny? Sam's father only lives two blocks from here and we had to meet in Brooklyn. Isn't that funny Mama?

FANNY: A riot.

YOUNG SAM: I'd like permission to call on your daughter . . . on Rose . . . with your . . . if you don't mind . . . Mama.

FANNY: He wants my permission. If I don't mind. He's here already and now he wants my permission. When?

YOUNG SAM: Well, I have ten days leave left—

FANNY: So, when?

YOUNG SAM: I'd like to come by . . . every day, Mama, if you don't . . . with your . . .

YOUNG ROSE: Please Mama, I want him to come.

FANNY (*pausing*): Okay, Western Union. Okay. But he better not leave me any surprise packages.

YOUNG ROSE: Oh Mama. He's good, Mama. Sammie, come and meet my sisters and my baby brother.

(*Music starts.* YOUNG ROSE *and* YOUNG SAM *take a stroll.* OLD ROSE *and* OLD SAM *pass them, sometimes framing them. Fanny's house disappears and comes back. Music stops.*)

YOUNG SAM: Rose, I know we've only known each other a week—but I wish you'd write to me—when I go back to Nicaragua.

YOUNG ROSE: Oh I will. I'd really like to.

YOUNG SAM: I don't have much longer to serve—and now—and now that I've—met you

YOUNG ROSE: How much longer—before—you come back?

YOUNG SAM: About a year.

YOUNG ROSE: Oh. That's long. That seems very—long—to me.

YOUNG SAM: But now that I met you and—your family.

YOUNG ROSE: I'd like to meet your family.

YOUNG SAM: You will, really, when I get back.

YOUNG ROSE: I'll—miss you.

YOUNG SAM: When I get back I'll get a job—I'll miss you too. I'll send you money—to save—for a ring. I'll really miss you Rose.

(*Music starts.* YOUNG ROSE *meets* YOUNG SAM *at the altar.* ACTOR *marries them.* OLD ROSE *and* OLD SAM *watch.* DETECTIVE *puts veil on* YOUNG ROSE *and holds her train.* YOUNG ARTIST *helps set up altar. Music stops.*)

YOUNG ROSE: I love you Sam. I hope you won't disappear like my father.

YOUNG SAM: I love you Rose. I hope you won't disappear like my mother.

(*Wedding music starts. All the following actions are framed at various times by* OLD ROSE *and* OLD SAM, *the* ANGERS, *or* YOUNG ARTIST. *Wedding picture:* OLD ROSE *and* OLD SAM *frame* YOUNG ROSE *and* YOUNG SAM, FANNY, *and* DETECTIVE. YOUNG ROSE *and* YOUNG SAM *waltz.* YOUNG ROSE *and* YOUNG SAM *go to bed; Rose's veil becomes their blanket.* YOUNG ROSE *and* YOUNG SAM *set up house. Veil becomes a tablecloth.* DETECTIVE *rolls up veil, hands it to* YOUNG SAM, *who hands it to* YOUNG ROSE, *who stuffs it under her dress.* YOUNG ROSE *is pregnant.*)

YOUNG ROSE: Sam, Sammie—I'm scared, I'm really scared. I hope I'm going to be a good mother.

YOUNG SAM: You will, Rosie, I'm sure you will. And I'm going to be a good father. I'm going to get another job. With two jobs I'll be able to make more—money. Our son will have everything. Everything. Everything—we didn't have!

(*As* OLD SAM *speaks,* YOUNG ROSE *turns upstage, takes "baby" out from under her dress, turns around holding it, gives "baby" to* FANNY. FANNY *and* YOUNG ROSE *exit, leaving* OLD ROSE, YOUNG SAM, *and* DETECTIVE *to watch* OLD SAM.)

OLD SAM:

> This was the man I was.
> And that was the plan I had.

I was strong then.
The child survived
and hid his fears
and hid his needs
and hid his sadness.
You know,
I think sometimes, if I had the chance,
I could have played the violin.
That's right, the violin.
That would have been my—instrument.
The sad sound of the violin.
But—I had no chance for that.
I . . . donned my . . .
(*Aside.*) That's a good word—right? . . .
I "donned" my manly—image
like my Marine uniform
like the "Blues."
And I became the man I needed to be.
I became the man
who could bite the world's head off
before the world could bite me—
anymore.
And I planned the family I never had.
I planned to give my child
the family I dreamed of
and then—GODDAMN!
I didn't know how to do it.
What did I know about being a father?
What did I know about—family?
What did I know
except what I knew.
So I did what I did best.
I worked my goddamn ass off
so that they would never want.
That was what I knew how to give.

And I gave it all.
That counts!

(*Music ends.*)

I gave it all.
That counts—doesn't it?

(OLD ROSE *comes and helps him offstage.*)

PART II

Music starts.

DETECTIVE: Mr. and Mrs. X have been married for more than fifty years.

ANGER I: What is it that keeps two people together?

ACTOR: Is that a trick question, like how fast is the train going if the engineer is named—Morris?

YOUNG SAM: Not Rose's father Morris.

YOUNG ROSE: Not Sam's brother Morris.

GROUP: Another (*singing*) Morris.

DUCHAMP: When you make a painting, even abstract, there is always a sort of necessary filling in. I wondered why. I always asked myself "why" a lot. And from that questioning came doubt, doubt of everything.

GROUP: What is Art?

DETECTIVE: What is Art?

DUCHAMP: What is What?

YOUNG ARTIST: What is Is?

MR. HIM: What did I do?

MRS. HIM (*speaking*): What do I do?

(*Singing.*) I buy shoes, lots of shoes.
> I buy them loose, I like them loose.
> I like the ease of soft, loose shoes.
> I buy blacks and browns and blues.
> I spend some time before I choose.
> Then when I think the shoes are right
> Not too loose, not too tight.
> Not too dowdy, not too bright.
> Not too heavy, not too light.
> Not too flat, not too high.
> I spend time and then I buy.
> I spend big bucks when I buy.

(*Spoken over music.*) When I buy shoes.

ANGERS: Lots of shoes.

MRS. HIM: I buy them loose.

ANGERS: But not too loose.

MRS. HIM: I like the ease of soft, loose shoes. I buy grays.

ANGERS: and greens

MRS. HIM: and blues.

ANGERS: Then when she thinks the shoes are right

MRS. HIM: Only when I think they're right
> When I'm certain I have no doubt

ANGERS: She takes them home and she takes them out.

MRS. HIM (*singing*):

> I take them home and I take them out.
> But they're not the same at second sight
> They're much too loose or just too tight.
> They're too dowdy or too bright.
> They're much too heavy or too light.
> The heel's too flat, the vamp's too high.

The damned waxed laces won't stay tied.
The left shoe pinches, the right one squeaks.
The rubber sole sticks, the inner sole slides.

(*Spoken over music.*) I can't imagine how I got these shoes.
I can't imagine who chose these shoes.
Whose were the feet that tried these shoes?
Who was the woman who bought these shoes?
They're royal blue, I hate royal blue.
I have nothing to wear with royal blue.
Who was the woman who bought these shoes?
Who wrote that check, who signed that bill?
Who was the woman who took these home?
These shoes are snake, I don't wear snake.
Who was that woman seduced by a snake?
It wasn't me, I swear it wasn't me.
Who was the woman who bought these shoes?
Who was that woman, it wasn't me?
I swear, I swear it wasn't—
(*Music stops.*)

MR. HIM: Hi hon I'm home.

(MRS. HIM *storms out.* YOUNG ARTIST *facilitates and imitates Duchamp's actions.* ANGERS *manipulate* MR. HIM *as in bed scene.* MR. HIM *and* DUCHAMP *carry scripts as in Detective's first scene.*)

This is what happened. First nobody liked me or they weren't interested in me or they didn't know I existed.

DUCHAMP: Nobody?

MR. HIM: Almost nobody. A few choice persons.

DUCHAMP: A few choice persons liked you?

MR. HIM: Yes, very few.

DUCHAMP: Very choice?

MR. HIM: Actually, yes, pretty choice.

DUCHAMP: That doesn't sound bad.

MR. HIM: It wasn't bad. I didn't say it was bad. I'm not talking about good or bad. I'm not even talking about me. I'm talking about circumstances.

DUCHAMP: I'm sorry, okay, go on, go ahead.

MR. HIM: Okay, okay, where . . . okay, where was I?

DUCHAMP: Choice persons.

MR. HIM: Oh yes. Well, they thought I had a broader appeal.

DUCHAMP: Who did?

MR. HIM: The few persons who knew about me thought other people would be interested if *they* knew about me and that I had a broader appeal.

DUCHAMP: What does that mean?

MR. HIM: A broader appeal?

DUCHAMP: Yes, appeal to more people?

MR. HIM: Yes, if they knew about me.

DUCHAMP: Did you want that? To appeal to more people?

MR. HIM: I don't know. If you do something you want someone to know about it.

DUCHAMP: Or not.

MR. HIM: Why not?

DUCHAMP: If it's private, your secret.

MR. HIM: It's not about me. It's about what I do. Or what someone does. It's about reputation.

DUCHAMP: You want more people to know your reputation.

MR. HIM: No, to know what I do. To know what I have a reputation for doing.

DUCHAMP: You want more people to know what you do?

MR. HIM: I don't know. A few people said more people would be interested in what I do if they knew about it.

DUCHAMP: And you wanted that.

MR. HIM: I must have. I didn't say no.

DUCHAMP: Unless you would like to think of yourself as the victim of a few choice persons.

MR. HIM: No, I think they were thinking of my good.

DUCHAMP: Or the good of what you do? Or their own good? Or the good of more people?

MR. HIM: Or something, I don't know, I didn't say no. I know that. I said it wouldn't work but that was to protect myself if it didn't work.

DUCHAMP: And this isn't about you.

MR. HIM: No, it could be about anyone. Substitute Trollope, Anthony Trollope.

DUCHAMP: Do you think people nowadays know Trollope?

MR. HIM: Okay, well then there the chosen few were wrong, right? More people didn't get interested or maybe

DUCHAMP: didn't stay interested. Is this—am I getting there? Is this still about broad appeal? About broader appeal? Is this about your broader appeal?

MR. HIM: No, No! It could be really about anyone, about any one. Substitute Queen—uh . . . substitute Queen—Elizabeth or the other Queen Elizabeth or Elizabeth—Taylor!

DUCHAMP: First nobody liked Elizabeth Taylor?

MR. HIM: Or Dustin Hoffman, try tiny Dustin Hoffman.

DUCHAMP: Or they weren't interested in Dustin—

Mr. Him: Hoffman, right—or Madonna.

Duchamp: Everyone was always interested in Madonna.

Mr. Him: No, no. We only knew when a few choice persons thought we would want to know.

Duchamp: Or when Madonna figured out that wearing her underwear on the outside would win—

Mr. Him: Which that French designer Gaultier figured out too—I mean—remember "I dreamed I was a something in my Maidenform."

Duchamp: Bra! Right, Madonna dreamed she was a rock star in her Maidenform bra! But this is all still about people, persons. Just substitute some name for your name and the game goes on.

Mr. Him: No, no. Try Nicaragua—go ahead—try!

Duchamp: First, nobody liked Nicaragua—

Mr. Him: Or were interested in it—try the homeless—try microwave ovens.

Duchamp: First, nobody liked microwave ovens.

Mr. Him: Or were interested in them.

Duchamp: Or they didn't really know they existed. And then a few

Mr. Him: Choice persons.

Duchamp: A few choice persons.

Mr. Him: Broader appeal, right.

Duchamp: I'm beginning to . . . is this like Adlai Stevenson?

Mr. Him: Well that's interesting isn't . . .? The chosen few were wrong twice! The better man didn't win. They couldn't make him president so they made him a myth.

Duchamp: Mithter Adlai Thteventhon. The mythtery of Mithter Thteventhon—wait—are you saying he wasn't great?

MR. HIM: No, I'm not, not at all. Great and popular are not the same—I mean it's great if you're both—but . . .

DUCHAMP: Maybe if Stevenson had worn his Jockey shorts outside his Brooks Brothers suit—right! (*He begins to leave, followed by* YOUNG ARTIST.)

MR. HIM: He did get some mileage on the hole in the sole of his shoe—that sounds like a song, doesn't it? . . . The hole in the sole—

ANGERS: There was a hole in the sole of Stevenson's shoe

MR. HIM AND ANGER I: which to his team made him seem just like me and you.

MR. HIM AND ANGER II: But he just couldn't generate enough romance.

ANGERS: Because he wore his shorts underneath his pants.

MR. HIM: Hon, where's my white shirt?

MRS. HIM (*entering*): I don't know, hon.

MR. HIM: Hon, I told you I needed my white shirt for Tuesday.

MRS. HIM: What's today, hon?

MR. HIM: It's Tuesday, hon.

MRS. HIM: Well don't get so excited, hon, what's wrong with your blue shirt? Hon?

MR. HIM: Hon, it's not white!

MRS. HIM: Well, hon, what's so important about white?

MR. HIM: Okay. Okay, hon, where's my blue shirt?

MRS. HIM: It's not there, hon?

MR. HIM: Hon! Where?

(*Music starts. Others return.*)

DETECTIVE: Mr. and Mrs. X have been married for more than fifty years. They loved each other at first sight. They courted, committed, engaged, married, became economically interdependent, relatively tolerant, and compromising.

YOUNG ARTIST: The mystery of compromise.

DUCHAMP: There's a difference, isn't there, between mystery and evasiveness, between mystery and ambiguity, between mystery and obscurity. There is a difference between what you intend and what you don't—intend and what you forgot to think about and what you never thought, never knew even—to think about.

YOUNG ARTIST: Half the mysteries in life could be cleared up if somebody would spill the beans.

MRS. HIM: You must stop calling me hon.

ANGERS: As if that's the problem.

MRS. HIM: You must never again call me hon.

MR. HIM: Whatever you say—dear.

ACTOR: I run the committee for keeping things a mystery! Unspill those beans.

MR. HIM: Dear—say you ever what.

MRS. HIM: Hon me call again never must you.

DUCHAMP, DETECTIVE, AND YOUNG ARTIST: Problem the that's if as.

MRS. HIM: Hon me calling stop must you.

GROUP: The mystery of words.

MR. HIM: Are you tired?

MRS. HIM: Tired's not the word.

MR. HIM: Are you hungry?

Mrs. Him: Hungry's not the word.

(*Entire company enters, talking as if in noisy restaurant.*)

Actor (Waiter): Would you like a beverage? I'm your waiter.

(*Group, including* Duchamp, *gathers upstage, watching.*)

Detective and Young Artist (*to* Waiter): We're waiting for a friend. (*Sees* Actor.) Hi, hiiii, We're over here. (*Music and talking upstage stops.*) I'm so glad we could get together.

Actor: Oh, I am too. (*Aside.*) Actually I'm not.

Detective and Young Artist: We've been wanting to hear about your new role.

Actor: And I'm longing to talk about it with you. (*Aside.*) Actually I'm not.

Detective and Young Artist: Acting must be so . . .

Actor (Waiter): Beverage?

Detective and Young Artist (*to* Waiter): No, thank you.

Detective and Young Artist (*to* Actor): Acting must be so fulfilling.

Actor: Yes, yes it is. (*Aside.*) I'm saying yes but I'm acting no. I'm acting as if acting isn't fulfilling. Actually I'm not.

Detective and Young Artist: I mean you play so many kinds of people and you're always so different.

Actor: How sweet and flattering of you to say so. (*Aside.*) I said that with a hint of irony in my voice as if I doubt their sincerity. (*To them:*) You're always so kind. (*Aside.*) And I'm doing that to protect myself in case they aren't sincere although I think they are. Actually I don't. (*To them:*) Acting is my life. Delving, revealing, reacting, and acting, acting, acting. (*Aside.*) Sometimes I don't know what the hell I'm talking about.

Actor (Waiter): Beverage?

DETECTIVE AND YOUNG ARTIST (*to* WAITER): No. Thank you.

ACTOR: One woman's honest search for theatrical reality. (*Aside.*) I'm acting sincere. (*To them:*) I'm sincere. (*Aside.*) I may, in fact, be sincere. Probably not.

DETECTIVE AND YOUNG ARTIST: Are there . . .

ACTOR: There are sometimes, *is,* sometimes, on stage, moments, *a* moment, when you know, you suddenly know. (*Aside.*) You know sometimes I lie and call it acting. (*To them:*) You suddenly know who you are. (*Aside.*) I'm acting like I really want to believe this. (*To them:*) Or if not, if you don't know *who* you are, you know *that* you are. (*Aside.*) I'm acting like this could be true (*to them:*) and acting becomes action and you— (*Aside.*) No, not them, me, me and I, I am entire and consumed, entirely consumed. (*All enter.*)

GROUP: Marcel Duchamp

YOUNG ARTIST (*to* DUCHAMP): I have the impression that every time you commit yourself to a position you undercut it by irony or sarcasm.

(*Music starts.*)

DUCHAMP: You're right. Because I don't believe in positions.

DETECTIVE AND YOUNG ARTIST: What do you believe in?

DUCHAMP: Nothing. The word belief doesn't mean anything. It's like the word judgment. I hope there won't be words like that on the moon.

GROUP: But you believe in yourself.

DUCHAMP (*shaking head*): No.

DETECTIVE AND YOUNG ARTIST: Not even that.

DUCHAMP: I don't believe in the word being.

GROUP: But you like words so much.

DUCHAMP: I like poetic words.

DETECTIVE AND YOUNG ARTIST: "Being" is very poetic.

DUCHAMP: No, not at all. Being is an idea.

YOUNG ARTIST: What is the most poetic word?

(*Music stops. Pause.*)

DUCHAMP: Maybe "backward."

(*Music starts.* OLD ROSE *and* OLD SAM *return. An* ANGER *brings on a table. They sit down to dinner.*)

DETECTIVE: Mr. and Mrs. X have been married for more than fifty years. They loved each other at first sight. They courted, committed, engaged, married, became economically interdependent, relatively tolerant, and compromising. They had one child. The mystery of being the only, the oldest

(*Repeated material is said slightly faster each time, slowing down for new information.*)

OLD ROSE: of being everything to them

OLD SAM: to them, everything

OLD ROSE: everything.

DETECTIVE: Mr. and Mrs. X had one child.

(*Music stops.*)

OLD ROSE: Mr. X went *out* to work.

OLD SAM: Mrs. X stayed home with the baby. How much did we pay that doctor?

OLD ROSE: What?

OLD SAM (*to* CHILD): She doesn't listen. (*To* OLD ROSE:) The doctor. The baby doctor. How much did we pay the doctor?

OLD ROSE: I don't remember. (*To* DETECTIVE:) Who can remember?

OLD SAM: We paid him. We paid him plenty. And the hospital. The private hospital. (*To* DETECTIVE:) We paid plenty.

OLD ROSE: And then my water broke.

OLD SAM: Your water broke. (*To* DETECTIVE:) It's true. Her water broke.

OLD ROSE: In the middle of the night.

OLD SAM: We had to get the police.

OLD ROSE: We couldn't get the doctor.

OLD SAM (*to* DETECTIVE): How could we get the doctor?

OLD ROSE (*to* DETECTIVE): Who knew where to get the doctor?

OLD SAM (*to* OLD ROSE): It was the night. (*To* DETECTIVE:) It was the middle of the night.

OLD ROSE (*to* DETECTIVE): The middle of the night—it's true!

OLD SAM: So we got the cops.

OLD ROSE: We were scared.

OLD SAM: Sure we were scared. They tied you—remember?

OLD ROSE (*to* DETECTIVE): To a stretcher. (*To* OLD SAM:) You remember?

OLD SAM: Sure I remember. (*To* DETECTIVE:) How could I forget? (*To* OLD ROSE:) They had to get you down three flights of stairs.

OLD ROSE (*to* OLD SAM): Over the banisters. (*To* DETECTIVE:) That's the truth.

OLD SAM: From one to the other. That was something. Those cops.

OLD ROSE: That was something.

OLD SAM: How could I forget? (*To* DETECTIVE:) You can't forget a thing like that.

OLD ROSE: She was almost ten pounds. (*To* DETECTIVE:) You were almost ten pounds.

OLD SAM: She was something. She was one big baby.

ALL MEN: The mystery of babies. (ACTOR *makes baby sound punctuating scene and underscoring key lines.*)

ALL MEN: The mystery of babies.

YOUNG SAM: Of having babies.

OLD SAM: The mystery of *a* baby

YOUNG SAM: of having

OLD SAM: of wanting

YOUNG SAM: of wanting to have

ALL MEN: a baby (*baby sound*)

ANGER I: the mystery of wanting to have a baby,

YOUNG ARTIST: a tiny

ANGER I: dependent

YOUNG ARTIST: a very tiny

ANGER I: very dependent

YOUNG SAM: iddy biddy

OLD SAM: widdoo, widdoo

ALL MEN: baby. (*Baby sound.*)

OLD SAM: The mystery

MR. HIM: of wanting to *have* one

OLD SAM: of wanting to *own* one

MR. HIM: of wanting to have one's *own*

ALL MEN: baby. (*Baby sound.*)

YOUNG SAM: I want to have a baby.

ALL MEN: Why?

YOUNG SAM: I want to hold it in my arms.

ANGER I: Here, hold mine.

YOUNG SAM: I want to *have* one, one baby.

ANGER I: Here, have *this* one. This *extra* one.

YOUNG SAM: No, I want to have my own.

ALL MEN: Why?

YOUNG SAM: To be like me.

OLD SAM: To look like you.

YOUNG SAM: Yes, yes, I want a baby.

(ACTOR *goes out.*)

OLD SAM: To look like you.

YOUNG SAM: Yes, yes, I want to look

OLD SAM: at that baby

YOUNG SAM: and see

ALL MEN: yourself.

MR. HIM: Yes, and my mother

ALL MEN: father.

MR. HIM: Yes, yes, and my mother's mother

ALL MEN: father's father.

MR. HIM: Yes, yes, yes, I want my baby to be

ACTOR (DOCTOR) (*coming back on, holding veil as baby*): your history

ALL MEN: Ohhhhhh.

MR. HIM: My history, yes.

ACTOR (DOCTOR): Your history and

MR. HIM: yes my history and

ACTOR (DOCTOR): your legacy.

MRS. HIM (*entering*): Yes, *my* legacy, *my* history and *my* legacy.

MR. HIM: Okay ho—

ALL MEN: *Dear.*

MR. HIM: Whatever you want.

ACTOR (DOCTOR): Here's your baby.

MRS. HIM: *My* baby.

ACTOR (DOCTOR): He's going to grow up (*Exits.*)

MRS. HIM: *Oh*—not too fast I hope.

GROUP: to be an artist.

MR. AND MRS. HIM: *Oh*—there must be some mistake.

(*Baby sound. All exit.* DUCHAMP *and* DETECTIVE *enter.* YOUNG ARTIST *follows* DUCHAMP.)

DETECTIVE: Mr. and Mrs. X have been married for more than fifty years. They loved each other at first sight. They courted, committed, engaged, married, became economically interdependent, relatively tolerant, and compromising. They had one child. Mr. X went *out* to work. Mrs. X stayed home. For thirty-five of their more than fifty years together, Mr. X left for work before six in the morning and never came home before eight at night, six days a week. On the seventh day, like God, he rested. (*To* DUCHAMP:) When did you make the decision to stop painting?

DUCHAMP: I never made it. It came by itself.

DETECTIVE: And you never had the longing to paint since then?

DUCHAMP: No.

DETECTIVE: You never touched a brush or a pencil?

DUCHAMP: No. I think a painting dies, you see. After forty or fifty years a picture dies. Sculpture dies.

GROUP: We don't believe that.

DUCHAMP: No one believes this, but I don't mind. I think a picture dies after a few years like the man

DETECTIVE: or woman

DUCHAMP: or woman who painted it. Afterwards it's called the history of art. And the history of art is what remains of a time in a museum. But it's not necessarily the best of that time.

DETECTIVE: So you stopped. (*Music stops.*) You took a walk. You disappeared. (DUCHAMP *and* YOUNG ARTIST *exit.*) The mystery of the disappearing Dada.

GROUP (*offstage*): Daddy.

DETECTIVE: Mom, where's Daddy?

YOUNG ROSE (*offstage*): Working.

DETECTIVE: Mom, where's Daddy?

YOUNG ROSE (*offstage*): Resting.

DETECTIVE: Six days a week she kept house and cared for the kid and on the seventh day she kept the house quiet and the kid quiet so God could rest. What did she do for fun? Did she have fun? (*All enter.*)

GROUP: The mystery of shopping for fun.

(*Music starts.*)

ACTOR (SALESPERSON): If I can help. If I can help. If I can be of any help.

YOUNG SAM AND YOUNG ROSE: Just looking.

OLD SAM AND OLD ROSE: Just looking.

DETECTIVE AND FANNY: Just looking.

MR. AND MRS. HIM: I'm just looking.

ALL: We're just looking.

ACTOR (SALESPERSON): Are you looking for anything special? Anything special? Anything in particular?

YOUNG SAM AND YOUNG ROSE: No, just looking.

OLD SAM AND OLD ROSE: No, no, just looking.

DETECTIVE AND FANNY: No, no, no, just looking.

MR. AND MRS. HIM: No, no, no, no, I'm just looking.

ALL: No, no, no, no, no, we're just looking.

ACTOR (SALESPERSON): Well, if I can direct you. If I can direct you. May I direct you?

YOUNG SAM AND YOUNG ROSE: No directing.

OLD SAM AND OLD ROSE: No, no directing.

DETECTIVE AND FANNY: No, no, no directing.

MR. AND MRS. HIM: No, no, no, no directing.

YOUNG SAM AND YOUNG ROSE: No.

OLD SAM AND OLD ROSE: No.

DETECTIVE AND FANNY: No.

MR. AND MRS. HIM: No.

ALL: No thank you, no directing, no direction.

YOUNG SAM AND YOUNG ROSE: Just looking.

OLD SAM AND OLD ROSE: Just looking.

DETECTIVE AND FANNY: Just looking.

MR. AND MRS. HIM: I'm just looking.

ALL: We're just looking.

ACTOR (SALESPERSON): Oh. Oh well. Did you have something in mind? Something in mind? Did you have anything—at all—in mind?

(YOUNG SAM *and* YOUNG ROSE *begin a round;* OLD SAM *and* OLD ROSE, DETECTIVE *and* FANNY, *and* MR. *and* MRS. HIM *enter in, in turn, at "no mind."*)

YOUNG SAM AND YOUNG ROSE: No, no, nothing in mind, nothing in mind, no mind, no mind, never mind, never mind, just looking.

OLD SAM AND OLD ROSE: No, no, nothing in mind, nothing in mind, no mind, no mind, never mind, never mind, just looking.

DETECTIVE AND FANNY: No, no, nothing in mind, nothing in mind, no mind, no mind, never mind, never mind, just looking.

MR. AND MRS. HIM: No, no, nothing in mind, nothing in mind, no mind, no mind, never mind, never mind, just looking.

ALL: We're just looking.

(*Music stops.*)

ACTOR (SALESPERSON): Well, if you see anything you think is fun I'm Miss Something.

(*Everyone starts to exit.*)

MRS. HIM: Oh—actually—I *do* need something for my husband. (*Music starts.*) A white shirt. (MR. *and* MRS. HIM *reenter with* ANGERS.)

ANGERS: So here we are,

MRS. HIM: we are so far,

MR. HIM: we are so far.

MRS. HIM: I think I'll change.

ANGERS: She'll change her life.

MRS. HIM: I'll be his good wife.

ANGERS: Good grief.

MR. HIM: The problem's solved.

ANGER I: He thinks he's saved.

ANGER II: Now she'll be well behaved,

MRS. HIM: I will be well behaved

ANGERS: Uh oh!

ANGER I: Here's the ointment.

MR. AND MRS. HIM: Where's the ointment?

ANGERS: Here's the fly,

ANGER I: Unless she learns

ANGER II: that who she is

ANGERS: is who she is.

ANGER I: Unless he learns

ANGER II: that what he does

ANGERS: is what he does.

MR. HIM: That what I do, I do.

MRS. HIM: That who I am, I am.

ANGER I: And greets his anger.

ANGER II: Greets her anger.

MRS. HIM: With a grin.

ANGERS: And learns to love.

MRS. HIM: To love.

MR. HIM: To love.

MRS. HIM: Unless I learn to love

ALL: to love the question (*singing*) "Why?"

MR. HIM: Why?

ANGERS: And learns to live.

MRS. HIM: To live.

MR. HIM: To live.

MRS. HIM: I just have to learn to live.

ANGERS: To live unfearfully with doubt and give up envy.

MRS. HIM: Why are other people so happy?

MR. HIM: So famous.

ANGERS: Give it up.

MR. AND MRS. HIM: Oh, I'm so happy for them.

ANGERS: And give up envy to care for other people's Art.

ANGER I: Unless she learns,

MRS. HIM: I'm learning.

ANGER II: He learns,

ANGERS: They learn,

MR. AND MRS. HIM: Our grapes are sour.

ANGERS: They'll not have power.

MRS. HIM: No power.

MR. HIM: No power.

ANGERS: They'll never have power.

(*Music stops.*)

MR. AND MRS. HIM: No power, no power.

ANGERS: They'll never have power.

(*All exit. Music starts.*)

DETECTIVE (*entering*): Mr. and Mrs. X have been married for more than fifty years. They loved each other at first sight. They courted, committed, engaged, married, became economically interdependent, relatively tolerant, and compromising. They had one child. Mr. X went *out* to work. Mrs. X stayed home. For thirty-five of their more than fifty years together, Mr. X left for work before six in the morning and never came home before eight at night, six days a week. On the seventh day, like God, he rested. Six days a week she kept house and cared for the kid and on the seventh day she kept the house quiet and the kid quiet so God could rest. Then things changed. Fanny, who always lived next door, died. It's time now to talk about Fanny.

OLD SAM: About how she was the center of it all.

DETECTIVE: And is.

OLD ROSE: And is still somehow in the center.

DETECTIVE: About being haunted. About being haunted by Fannie's last days.

(*Music stops.*)

OLD ROSE: Doctor, there's something wrong with my mother. She says sometimes time passes and she can't remember.

ACTOR (DOCTOR): Well dear, those are little strokes.

FANNY: That's really what the doctor said. "Little strokes." It don't sound so bad. Big sounds bad.

OLD ROSE: Will it get worse?

ACTOR (DOCTOR): Well dear, you never know.

FANNY: That's what the doctor really said. "You never know." It didn't sound so bad. At least fifty-fifty.

ACTOR (DOCTOR): It's in God's hands, dear. (*Exits.*)

FANNY: That doctor really said that. "God's hands." I shoulda known I was in big trouble. Goddammit, if it's in God's hands, why am I paying so much to this doctor?

DETECTIVE: Did the doctor say what to do about it?

OLD ROSE: The doctor gave her something. A pill, more pills.

FANNY: I remember. That stupid gave me more pills.

DETECTIVE: Did you take them?

FANNY: Sometimes I took them. Sometimes I forgot. Maybe I was having a little stroke.

DETECTIVE: When did Fanny start dying? Was it then? Those little disappearances. Little deaths. Where did you go?

FANNY: Don't ask stupid questions Detective Big Shot. If I went someplace good I woulda sent you a post card.

OLD ROSE: All right. It's supper time. Come to the table.

OLD SAM: I don't remember where I sat.

OLD ROSE: At the head of the table where you always sit.

FANNY: Wait a minute, I remember this. It was Sunday and the day kept going away and coming back.

OLD ROSE: Mama, please eat something. But watch out for the bones.

FANNY: I said to somebody—to who?—I said, "Why is this happening to me?"

DETECTIVE: You said it to me.

FANNY: And did you have an answer Miss Big Shot Detective?

Old Rose: C'mon. Before everything gets cold. I made everybody's favorite.

Detective: I'll have some of that. Not too much please.

Old Sam: Try some of this.

Old Rose: Here try this.

Detective: Just not too much please.

Old Sam: I hope you didn't come to not eat.

Old Rose: Leave her alone, maybe she's on a diet. Look in your own plate.

Detective: This is when everybody stopped talking.

Old Rose: We saw what she was doing.

Detective: You kept putting food in your mouth. You didn't chew. Just more food. And then more. And then more. Why? Why did you do that?

Fanny: What do I know? I think I sat down—I know I sat down and the day went away, and went away, and went and went. I know I wasn't so hungry for your mother's cooking.

Old Rose: Mama, be nice.

Fanny: The day went and went, and finally went and never came back.

Old Rose: I pulled the food out of your mouth. I put my fingers in your mouth to pull out the food.

Fanny: And you pulled out my teeth. In front of everybody. And you slapped me in the face—don't think I forgot that.

Detective: I held you in my arms and I tried to keep you from falling off the chair. You were looking into my eyes. You were looking right into my eyes and I told you not to be scared. I told you everything would be all right.

FANNY: That shows how much you know. Maybe *you* should be a doctor. Wait a minute—who called the police?

OLD SAM: I did. I called emergency.

FANNY: What for? What did you have to do that for? You couldn't drive me?

OLD ROSE: Mama, we were scared. We didn't know what happened. We didn't know.

FANNY: Yeah, I know. But that's when I started to get mad. Everywhere was strangers. I had so many daughters but they left me with strangers. That made me really mad.

DETECTIVE: C'mon, you were always mad. You had a hard life and you married the wrong man and you were an angry woman.

FANNY: So now you're a *head* doctor, Lady Big Shot. If you're so smart why didn't you fix me up instead of sitting and yelling stories from the newspaper at me.

DETECTIVE: You knew. Goddammit you knew I was there.

OLD ROSE: Watch your language. You're talking to your grandmother.

DETECTIVE: You knew I was there in the nursing home. In that damned yellow room. I was trying to get through to you. I didn't know if you could hear me.

FANNY: They could hear you in Poughkeepsie. Just because I couldn't talk back didn't mean I was all of a sudden deaf.

OLD ROSE: Did you always know when we were there?

FANNY: How should I know? And if I didn't know, then how would I know? Anyway, sometimes I was visiting with my mother, or with Ida. I even saw my old friend Mary. Rosie, you remember Mary. She didn't look too bad.

OLD ROSE: But Mama, they were dead.

FANNY: So, what was I? You call that living? And besides, ain't you here with me right now?

DETECTIVE: Fanny spent two years in that nursing home.

FANNY: "Spent" is a good word Big Shot. All the money it took my whole life to save got "spent." All the time I had left got "spent." I spent it till I used it up.

(DOCTOR *enters.*)

OLD ROSE: Doctor, there's something wrong with my mother. She's having trouble breathing.

ACTOR (DOCTOR): Well dear, she has pneumonia.

OLD ROSE: Will it go away?

ACTOR (DOCTOR): Well dear, you never know.

OLD ROSE: Will she live?

ACTOR (DOCTOR): It's in God's hands dear. (*Exits.*)

FANNY: Goddamn, how much did you pay that idiot?

DETECTIVE: They moved Fanny from the nursing home to the hospital and her anger turned to fury.

FANNY: Why didn't you stop them? Why didn't one of you stop them? Why didn't someone stop them from putting all those tubes in me—in my arms—taped to my face—down my throat—why didn't you stop them when they tied me—when they tied me up?

OLD ROSE: Mama, you were tearing out the tubes. Mama, please, we didn't want you to go.

FANNY: So, you tried to tie me to the world.

DETECTIVE: We weren't smart. *I* wasn't smart.

FANNY: No my sweet child, you were not smart.

DETECTIVE: And Fanny died.

(Preparation for the funeral procession.)

FANNY: Now, I wanna know—how much did that coffin cost? And whose idea was it to put makeup on my face for the funeral and why did you let them put that goddamned ugly blouse on me?

(Music starts. Funeral procession begins. The entire company, led by OLD ROSE *and* OLD SAM, *who head slowly back toward their TV set.)*

DETECTIVE: Mr. and Mrs. X have been married for more than fifty years. They loved each other at first sight. They courted, committed, engaged, married, became economically interdependent, relatively tolerant, and compromising. They had one child. Mr. X went *out* to work. Mrs. X stayed home. For thirty-five of their more than fifty years together, Mr. X left for work before six in the morning and never came home before eight at night, six days a week. On the seventh day, like God, he rested. Six days a week she kept house and cared for the kid and on the seventh day she kept the house quiet and the kid quiet so God could rest. Then things changed. Fanny, who always lived next door, died. The only child grew up and moved out. They were sorry to see her go, but go she went, and Mr. X grew old, grew ill, retired, and moved in.

(OLD ROSE *and* OLD SAM, *who have previously always faced upstage when at TV set, now face audience.)*

OLD SAM: Rose, Rosie

GROUP: Wake up Rose

OLD SAM *(to self)*: I'm Sam, I am Sam. What's left of him, that's what I am. I was your man. I was *a* man. *(To* ROSE:) Rose, Rosie.

GROUP: Wake up, wake up Rose.

OLD ROSE: What? Sammie? Are you all right? Do you need something?

OLD SAM (*to self*): I'm Sam, I am Sam. God damn. I am a man. (*To* ROSE:) I love you, I love you Rosie.

GROUP: He still loves you Rosie.

OLD ROSE: What are you—crazy? Why all of a sudden do you love me?

OLD SAM: My head clears. It's when my head clears, like those pills, like a decongestant, Rosie, you know?

OLD ROSE: What? Sammie, what are you talking about?

GROUP: He's making love Rosie.

OLD SAM: A decongestant! A god damn . . . capsule! Every once in awhile my head clears. And I remember how I *loved* you. I *know* I love you. (*To self:*) Sam, I am Sam, I am Rose's husband Sam. (*To* ROSE:) I feel the feeling of loving—of loving you.

GROUP: He still loves you Rosie

(*Pause.*)

OLD ROSE: I love you. I love you too Sammie.

GROUP: She still loves you Sammie.

(*Music stops.*)

OLD ROSE: So (*pause*) what do you say? Are you hungry? Do you want something to eat? Can I make you a sandwich?

(OLD ROSE *and* OLD SAM *move slowly, like old people, back to face* TV.)

DETECTIVE (*to* DUCHAMP): In an interview you said there's one question which you're never asked and which you'd love to be asked, namely—

GROUP: How are you?

DUCHAMP: Thank you for asking. Actually, I'm doing very well. I undergo the troubles which bother all people at my age. Watch out! But otherwise, I am very happy.

DETECTIVE: Do you think about death?

(*Music starts.*)

DUCHAMP (*laughing*): As little as possible. You think about it from time to time, at my age, when you have a headache or heartburn. You imagine the worst. You think about it as you lose your friends—the people who knew the world as you knew it. It's true—then death appears.

GROUP: Death appears.

DUCHAMP: Despite yourself you're impressed—

GROUP: Wait.

DUCHAMP: by the undeniable fact

DETECTIVE: This sounds like a conclusion.

DUCHAMP: that you're going to completely disappear.

GROUP: Of sorts.

(*Music continues. The stage slowly empties of actors till only* OLD ROSE *and* OLD SAM *are left, watching TV. They are holding hands. Lights fade.*)

mac wellman

SINCERITY FOREVER

JUDY (Amy Brenneman) and MOLLY (Leslie Nipkow) enjoy a beautiful summer's night in Hillsbottom, USA.

The obsessive, lewd, manic flow of speech that takes over the small-town souls of *Sincerity Forever* is a kind of mordant self-parody, a playwright's mocking tribute to the mystery of playwriting itself. As every playwright knows, the art consists of not writing the lines yourself but stepping aside to receive them as they come from the characters' mouths. The imaginative center, not the conscious one, is in charge. Every artist knows and cherishes this experience; the inartistic misunderstand and fear it. It's the peculiar misfortune of Americans to live in a country that suppresses its own imaginative voice. *Sincerity Forever* is a meta-play built on the matrix of that suppression: Locked in by prejudices, fears, angers, and a complacency born out of pure defensiveness, Wellman's characters can only speak their deepest feelings when their souls are possessed by cosmic furballs — and one should note, in this context, that real furballs are produced when a cat's been nuzzling itself too much, and the stray bits of its own fur lodged in its throat clog its craw.

Only when their spiritual craw is clogged this way can Wellman's Americans discuss, in even the crudest terms, their sexual impulses, the state of the world around them, how they perceive their place in the universe. Unfree in themselves, they can only find relative freedom in a manic viciousness that literally makes them — in one of the playwright's slyest dealings with text — interchangeable parts. Which is what their conformity has already reduced them to on the bland surface level, and what the play's Christ figure keeps trying to awaken them from.

The presence of Christ in what is fundamentally an un- (but not anti-) religious play has of course raised hackles among people who believe that Jesus is their personal property and that dramatic discussion of what he means to us is not part of free speech. Wellman's play is dedicated to its inspirations, Senator Jesse Helms and Reverend Donald E. Wildmon; naturally Wellman sent both men copies, resulting in the correspondence which follows. Interestingly, the *Journal of the American Family Association,* Wildmon's newsletter, published without the copyright holder's permission a large segment of JESUS H. CHRIST's final speech, in violation of Wellman's copyright, in an article headlined PLAYWRIGHT USES $15,500 GRANT TO WRITE PLAY DEPICTING JESUS AS A FOUL-MOUTHED BIGOT. According to Wildmon, "The play, filled with obscenities and profanities, is only the latest example of anti-Christian bigotry funded by the NEA. The NEA is a government agency supported by tax dollars. . . . In order to lessen the offensiveness of the script, we have edited the obscenities in Mr. Wellman's play." The AFA also published an excerpt from the cover letter, in which the author said he sent Wildmon the play "With my compliments, for the fine job you are doing of destroying civil liberties in These States."

One would think the letter, and the speech, might lead a reasonably literate person to conclude that Wellman, and not Wildmon, had the deeper understanding of Jesus's actual teachings. But Wildmon knows enough about the relative illiteracy of his flock, and their unquestioning obedience, to quote without fear. In fact, the two—the ignorance of the semi-literate and a blind obedience to received ideas—are closely linked. After all, as Brecht said, "If the cows could get together and discuss things, the slaughterhouse wouldn't last long." So the one alternative Americans have to the arid schematism of life as the Wildmons see it is the relentless obscenity of—cosmic furballs. Or, as Freud called it, the return of the repressed. There ought to be better answers, but in the meantime there is Wellman, standing puckishly aside while his characters pose the question, in a fine frenzy of splendidly raffish, torrential, eloquence.

American Family Association
Mr. Donald Wildmon
P.O. Drawer 2440
Tupelo, MI 38803

Brooklyn,
6 October 1990

Dear Donald,

A friend (and I have many among the semi-terrorized denizens of your "flock") recently sent along a copy of September's issue of your AFA Journal. I was most shocked by the title of the article about my play, since you claim my play refers to Jesus as a "foul-mouthed bigot." But it is you, Donald, who is the foul-mouthed bigot. It is you who has twisted the words of the Gospels to support your equally twisted dreams of power, dominion, and exclusion. I have said over and over, privately and in interviews about you and your organization, that what you call religion boils down to organized bigotry, pure and simple. A bigot, for your information (since you don't seem to know), is a person who is intolerant, particularly of other people's beliefs and ways of life. It is you and not Jesus— neither the one of my play nor the historical person—who hates gays and lesbians, black people, Jews, and everyone else who isn't lily-white, born-again, and xenophobic like you. I found it interesting that when you printed a large part of the last scene of my play you neglected to mention to your readership that Jesus H. Christ is a black woman, and that the speech he gives is a rewrite of the Sermon on the Mount; but perhaps you are not familiar with the Sermon on the Mount, and surely the idea of an African-American Jesus has haunted

the bad consciences of people like you all the way back to
Edgar Allan Poe and Nathan Bedford Forrest.

Furthermore, I was intrigued by your intense hatred of the
rich and colorful language of the common people, a language
used—I would guess—by 90% of the American people 80% of
the time, ever since the Founding Fathers. Furthermore, I
would suggest it is you—not me—who is corrupting the
language of the tribe: for it is you and your kind who dress
up hatred in the language of love, and lies in the language of
truth. And what hatred and lies! Do you <u>know</u> any
homosexual people? Has it ever occurred to you that they
have defended this country in its wars, time and time again?
that they pay their taxes and that they vote? and that they
are not proscribed in the Constitution, or anywhere in the
Bill of Rights, from sharing in our civil rights and liberties?
What is the origin of these "community standards" for which
you claim to be the spokesman? Who authorized you to
speak as the self-appointed moral dictator for your own
community? Who authorized you to lay down the moral
standard for communities you have never visited and have
no meaningful knowledge of? I do not recognize your church,
because your church is based on lies, pure and simple. The
Bible is a great book, a very great book indeed; it was
conceived and written by some of the most inspired men and
women who ever lived. But you have ignored the whole
marvelous textual complexity of the Good Book, and have
committed the sacrilege of treating it all as some moronic
tract like the <u>Protocols of the Elders of Zion,</u> a vehicle for
marginalizing minorities and subjecting them to slander and
vilification. I repeat, it is you, not me, who is the
foul-mouthed bigot; and certainly not the Jesus H. Christ of
<u>Sincerity</u> <u>Forever,</u> who merely enjoins people not to be "so
goshdarned pleased with theyselves" and not to put "words
in my mouth concerning they fears."

Since you appear to possess no mind, I don't expect to change it; but what really puzzles me with you and your kind is where your heart went? Don't the real sufferings of real people, the chronic poor, the homeless, those dying of terrible diseases like AIDS, and so on, and so forth—doesn't this immense pain ever intrude into the bland and empty precincts of your consciousness? Are you truly capable of feeling nothing <u>real</u>!? Or is the only reality you know the turning of political wheels and widgets, chiseling little old ladies and those who don't know any better out of their hard-earned dollars with your inane and bigoted and cheesy newsletters and evangelical TV fakes and goons?! I guess not, and that both saddens and angers me, as it would any Jesus H. Christ, whether imaginary or historical.

I cannot help but imagine that you are a disappointment to the creator; a polecat or a cockroach has more divine spark than you and all your holy rollers. And thanks for reprinting Scene Eight from my play, but next time you do why not think about paying me? But I'm sure your hopelessly incurable and chronic stinginess has infected that part of your operation as well. But please, please, do observe my line breaks the next time you print anything of mine. That really gets my dander up. So long, Donald, keep those hellfires burning bright . . .

Sincerely,

Mac Wellman

Senator Jesse Helms
U.S. Senate
Room SD-403,
Washington, D.C. 20510

5 July 1990

Dear Jesse,

Since the enclosed play, Sincerity Forever, is dedicated to
you (and Mr. Wildmon), I felt you ought to have a copy. With
my compliments, for the fine job you are doing of destroying
civil liberties in These States.

Save the Republic!

Mac Wellman
(1990 NEA Recipient)

NATIONAL
ENDOWMENT
FOR
THE ARTS

WASHINGTON
D.C. 20506

A Federal agency advised by the
National Council on the Arts

September 11, 1990

Dear Mr. Wellman,

It has been brought to my attention that a manuscript page
of your play, <u>Sincerity Forever</u>, contains the following
statement which is erroneous with respect to the Arts
Endowment:

> <u>Sincerity Forever</u> was made possible by generous
> support of the NEA, NYFA, The John Simon
> Guggenheim Foundation, and is the first flower of the
> Roger Nathan Hirschl Playwriting Award.

You received a Theater Program Playwright Fellowship
grant of $15,500 for Fiscal Year 1990, covering the period
April 1, 1990 to December 31, 1991. However, I
understand that this play was actually the direct result of a
commission you received from the Berkshire Theatre
Festival under the newly founded Roger Nathan Hirschl
Playwriting Award.

Therefore, to correct the above cited error, the Endowment

requests that you remove credit to the National Endowment for the Arts from the relevant page (headed: <u>Sincerity Forever</u> <u>persons of the play</u>:) of all copies of this play. Also, please confirm to me in writing that this step has been taken.

Thank you for your attention to this matter.

Sincerely,

Randolph McAusland
Deputy Chairman for Programs

cc: Jessica Andrews

The National Endowment for the Arts
Mr. Randolph McAusland
Deputy Chairman for Programs
1100 Pennsylvania Avenue NW
Washington, D.C. 20506

Brooklyn,
30 September 1990

Dear Mr. McAusland,

I am responding to your letter of 11 September 1990, in
which you requested that I remove credit to the National
Endowment for the Arts from the Persons of the Play page of
all copies of my play, Sincerity Forever.

In accordance with your wishes, I shall attach a statement
to all copies of Sincerity Forever which will make known to
all who are interested the nature of your request and will
correct my error. But I thought, perhaps, it might be
sensible for me to explain why I credited you in the first
place. I began Sincerity Forever in early January 1990, as
you mentioned, under the auspices of the Roger Nathan
Hirschl Playwriting Competition Commission. However the
play had been in my head for some time; I would have
written it in any case, whether or not I had received the
Hirschl Commission. Since I received several grants and
fellowships this year and used monies from these grants
and fellowships to live while at work on the writing and
rehearsal of Sincerity Forever, I did not feel I was being
remiss as a 1990 NEA Fellowship recipient in thanking you
for the Fellowship.

Certainly it was not my intention to contravene the will of the authorities. I keep thinking of Kafka: A cage went in search of a bird.

Sincerely,

Mac Wellman

Mac Wellman

This one's for Jesse and the Wildman

PRODUCTION NOTES

Sincerity Forever was first produced as the winner of the first Berkshire Theatre Festival Roger Nathan Hirschl Playwriting Award. The play premiered in 1990 at the Festival's Unicorn Theatre under the direction of Richard Caliban; music composed by David Van Tieghem; sets by James Youmans; costumes by Mary Myers; lighting by Kenneth Posner.

The cast included (in order of appearance): Angie Phillips, Kate Forbes, Jason Duchin, Tom Hildreth, Ntare Mwine, Mark Singale, LuAnn Adams, Tom Simpson, Ariane Brandt. *Sincerity Forever* was then dedicated to Senator Jesse Helms: ''. . . for the fine job you are doing of destroying civil liberties in These States.''

Sincerity Forever was produced in November and December 1990 at Brooklyn Arts and Cultural Association (BACA) Downtown as part of the 1990 Fringe Series. It was directed by Jim Simpson; produced by House Frau, Inc.; music was composed by David Van Tieghem; sets and lights were designed by Kyle Chepulis; costumes were designed by Claudia Brown.

The cast was: Amy Brenneman, Frank Deal, Zach Grenier, Jan Harding, Patrick Kerr, Steve Mellor, Dan Moran, Leslie Nipkow, Kenya Scott, David Van Tieghem.

Sincerity Forever was made possible by generous support of the NEA*, NYFA, the John Simon Guggenheim Foundation, and is the first flower of the Roger Nathan Hirschl Playwriting Award.

---

*See Author's Note and Correction, p.96.

AUTHOR'S NOTE AND CORRECTION

The National Endowment for the Arts has requested that I remove credit to them for my play *Sincerity Forever*, although I received a 1990 Playwriting Fellowship. Accordingly, the author would like to amend the error of his ways: I was wrong, *Sincerity Forever* was not made possible by the generous assistance of the NEA. I don't know what I was thinking . . .

—Mac Wellman
September 30, 1990

CHARACTERS

JUDY, a sincere young person and member of the Invisible
   Nation

MOLLY, ditto

TOM, ditto

HANK, ditto

GEORGE, ditto

LLOYD, ditto

MELVIN, ditto

TWO FURBALLS, of the tribe of Belial and Abaddon

JESUS H. CHRIST, a young African-American woman who
   carries a very heavy suitcase

*The occasional appearance of an asterisk (*) in the middle of a
speech is used by the playwright to indicate that the next speech
begins to overlap at that point. A double asterisk (**) indicates that
a later speech (not the one immediately following) begins to overlap
at that point. The overlapping speeches are all clearly marked in the
text.*

Dogs bark at a person whom they do not know.

—Heraclitus

A beautiful summer's night in the outskirts of Hillsbottom. Two girls sit in a parked car talking about things. Both are dressed in Ku Klux Klan garb.

JUDY: Molly, do you know why God created the world the way he did? So complicated, I mean.

(Pause.)

MOLLY: Nope.

JUDY: Because I've been thinking about it, and I just get more and more puzzled.

MOLLY: So do I.

JUDY: Because if there is a divine plan it sure doesn't look it, very divine, that is. Or planlike. It looks kinda like a mess.

MOLLY: Most of the time, when I think about big things, things like God, and the end of nature, and global warming, and so on, I feel like I don't know anything at all.

JUDY: That's just how I feel. Like I don't know anything. It's really scary. I mean I don't know the name of the state capital. I don't know what my dad does at work. I couldn't name more than two or three South American countries, and I'm not much better when it comes to Europe.

MOLLY: I don't know the difference between good art and bad art. I haven't a clue what a "hostile takeover" is, nor why junk bonds are junky. I mean why would anybody want them if they're worthless? It doesn't make any sense.

JUDY: I don't know why the sky is blue, and I don't know what "blue" is, and I don't know why I don't know. (*Pause.*) I don't know anything. I mean, when you come right down to it, I don't know a blessed thing, and you know? I don't care, I don't care that I don't know anything because I strongly suspect that nobody else knows anything either.

MOLLY: You think they're just pretending?

JUDY: I think they're all faking it, particularly our parents, our teachers, our social betters, people in positions of authority, and celebrities on TV, and in the halls of Congress, in the churches and klonvocations, and on the radio, even in the middle of the night, when we are all asleep, except Poky the cat. Poky the cat knows. (*Long pause.*) Sometimes I wonder if I'm really named Judy, and that freaks me out, because if I am not then who am I, and if I don't have a real name what am I? Maybe I don't exist and this is some kind of a cruel joke my family is playing on me, and I wouldn't put it past them, particularly Dexter, my brother. He says he has a crush on you. But I don't know if Dexter's capable of such a thing, he's such a klutz he couldn't spell I.Q. if you spotted him the "Q," and he doesn't know much of anything, any more than I do. I know that for a fact.

MOLLY: Judy, I think probably God has a plan for all things, and I think the proof of this plan is in the pudding. I mean, why else would we not know anything, unless there were an intelligent being out there, somewhere, whose cunning idea it was that you and I, Judy and Molly, should be forever ignorant of the true nature of things, ignorant forever in absolute sincerity. Does Dexter really have a crush on me, or did he just say he did?

JUDY: I think the absolute sincerity part of it is the most important, because it's real hard not to know anything unless you are perfectly sincere about it. I can't remember whether he told me he had this crush on you, or I just dreamed it up, or came to that conclusion because he asked what your name was.

MOLLY: I think there is this mystic furball that has infected the whole town with its poison of ignorance, and that's why none of us know anything. And this mystic furball must be found and destroyed.

JUDY: What's a mystic furball?

MOLLY: I don't think I can explain.

JUDY: How could it make us not know anything?

MOLLY: I don't know.

JUDY: Then why did you say it did?

MOLLY: That it did what?

JUDY: You know. Make us dumb.

MOLLY: It didn't make us dumb. It made us ignorant. They aren't the same.

JUDY: But how did it do this?

MOLLY: How do I know? It was just an idea, a shot in the dark, you don't have to get so worked up about it all, you know.

JUDY: Sorry.

MOLLY: Judy.

JUDY: Yes, what is it?

MOLLY: What if, maybe, I only think I'm Molly and that in fact I'm Judy and you're Molly and that somehow we got all mixed up, tragically, walking back from school, and the mystic furball did it to us to prevent us from finding his hiding place out in the backyard, or behind the garage, or under the pile of dead leaves beside the doghouse, or behind the elm tree, or up on the roof above the dormers, or on the weather vane on top of the barn, over there, Mr. Whatsisname's barn, or deep in the ground, where the standpipes are, where we're not supposed to go, near the toxic waste dump site, where some pretty creepy stuff is supposed to be leaching into the subsoil and will eventually contaminate the groundwater and all the people for miles around will have to go around in plastic bags, on tippy toes.

JUDY: What makes you think you know all this stuff?

MOLLY: I don't.

JUDY: Then why did you say it?

MOLLY: Overheard someone at school. Guess I got carried away.

JUDY: But who said it?

MOLLY: Who said what?

JUDY: The stuff about the furball?

MOLLY: George, or Lloyd. You know, the gawky string-bean guy, the guy who said he pissed on a skunk.

JUDY: That was Lloyd, not George.

MOLLY: That's what I said.

JUDY: That's not what you said.

MOLLY: That is too.

JUDY: That is not.

MOLLY: But the most important thing is not what you know, but whether you're sincere or not. That's what I think.

JUDY: That's what I think too. If I don't know anything else I know that. I think . . .

MOLLY: Sincerity forever.

JUDY: Right.

(*Blackout.*)

*Two guys sitting in another car. Talking. They also are decked out in Klan
garb. Nice night, moon, bugs. A woman with a heavy suitcase approaches,
but stands off a bit in the bushes, unseen. This is* JESUS H. CHRIST. *She
holds a long, black staff.*

TOM: Hank, you're so fucking dumb, you're as dumb as the north end
of something headed south. Something kinda all time monster stupid.

HANK: Guess I am. But shit, you don't know much of anything
yourself, Tom. You got to admit. When it comes right down to it.

TOM: Hank, you're right about that. But I got sincerity. You, you
don't have no sincerity. Plus, you don't know nothing. That's a
heavy weight to bear.

HANK: I always was a devious son-of-a-bitch. So I guess you're right.
The way I look at it, this is the hollow time of humanity. It don't matter
if we don't know nothing, because we are looking for an event, an
event that will change all this weirdness, all this mediocre everydayness
into something higher. Meaningful. And transcendent. Just because I
was never good at chemistry or economics or algebra, and flunked out
of Hillsbottom Junior College don't mean moosedick. It don't mean
moosedick because I have a special thing inside my head, here, under
this pointy hat. And this thing which I am referring to is my infinitely
precious human soul, which is worth more than knowledge, because
what you know is subject to the corrosive work of time, dry rot,
entropy, alien juju, and the works of those who fear not God and all his
works, through the malign agency of the devil who labors in the fiery
furnace of hell, knitting together the warp and woof of human
delusion. And that ain't beanbag.

TOM: I say a skunk is a skunk is a skunk and he ought to be rooted
up, and took out and shot, and left to rot by the side of the road.
You're not talking normal, Hank.

HANK: I say that I worry a lot about things like nontemporal unaccountability and infinite regress and the fiery pit. I worry a lot about hell, and where it is, and what it looks like, and who lives there, and who receives which torment, and what these torments feel like, since if I was capable of feeling the true nature of these torments for even the fraction of a second I might know how to amend the howling madness of my ways, even though I'd most like remain for sure an ignorant cuss and not worth a crap in the scale of things, not worth a mote in the eye of the least of the angels in the radiant economy of heaven. (*Pause. Looks puzzled.*) Now, what the hell was it I was driving at?

TOM: You were saying you would sure bust your ass to amend the error of your ways.

HANK: That's it, that's what I would do, take up my load and run with it till, till I find someplace where I could dump it down, where it would be safe, and I would be free of these insane dreams of fur . . . fur and furrrrrrr . . .

TOM: Fur?

HANK: Fur, and furballs.

(*Pause.*)

TOM: Hank, there's something the matter with you. Something not right, something wrong inside your head, with your brain.

HANK: I am John Q. Fedup is what is wrong with me. I got a whole lot of lead weights bearing down on me, inside my head, under this pointy cloak. You couldn't imagine what it's like having this infernal thing inside you, this damned, eternal, Christian soul. This life sentence for eternity, which I never asked for, because like I said, I confess to not knowing a damn thing, nor the subtle ramifications of this not knowing, because all such not knowing is as bad as knowing, and I would rather be rid of both than go to heaven even, which is my dark secret and a bad thought, but it's the truth, so help me God. I mean, why is this heaven any better than hell? I mean, really, *why!?* I don't mean to be a wiseass, I'm just curious, that's all.

(*Pause.*)

Tom: Hank, you're a snake is what you are, a viper. Here you sit, wearing your human flesh, wearing the cloth of creation * and you dare . . .

Jesus: Pardon me.

Tom: Pardon me, ma'am. We are having a little conversation. (*He continues talking with* Hank.) The garment of flesh which the good Lord bequeathed unto you, and you find nothing better in your heart than to soil it with this doubt, this badass cynicism. No wonder you say you don't know nothing. Now. Now me, I, too, may be as dumb as a post, and unclear about the multiplication table, the boundaries of more than a half dozen states, and unable to repair my own toilet, but dammit, Hank, if the English language was good enough for Jesus H. Christ then it's good enough for me. Furthermore, I do not feel compelled by reason to accept this theory of evolution, nor the periodic table of elements, nor the theory of global warming, nor the supposed crimes against the Jews attributed to one Rudolf Hitler. Nor the spherical nature of the earth, because it's against the law of nature and we would fall off for sure and my motto is: never explain, never apologize. As for the dead, they got no rights. So, I too am John Q. Fedup, and we'll both have a heap of company, in this regard, in the happy land to come. Or the other place, which is where your soul, sure as hell, shall end up if you don't get a hold on yourself and cut out this bonehead crap and act normal like a man should and just get on with it. Now what can I do for you, stranger?

(*Pause.* Jesus *puts down her heavy bag and the earth trembles. Pause.*)

Jesus: This wouldn't be the town of Hillsbottom, would it?

Tom: It might be, and then it might not be.

Hank: What do you got in that there weighty box?

JESUS: Weaseldervishbullcrushing machinery.

HANK: She's crazy.

JESUS: You want to answer my question, Bud?

TOM: Go fuck yourself.

JESUS: You amaze me, gentlemen. Even though, even though nothing that was, was done did without my sayso it seems like nobody roundabout here don't know it, and that's a fact. You set there, in that wreck of a Ford, smiling like you just ate a five-hundred-pound canary, when you are in a parlous state. That's right, because there is a furball here in Hillsbottom. I can detect it with my apparatus. Maybe even two. I cannot only detect 'em with my apparatus, I am able to destroy 'em with my mind, because this furball is no ordinary furball, no, it am a mystic furball, nay, a monster furball, of the tribe of Abaddon and Belial, and are therefore a spirit of negation, and this furball don't give a crap whether you cling to the angel of you ignorance, this furball am bodacious and am like to bust down boundaries between things, things dear to you, and this despite the innocence of your down-home cracker ignorance, because this time ignorance won't save you as it used to was in the pretty times done did, so many times afore, during the Season of Dread and the Season of Bloating, when the mighty leviathan (*pause*). But I see you gentlemen are not taking this serious, as you should. I see you are mocking me, in your heart, with your vileness and pride and lust and superstition and greed and moron stupefaction, and I feel had. I feel like a loyal lover who has been rejected, and who has wearied of the object of her love, and therefore feels a disappointment. Do you know what hell is like? For I have been to the place, and know what it looks like.

TOM: Yeah, you've been to hell, and my name is Edsel Ford.

JESUS: Surely, I have been to hell and know the place, for it was I who caused it to be riven.

(*Her staff turns into a snake. She begins to go offstage.*)

HANK: Oh yeah, what does it look like?

JESUS: Hell looks very much like Hillsbottom.

(*She goes out. Pause. They laugh.*)

Another wonderful night, but strange. Two lovers in a parked car. They, too, are arrayed in the Klan way. In the bushes a FURBALL *spies upon them.*

JUDY: Do you believe that terrible things always have to happen, or not? I mean, if it's possible for some really gross and disgusting event to happen, do you think it has to, or not, which?

GEORGE: Never really thought about it.

JUDY: Neither did I, until right now.

GEORGE: The way I look at it, we must all have a purpose, a purpose that God keeps hidden from us.

JUDY: How do you mean?

GEORGE: Well, if God informed us upfront of why we were put on earth there wouldn't be any surprises in it. God must've felt he needed to liven things up, by keeping the true purpose of all this hidden. Secret, and stuff.

JUDY: Sometimes, I do wish He had made it a little clearer, though. I mean like with car crashes. Child abuse. The divorce rate, and stuff. The sacred and mystical rights of the unborn. Like the plutonium seepage problem near West Hillsbottom, all those people downwind with growths, and how you're not supposed to drink the well water in East Hillsbottom, and stuff.

GEORGE: That's not been proven.

JUDY: That's not proven, but it's suspicious. People say it is very likely a big worry.

GEORGE: It has not been scientifically proven, otherwise those in charge of the facility would come out and say so. This is not a case of God's will being murky or his plan for us, it is just a case of the evidence not being all in.

JUDY: If the evidence were all in, would it make any difference, as far as God's will goes? That's what I mean.

GEORGE: I don't think so, because nuclear pollution might still be a part of God's design, I mean his plan for Hillsbottom. We might not be able to fathom that plan, is all.

JUDY: Then we're better off not knowing that plan.

GEORGE: That's a deep thought. I think you have a deep mind, Judy.

JUDY: George, I feel so reverent when I think of all the things I don't know, and how majestic the summer sky is at night, and how much God must love us, how much he must have cared all along, millions of years ago, before he had any idea that you or I might exist.

GEORGE: You know, I've been thinking about you all week.

JUDY: I didn't think you liked me.

GEORGE: I told Carol I had a crush on you, and I'd kill her if she told anyone.

JUDY: I can't believe it. I thought I was the one with the crush.

GEORGE: I thought you thought I wasn't part of the "in" crowd.

JUDY: I can't stand those guys. They're such snobs. I can't stand conceited people.

GEORGE: Neither can I. People who think they're better than you, just because they drive a Corvette their father gave them. Like Ralph.

JUDY: I can't stand that.

GEORGE: But you went out with Ralph for six months.

Judy: Even then I couldn't stand that about him. First I had a crush on him because I thought he was cute and stuff. But pretty soon I wised up and realized he wasn't sincere. Actually he was a jerk, and just did things to impress his friends. Like Chainsaw and Dragonwagon. Gross. And the furball guy. Whatsisname. Actually I only went out with him because he drove a red Corvette. Red's my favorite color.

George: I thought you were madly in love with him.

Judy: I wasn't.

George: Are you sure?

Judy: What are you talking about? You're the one who was making googly eyes all over Susan Hanahan all during the field trip to the . . . museum. Was it the museum?

George: No, it was the nuclear power plant. It was in the cooling unit.

Judy: Well, you were the one who * was making eyes at her.

George: I was not making eyes at Susan Hanahan. I was only trying to make sure she had someone who could give her the lowdown on who to hang out with. I did not find her attractive. I found her pathetic, actually. But that was before I realized she had this crush on that slob Randolph. Can you believe it?

Judy: I still cannot believe that. I still cannot believe anyone could possibly have a crush on someone so nerdy and insincere as Randolph.

George: It's bad enough to be nerdy and insincere, but to be nerdy and insincere like Randolph is enough to make a person positively gag.

(*Pause.*)

Judy: I have a crush on you.

George: I have a monster crush on you. (*They laugh.*)

Judy: I didn't think anything like this would happen. I just thought you thought you were doing me a favor because my friends aren't as cool as your friends.

George: Your friends are just as cool as my friends. I figured you might not go out with me, well, on account of how I don't know anything, and your dad being this famous pervert and all and socially unacceptable and stuff, not that any of it means moosedick to me, hell, my whole family went bankrupt and stuff. We aren't exactly the country club set.

Judy: George, I don't care about what all those snobs think. I think you are a very sincere person, and that is the most important to me.

George: Really, Judy?

Judy: Yes, George, it is.

George: I've never felt this good before.

Judy: Neither have I. It's really wonderful. (*Pause.*) Do you believe in God, George?

George: I didn't used to think I did, but when I think about us, and all the terrific feelings I have for you, then I think there must be a God, a god who has arranged for everything to work out perfectly, the way it should.

Judy: I feel that way too. I feel very sure that you will accomplish wonderful things in your life, George, and that you will go to heaven.

George: I don't know, Judy, sometimes I feel I'm not up to life's challenges.

Judy: Just because you've had some rough times doesn't mean you won't be up to the challenges of life. I think you've been very brave. And your dad was really looked up at, that's what my mom said. And Dad, too, before he got strange. They said your dad was the best Kludd they ever had at the big klonvocations. It must've been real hard to have him go like that.

George: Jdark, he said, and croaked.

Judy: What?

George: At the hospital. That's what he said. Jdark, and then he rolled over and died. Terminal furball. Furball in the windpipe.

Judy: Oh, that sounds awful.

George: I meant tail pipe. There was this furball that somehow got lodged in the tail pipe of his Ranchero. Did something bad to the whatchamacallit. The throttle spring thing got sprung, got wedged, somehow, on full. Brakes locked, spun out. He could've put the clutch in, but he didn't. Stubborn cuss. Took the steep hill up by Route Seven at fifty-five. Old Pancake Road up by Sandman's Creek. He made the first turn, witnesses say, somehow. No one ever did it that fast before. That's what they say.

Judy: He must've been quite a man.

George: He went into the hairpin turn on top of Old Boabdil at seventy. Took out a ninety-year-old oak with him and tore off the edge of Dead Man's Gulch. The drop is about five hundred feet. Into the rapids just beneath the falls. It took them three hours to cut him out of the wreck. He was still alive. They took him to the county hospital, but he wasn't conscious anymore. They called us and we got there just in time. He woke up, just before he passed on. Jdark, he said and croaked.

Judy: That's so tragic, George.

George: Jdark, he said. That was all.

Judy: Hold my hand, George. (*They hold hands. Pause.*) Life is so mystical sometimes.

(*The spying* Furball *goes away. Blackout.*)

Another nice night, another parked car. Two FURBALLS *sit in the car, bitching.*

FURBALL ONE: Shit.

FURBALL TWO: Fuck it.

ONE: Shit on you, fuckhead.

TWO: Shit on you, why don't you fucking get off my case, you moron.

ONE: Fucking dickbreath is what you are. Fucking monster crapface.

(Pause.)

TWO: I dunno, this fucking town, this fucking town is driving me crazy. "That's so tragic, George . . ." "Jdark, he said. That was all . . ." "Life is so mystical sometimes . . ."

ONE: Fuck, I'd like to fucking fuck all these fucking pussies till they turn puke green and belly up, the stupid fucks. *(Pause. Both* FURBALLS *pick their noses.)*

TWO: I mean, I really can't stand this fucking place; it's like an itch you can't scratch, a scab that's driving you crazy, or a really gross and disgusting bald spot on the head of somebody you really can't stand; it's kinda like the sort of cheerful, nerdy music they're always playing on public radio: sorta bubbly, sorta goofy, sorta upbeat, you know? But really dead and empty inside. I mean, the whole fucking place rubs my fur the fucking wrong way; I mean, it's all so fucking decent and god-fearing and goody-two-shoes and law-abiding and thankful and smarmy and sentimental and full of wishful thinking and sugar-coated bad faith and chintzy, cheesy, boring mediocrity it makes me want to gag. I mean all these totally square fuckheads who only care about God and family and communication and community and law

and order and morality and safe sex and global warming and Jesus
H. Christ and the whole moldy, worn-out crock of shit. It makes me
want to spew and leave my lunch all over their well-manicured
lawns. I mean, these fucking losers don't have a clue! Fucking
smart-ass bigots and liars and cheapskates and schemers and conni-
vers and empty-headed purveyors of the empty hoax of the American dream. I mean, it makes me sick with laughter, all their fake
ideals and cant and bullshit and stupid rigmarole and mindless,
conventional functional-fixedness, conformity, and lack of spunk.
Middlebrow, mainstream, heavy-handed, hypocritical, slimy, rubber-
ized, saccharine, homogenized, namby-pamby, cretinized, dull,
repetitive, unavowed, moronic, jerky, overdone, hackneyed, effemi-
nate, creepy, flabby-minded, suburban, knee-jerk, bogus, flatulent,
slimeball, cornball, reject, slipshod, uncouth, yahoo, fruitcake,
wishy-washy, deaf-and-dumb, bloated, numbskull, puke-faced, flat-
footed, goofy, dilapidated, superannuated, depraved, psychotic, pe-
destrian, rebarbitive, and totally uncool, unhip, and unfun. All of it,
deeply insincere. (*He shudders. Pause.*)

ONE: Who the fuck do you think you are, you fucking meatball? Just
look at you! What have you ever done to justify your existence,
furface? What makes you think you're so hot? What did you ever
accomplish? What right have you got to rant and rail about the
cheesy inhabitants of Hillsbottom when you aren't one iota better
than them? What new and time-saving machines have you invented?
What money have you heaped up and saved through your diligence
and industry and perspicacious shrewdness? What new idea has
shuddered, stumbled, and lurched forth from the monastic stillness
of your furry brain? What histories have you penned, chronicling the
hidden purpose behind the vast scenes of horror and pandemonium
of human action, scenes hitherto thought meaningless, dark, and
inaccessible to the light of reason? What foodstuffs have you planted
and hoed, nurtured with your own furry meathooks, through your
own furry labors, and by the sweat of your furry brow, and pro-
cessed, bottled, and crated up for the common good? What beautiful
works of art have you imaged in the fiery furnace of your furry,

esemplastic imagination, then chopped and hewn out of what hardwood, or cut out of what whole cloth, and polished to a "T," thereby winning cries of wonder and astonishment from crowds of admirers, wherever they assemble, in parks, museums, traffic islands, and in malls and movies theaters? What humble, odious, but high-minded and necessary public service have you rendered, toiling in obscurity, all for the good of others, with no recompense expected or asked for, within the heroic purity of your innermost heart? What joys have you given others, in the form of small gifts or meaningless little gestures of basic human goodwill and positive-mindedness, which might—if only for a moment—lighten the load of those less fortunate than you, those even more bestial and craven, those lost in blind despair within the horrid attics of existence, driven crazy by bats, skunks, and rodents in the insulation and under the floorboards; those whose destiny is other than yours, the overlooked, the undervalued, the unsightly, the woebegone, the mocked and scorned, the deprived, the damned, the doomed, the dead. All of 'em, fuckheads.

Two: No cigar, Furry. The dead don't got no rights.

One: Don't give me no "No, cigar, Furry." I am more different from you. For I confess that, although I am a furball of monster magnitude—a hellacious, badass furball!—I am sincere.

Two: Fuck you, I am bigger than you, and I can whip your furry ass any time I want. I am smarter than you, a better bowler, and will take you on any time at blackjack, craps, or Chinese checkers. I am a better dancer, am more better in bed, a flashier dresser, and have more best-looking shoes than you. I got more important stuff on my mind than you, and do not waste my breath on what is common and low class. My friends are more interesting than your friends, and they are more fun to hang out with. My house is in a more better neighborhood, and your house is a wreck and poorly furnished and I would walk right by without saying "hello" if it were not for wanting to do you a favor on account of you being such a miserable, washed-up, jerkoff, has-been, pathetic loser, and that's a fact. I got more money than you, and have heaped up more valuables, foodstuffs, and loot. My wine cellars overflow with highclass swill, and I got whole warehouses of stuff, pretty damn hifalutin' type stuff, stuff the likes of which you never laid eyes on owing to your lack of class, and general cussidness. And what's more I speak my mind more better than you because God loves me and mine better than you and yours and no wonder! because, like, I mean, you ever take a good close look at yourself, man? why, you are *ugly*, and when I say ugly I mean your kind of ugly gives whole new meaning to the higher concept of "ugly"; what's more, I am superior to you in all other respects, and if I have a fault it is that I have lowered myself somewhat by even bothering to associate with one such as yourself, someone whose sense of self-esteem lies buried somewhere, somewhere remote, buried butt-up beyond the barbed wire and towers of redemption. A total dickhead.

(*The* FURBALLS *scowl at each other. Blackout.*)

S C E N E   F I V E

Another wonderful night, but strange. Two lovers in a parked car. They, too, are arrayed in the Klan way. In the bushes a FURBALL *spies upon them.*

LLOYD: Do you believe that terrible things always have to happen, or not. I mean, if it's possible for some really gross and disgusting event to happen, do you think it has to, or not, which?

TOM: Never really thought about it.

LLOYD: Neither did I, until right now.

TOM: The way I look at it, we must all have a purpose, a purpose that God keeps hidden from us.

LLOYD: How do you mean?

TOM: Well, if God informed us upfront of why we were put on earth there wouldn't be any surprises in it. God must've felt he needed to liven things up, by keeping the true purpose of all this hidden. Secret, and stuff.

LLOYD: Sometimes, I do wish he had made it a little clearer though. I mean like with car crashes. Child abuse. The divorce rate, and stuff. The sacred and mystical rights of the unborn. Like the plutonium seepage problem near West Hillsbottom, all those people downwind with growths, and how you're not supposed to drink the well water in East Hillsbottom, and stuff.

TOM: That's not been proven.

LLOYD: That's not proven, but it's suspicious. People say it is very likely a big worry.

TOM: It has not been scientifically proven otherwise those in charge of the facility would come out and say so. This is not a case of God's will being murky or his plan for us, it is just a case of the evidence not being all in.

LLOYD: If the evidence were all in, would it make any difference, as far as God's will goes? That's what I mean.

TOM: I don't think so, because nuclear pollution might still be a part of God's design, I mean his plan for Hillsbottom. We might not be able to fathom that plan is all.

LLOYD: Then we're better off not knowing that plan.

TOM: That's a deep thought. I think you have a deep mind, Lloyd.

LLOYD: Tom, I feel so reverent when I think of all the things I don't know, and how majestic the summer sky is at night, and how much God must love us, how much He must have cared all along, millions of years ago, before He had any idea that you or I might exist.

TOM: You know, I've been thinking about you all week.

LLOYD: I didn't think you liked me.

TOM: I told Carol I had a crush on you, and I'd kill her if she told anyone.

Lloyd: I can't believe it. I thought I was the one with the crush.

Tom: I thought you thought I wasn't part of the "in" crowd.

Lloyd: I can't stand those guys. They're such snobs. I can't stand conceited people.

Tom: Neither can I. People who think they're better than you, just because they drive a Corvette their father gave them. Like Ralph.

Lloyd: I can't stand that.

Tom: But you went out with Ralph for six months.

Lloyd: Even then I couldn't stand that about him. First I had a crush on him because I thought he was cute and stuff. But pretty soon I wised up and realized he wasn't sincere. Actually he was a jerk, and just did things to impress his friends. Like Chainsaw and Meatball. Gross. And the furball guy. Whatsisname. Actually I only went out with him because he drove a red Corvette. Red's my favorite color.

Tom: I thought you were madly in love with him.

Lloyd: I wasn't.

Tom: Are you sure?

Lloyd: What are you talking about. You're the one who was making googly eyes all over Susan Hanahan all during the field trip to the . . . museum. Was it the museum?

Tom: No, it was the nuclear power plant. It was in the cooling unit.

Lloyd: Well, you were the one who * was making eyes at her.

Tom: I was not making eyes at Susan Hanahan. I was only trying to make sure she had someone who could give her the lowdown on who to hang out with. I did not find her attractive. I found her pathetic, actually. But that was before I realized she had this crush on that slob Randolph, can you believe it?

Lloyd: I still cannot believe that. I still cannot believe anyone could possibly have a crush on someone so nerdy and insincere as Randolph.

TOM: It's bad enough to be nerdy and insincere, but to be nerdy and insincere like Randolph is enough to make a person positively gag.

(*Pause.*)

LLOYD: I have a crush on you.

TOM: I have a monster crush on you. (*They laugh.*)

LLOYD: I didn't think anything like this would happen. I just thought you thought you were doing me a favor because my friends aren't as cool as your friends.

TOM: Your friends are just as cool as my friends. I figured you might not go out with me, well, on account of how I don't know anything, and your dad being this famous pervert and all and socially unacceptable and stuff, not that any of it means moosedick to me, hell, my whole family went bankrupt and stuff. We aren't exactly the country club set.

LLOYD: Tom, I don't care about what all those snobs think. I think you are a very sincere person, and that is the most important to me.

TOM: Really, Lloyd?

LLOYD: Yes, Tom, it is.

TOM: I've never felt this good before.

LLOYD: Neither have I. It's really wonderful. (*Pause.*) Do you believe in God, Tom?

TOM: I didn't used to think I did, but when I think about us, and all the terrific feelings I have for you then I think there must be a God, a god who has arranged for everything to work out perfectly, the way it should.

LLOYD: I feel that way too. I feel very sure that you will accomplish wonderful things in your life, Tom, and that you will go to heaven.

TOM: I don't know, Lloyd, sometimes I feel I'm not up to life's challenges.

LLOYD: Hold my hand, Tom. (*They hold hands. Pause.*) Life is so mystical sometimes. (*The spying* FURBALL *goes away. A long furry pause.*) So, it was you pushed Carol down the well.

TOM: I told Carol I had a crush on you, and I'd kill her if she told anyone.

(*Pause.*)

LLOYD: Tom, you a wicked awful son-of-a-gun.

TOM: Man's got to do what he got to do.

(*Pause.*)

LLOYD: The miracle at Horsedark, ever thought about that?

TOM: You ask me, it was all done with mirrors.

(*Pause.* LLOYD *takes his hand away.*)

LLOYD: Tom, there's something the matter with you.

(*Slow blackout.*)

SCENE SIX

Another nice night, another parked car. The two girls sit in the car, bitching. They've been corrupted by the presence of FURBALLS *in Hillsbottom.*

JUDY: Molly, do you know why God created the world the way he did? So complicated, I mean. (*Pause.*)

MOLLY: Shit on you, why don't you fucking get off my case, you moron.

JUDY: Because I've been thinking about it, and I just get more and more puzzled.

MOLLY: Fucking dickbreath is what you are. Fucking monster crapface.

JUDY: Because if there is a divine plan it sure doesn't look it, very divine, that is. Or planlike. It looks kinda like a mess.

MOLLY: Fuck, I'd like to fucking fuck all these fucking pussies till they turn puke green and belly up, the stupid fucks.

JUDY: That's just how I feel. Like I don't know anything. It's really scary. I mean I don't know the name of the state capital. I don't know what my dad does at work. I couldn't name more than two or three South American countries, and I'm not much better when it comes to Europe.

MOLLY: I mean, I really can't stand this fucking place; it's like an itch you can't scratch, a scab that's driving you crazy, or a really gross and disgusting bald spot on the head of somebody you really can't stand.

JUDY: I don't know the difference between good art and bad art. I haven't a clue what a hostile takeover is, nor why junk bonds are junky. I mean why would anybody want them if they're worthless? It doesn't make any sense. I mean, the whole fucking place rubs my fur the fucking wrong way. I mean, it's all so fucking decent and god-fearing and goody-two-shoes and law-abiding and thankful and smarmy and sentimental and full of wishful thinking and sugar-coated bad faith and chintzy, cheesy, boring mediocrity it makes me want to gag. I mean all these totally square fuckheads who only care about God and family and communication and community and law and order and morality and safe sex and global warming and Jesus H. Christ and the whole moldy, wornout crock of shit. It makes me want to spew and leave my lunch all over their well-manicured lawns.

MOLLY: I mean, these fucking losers don't have a fucking clue. Fucking smart-ass bigots and liars.

JUDY: You think they're just pretending?

MOLLY: I think they're all faking it, particularly our parents, our teachers, our social betters, people in positions of authority, and celebrities on TV, and in the halls of Congress, in the churches and klonvocations, and on the radio, even in the middle of the night, when we are all asleep, except Poky the cat. Poky the cat knows. (*Long pause.*) Sometimes I wonder if I'm really named Molly, and that freaks me out, because if I am not then who am I, and if I don't have a real name what am I? Maybe I don't exist and this is some kind of a cruel joke your family is playing on me, and I wouldn't put it past them, particularly Dexter, your brother. He says he has a crush on me. But I don't know if Dexter's capable of such a thing, he's such a klutz he couldn't spell I.Q. if you spotted him the "Q," and he doesn't know much of anything, any more than I do. I know that for a fact.

JUDY: Who the fuck do you think you are, you fucking meatball? Just look at you! What have you ever done to justify your existence, furface? What makes you think you're so hot?

MOLLY: I think the absolute sincerity part of it is the most important, because it's real hard not to know anything unless you are perfectly sincere about it.

JUDY: Sorry.

MOLLY: Judy.

JUDY: Yes. What is it?

MOLLY: What if, maybe, I only think I'm Molly and that in fact I'm Judy and you're Molly and that somehow we got all mixed up, tragically, walking back from school, and Judy . . . (*A furry pause.*) Fuck you, I am bigger than you, and I can whip your furry ass any time I want. I am smarter than you, a better bowler, and will take you on any time at blackjack, craps, or Chinese checkers. I am a better dancer, am more better in bed, a flashier dresser, and have more best-looking shoes than you. I got more important stuff on my mind than you and do not waste my breath on what is common and low class. My friends are more interesting than your friends, and they are more fun to hang out with. My house is in a more better neighborhood, and your house is a wreck and poorly furnished and I would walk right by without saying hello if it were not for wanting to do you a favor on account of you being such a miserable, washed-up, jerk off, has-been, pathetic loser, and that's a fact. I got more money than you, and have heaped up more valuables, food-stuffs, and loot. My wine cellars overflow with highclass swill, and I got whole warehouses of stuff, pretty damn hifalutin' type stuff, stuff the likes of which you never laid eyes on owing to your lack of class, and general cussidness. And what's more I speak my mind more better than you because God loves me and mine better than you and yours and no wonder! Because, like, I mean, you ever take a good close look at yourself, man? why, you are *ugly*, and when I say ugly I mean your kind of ugly gives whole new meaning to the higher concept of "ugly"; what's more, I am superior to you in all other respects, and if I have a fault it is that I have lowered myself somewhat by even bothering to associate with such as yourself, someone whose sense of self-esteem lies buried somewhere, some-where remote, buried butt-up beyond the barbed wire and towers of redemption. A total dickhead.

(*Pause. The girls look surprised by their little episode of unpleasantness.*)

MOLLY: Judy, I think there's something the matter with you.

JUDY: I think there's something strange going on. Something strange is trying to take over Hillsbottom.

MOLLY: But how could that be?

JUDY: We're good people. Good people shouldn't be talking like this. Good people should talk normal. Good people should act sincere.

MOLLY: Judy, I'm afraid.

JUDY: Something bad's gotten into us.

MOLLY: You have to have faith.

JUDY: Faith. (*She looks stunned.*) Yeah.

MOLLY: Judy, I just had a bad thought.

JUDY: I had a bad thought too.

(*Blackout.*)

Nice night, just as before. Same old moon, but strange. Bigger and mean-looking. The girl and boy of the first love scene, GEORGE *and* JUDY, *sit in car. They don't feel so hot.* CHRIST *observes them from the tall weeds, hidden.* MELVIN, MOLLY, *and* TOM, *unseen by audience, hide in car.*

JUDY: I don't feel so hot.

GEORGE: Neither do I.

JUDY: I don't feel so hot, and I think it's your fault. (*A nasty pause. They get out of the car.*)

GEORGE: It's not my fault, Judy. You're just pissed because I remind you of Melvin, your previous, jerky, boyfriend. Melvin, who was a total toad, if you ask me, but we aren't the same. * (JUDY *overlaps.*) I am a normal, sweet, good-looking, small-town-type American guy, whereas this Melvin is a true goon, a desperate loser, the kind you wouldn't trust to change a flat tire because he'd be likely to go and do something weird, ** (MELVIN *overlaps*) something uncoordinated, and not put the nuts on right, him being a somewhat alien type of fellow, the artistic type, a member of the glee club, if you get what I mean, a real limp wrist of the first water, and not like me.

(MELVIN *climbs up out of the car, and goes after* GEORGE. MOLLY *climbs out after him.*)

JUDY: No, no, no, you got it all wrong, and if I have to explain myself then clearly we have been proceeding along the foggy road of illusion, and there is an absence of trust. And how dare you bring up Melvin, who was kind enough to listen patiently to me when I had my crisis of faith, you probably forget, when Dad kept asking me to dance at the Prom, embarrassing me, us all, so that we had to ask the authorities to take him away to the asylum because of his sudden, twisted sickness; and you paid no attention, and kept jitter-bugging with Molly, who you know full well was my best friend, and this when I had my eye on you, and you had your eye on me, at least that's what you said when we got lavaliered two days later, and you took certain liberties, so that I had to admit some fairly unpleasant details of my personal life at confession and Father Greenblast was clearly shocked because he had never heard of such things being done at such a young age, in full knowledge of sin, death, and perpetuity, upon the body of one such as me, innocent, by one such as you, George, clearly a boy of too much experience to say he was normal. So when I lost my faith, that was a premonition of now, and now my soap bubble of hope is burst thanks to you, thanks George, thank you so much. (*She sits down and cries.*)

MELVIN: Well, I am John Q. Fedup, and if you ask me I think you're all a bunch of snobs, conceited assholes and, yes, Judy I admit I had this powerful crush on you and, no, I didn't expect nothing from you but you could've, you know, just had the courtesy to return my call, 'cause I know your mom was lying through her teeth when she said you were out, at hockey practice. I mean, I tried being nice, even though it was your Uncle Sedgewick who fired my dad—betcha don't even know that!—at the vee-belt factory in Horsedark, near the county morgue, and that was the beginning of the end for him, he took to drugs and banjo playing with Mrs. Whatshername, the second grade teacher at Horsedark School. I never forgot that, how one of you people did that to one of my people, and it galled me. It heaped me. It's worked me up into a fierce, semicramped state, and my heart wants to barf and blow up. (*Pause.*) But I wasn't good enough for you, and you start up with this faggot George creep, this cross-eyed, greasy, Asiatic mongrel, why, his people lived in yurts when my great uncle Williamson Hartbuckle played left guard on the same team as Red Knuckles. Why, he's such a loser he don't even know who Big Red Knuckles is, nor what he done, nor where he growed up, nor what sport he played, nor what his records are, nor which of them are still standing, nor what became of him after the sad accident, nor what his number is that was retired last year in a ceremony up in Horsedark.

MOLLY: How dare you insult me, you whorish slut, who I thought was friend to me when that was clearly an Easter Bunny of mistruth? Do you have moisture on the brain or a growth on the organ of your human reason? You seduced George from me, the turkey, even before we began going out, and you did this out of bitterness and rancor against me because you knew me and my family come of fine, old Aryan stock, and of Eldbended the longbow with the best, in the Black Forest with Hermann and Wolfius and their blond beasts, and our men stand over six feet tall and our genes are strong, like our white, gnashing teeth. (*Pause.*) And if we do not dance the hokey-pokey it is because we despise the hokeypokey and all things common. For we are strong. And furthermore we are more sincere than you, less afflicted with bad thoughts of sex, crime, embezzlement, and bank robbery Thank God. (*She stands, fiercely. Pause. All are suddenly still. All start up together. Loud.*)

JUDY: What a miserable creep you are, Melvin, * , ** (GEORGE *and* MOLLY *are overlapping*) to bring up this insulting garbage, and who cares what you feel, you and your swinish, low class family. Why, if I had my way there would be local legislation passed forbidding you and your swinish family from ever spreading your alien, swinish tents and campfires in Hillsbottom. We are a humble, modest people and we do not nose our normal, modest, American noses into other people's lives unless there is the threat of alien contagion, as in your case, which was only prompted by your alien nosing into our ways, which have always been prompted only by the spiritual promptings of our lives, spiritual lives which are far too delicate and intellectually sophisticated for your carnal lips, brains, and feral understandings. You are of the tribe of Belial and Abaddon and must be taught the rule of law. We have tried to teach you this rule of law, but to no avail. You even have spoiled our night of love, here under the magic influence of the summer moon, because you cannot leave be, but must always be tampering with the divine economy of the world, which rules all things, and compels George and me to this spot, to observe our ancient prelapsarian rites, under the furry mantle of heaven. Spite thee, devil! Get thee behind me, Satanist!

GEORGE: Molly, Molly, Molly, for Christ's sake, hear me, I too am of Wotan's mighty crew. Why, therefore, would you not have me when you might've, out back behind the hot dog stand, after we, the Hillsbottom Huns trounced the team from Isle of Hogs, and I could see in your eyes what you wanted, yes, even as your lips denied me, and we were removed from Grace, and expelled into the desert of unsatisfaction and cultural wobble. This, wobbly-legged with lust and lack of satiety, even as the cool night beckoned. (*Pause.*) And then you start up with that miserable, slick Norton guy, what a slick, jive-ass he was, no class at all. I mean, what'd he have that I didn't; he didn't have no red Camaro, and he talked funny too, like some abject weirdo from out of state, some abject, suspect, reform school retard from outer space, who didn't have a clue how to be cool. I mean, not a clue. And what the fuck do you want me to do? Wait till the end of time till you put out? I mean, like get serious. (*Pause.*) And Judy, you ask. She was strictly a party-time girl, yes, I confess it, which is why I asked her to go out, even though she is beneath me. Hell, we all know how beneath me she is! So I guess you could say I was dealing with this crippling emotional affliction (which you caused incidentally), and so where was I to turn, but this scag, Judy, the truly scaggiest of the scaggy. But to her credit she was not too proud, she was not too proud to boff me. Yes, Molly, she boffed me after gym practice, repeatedly, and in the custodian's room during the junior prom, and at the mall, in a dark place, off-limits, near the miniature golf course, and in her room, at her house, and in my room, at our house; and, Molly, I think God would approve this boffing because even though Judy is a dirty, scaggy slut she is sincere, which is more than I can say for you, Molly, yes, you who gave me a hurt that will not heal. Ever.

MOLLY:

Wotan protect me from this horde
of vicious, hellish, monsterific bipeds
in sheep's clothing.
May Wotan protect me from these creepy dickheads.
May Wotan bury his steel hatchet in their faces.
May Wotan fry them in his black skillet.
May Wotan howl over their broken limbs.
May Wotan stretch them up the rack,
    over the white-hot coals.
May Wotan rip their impious eyes from their ugly heads.
May He chant the sacred mystic syllables of our tribe.
May He prepare oils and greases for the holy jamboree.
May He rattle chains and swing the war club
    to terrify their ancestral spirits.
May He rout their armies and scatter
    the fleeing.
May He show no mercy when it comes to
    extermination.
May His revenge be relentless and exacting.
May He darken the skies with smoke of their
    burning dead.
May He place stones on their bleached bones.
May He curse the dead.
May He melt what is solid.
May He avenge the bad thought.
May He stomp and groan, horribly.
May He roar.
May He piss on their
    dreams.
May He shut his eyes.
May he (*pause*)
May He do what he must do.
May he fuck them in the head
    till they die. Amen.

(*A furry pause.* TOM *appears from out of the car.*)

TOM: Well, that's it. I guess none of you are really my friends after all. I plumb well knowed and misknowed all along, yup, cause if'n I were wrong you all woulda been more kindly roundabout here like most, and not up and be all so goshdarn high and mighty 'cause I never done a bad thing to none of you either and if the good Lord would hear me He would take you all up with one hand and fling you down with the other, and stomp on you good with him big furry feet, splat like that, till you were all one big red splotch, 'cause none of you ain't half as sincere as I used to was. So there. Good riddance.

(JESUS H. CHRIST *appears, with her heavy suitcase.*)

CHRIST: Shut up, cracker. (*Pause.*) Git away from that there Ford, you fools. Move your dumb asses, I say. (*They move away.*) Okay, my furry friends, you can come out. (*Pause.*) I'm going to torch the Ford if you two don't climb out of that heap pronto. (*Pause.*) I mean it. (*Two* FURBALLS *climb out of the car.*) That's better. (*She laughs. The* FUR-BALLS *make rude noises at her and give her the finger.*) All you crackers so fucking dumb you don't never see what's going on. Fucking furballs driving you crazy, man, and you can't see a thing. You fucking blind dickheads, all of you. (*Pause.*) And you, beat it. (*Pause.* FURBALLS *stiffen.*) I'm giving you five seconds to get the hell out of here, otherwise I'm gonna set fire to both of youse, and when you're all burnt up I'm gonna piss on both of youse. You understand what I'm saying? BEAT IT! (*The* FURBALLS *split.*) Who the fuck are all of you anyhow? You talk like you know what sincere is, and you don't know moosedick. Why should I bother my ass with a bunch of suck ass, jerkoff spit bags like you? You tell me. This world was not one of my Father's happier creations, I can tell you. I have this from the horse's mouth. He's John Q. Fedup on the subject of planet Earth. He has constructed other, fairer, more interesting worlds than this, whole other universes than this. (*She strikes the ground with her staff and the two girls stand and sing.*)

JUDY AND MOLLY (*singing*):
  I sing because I'm happy.
  I sing because I'm free.
  For His eye is on the sparrow,
  and I know He's watching me.

(*Blackout.*)

CHRIST *speaks to the company, assembled at her feet, including the* FURBALLS.

CHRIST: Do you think I came here to reconcile you, brother to sister, father to son, mother to mother-in-law, second cousin twice-removed to step-aunt from out of state, Cincinnati maybe? Furball to furball? Shit-ass no! I came here to raise badass, obstreperous, antisocial, pestiferous, brutalitarian, loudmouthed and chaotic bloody hell. The roaring kind! You swinish, mealy-mouthed bunch of hypocrites wouldn't know the Lord God of Hosts if he swope down and bit you on the ass. All you care about is what you look like, what you look like in a mirror, a mirror some monster furball dreamt up for you to look at to make you blind. America, you got your eyes open so wide you can't see a fucking thing. America, you're crazy if you think your limpdick, milksop, harebrained Christianity has anything whatsoever to do with Jesus H. Christ, because that's who's standing here before you in the dusty ruination of the open road, because the whole point of what I am about is to shake up belief, to shake up belief and make people stop being so gosh-darned pleased with theyselves, and take a good look at what a sorry place this world is, what with all the jive-ass bullslinging and endless justifying. And mudslinging. And monumental cheapness of heart and moral stinginess. Furthermore, whosoever puts words in my mouth concerning they fears of the so-called cabal of international faggotry, the scourge of the children of Ham, and the Hebrew contagion—(*with irony*) different folks who ought to be viewed with a skeptical eye as total washouts at maintaining correck social decorum and avoidance of the misnormal—all those who puts words in my mouth concerning these things I have no use for. What the fuck do I care who fucks with who? They fucking is they own concern, and may they use it wisely, and well. Furthermore, whosoever puts words in my mouth, he too fucks with me in the abstrack sense; therefore, I do not like him, because . . . because, you go figure: If'n I, Jesus H. Christ, had any desire to speak your language, the debased patois of late capitalism, I woulda done so roundabout here likemost, right from the start; but I didn't, so I don't; I won't give you the satisfaction. Because I got nothing to say to you, America. America, I have nothing to say. I prefer the language of furballs, although they are a wicked awful bunch, and spirits of negation, and the mere sight of 'em like to make my skin crawl. I prefer their language because you so much despise it. No, all I wanted, pure and simple, was to create a context for something powerfully human, great, and beautiful, it being the state of nature to leave off with telling who to do what, X in the name of Y, for no other reason than general cussidness. The door opens on your side, I always say—I can't open it! I mean, the handle's on your side and if you don't want to see that, tough shit, it's your problem and none of mine. Face it, you a sleazy, lying, conniving bunch of dickheads. If you fuck up, it's your fault, not mine. And if I had to do it all over again, I'd give the whole matter serious thought. Because of doubts I now possess about the entire enterprise. Because, you know what I got in this bag, do you? (*Pause.*) I mean, do you know what this load is which I have chosen to lug with me all down through the ages, through the peaks and canyons of oblivion, up to now, do you?

GEORGE: Nope. *

JUDY: No, we don't, ma'am.

CHRIST: OF COURSE YOU DON'T, DICKHEADS. BECAUSE you lack imagination, wit, manners, and any sense of humor. (*Pause.*)

Because anything simple and decent escapes you. (*Pause.*) Because you get lost in insane manias that devolve into nightmares of control, slaughter, rapine, and nontemporal unaccountability. You get lost in dumb-ass things like sincerity and infinite regress. Sincerity!? I'll tell you about sincerity! It's not about all the hooting and hollering. It's about the stillness after all the hooting and hollering has stopped. (*Pause.*) WHAT THE FUCK DO I CARE ABOUT YOUR FUCKING SINCERITY!? You can go shove your fucking sincerity up your tail pipe. (*Pause.*) In here is the quietest poem ever written. And it is heavy. It is really, really heavy. You (*to* GEORGE), you meathead, yes you, you want to try to pick it up? (*Pause.*) Go on. Just try. Pick it up. (GEORGE *tries and can't do it.*) I am Jesus H. Christ *and* I am Jane Q. Fedup. (*Pause.*) When your time comes, you too, each one, will cry out, "jdark," and be gone. You're looking for the wrong event, that's what you're looking for. (*Picks up the suitcase.*) Wake up to the hollow time that is, because that's where your parlous asses are, each and every one. (*She goes. Long pause.*)

MOLLY: The Lord giveth and the Lord taketh away.

TOM: Who was that African-American babe?

(*Blackout.*)

richard greenberg

THE AMERICAN PLAN

LILI (Wendy Makkena) and NICK (D. W. Moffett) grow wary of each other despite an idyllic sanctuary in the Catskills.

The gentleness and subtlety of *The American Plan* are such that one might almost miss the daring with which it subverts convention. Here are these nice people, so unhappy, so familiar to us from other bittersweet romances set at lakeside resorts in the summer. Everything would be fine and absolutely predictable if Greenberg didn't have the temerity to show us, with all the graphic shocks a skilled plot-builder can command, exactly what makes the nice people so unhappy, what they're avoiding, why they lie to each other, and— most distressing of all—what they might have done about it if they had chosen to. Under the unruffled surface of a soft, tender 1950s play, Greenberg's perception is hard, as coldly precise as surgical steel, but throbbing with hot anger as well as warm compassion for his hapless and misguided souls.

"I only wanted to show everyone," said Chekhov, "how empty and useless their lives were, so they would all cry, 'We must do something.' " The 1950s Broadway plays that allegedly took Chekhov as their inspiration turned his anger at the useless emptiness of upper-class lives into a kind of blasé reinforcement: Oh, alas, our lives are so empty and useless, don't we suffer glamorously, fa la. Using iconic scenes, moments, and characters from the period as pathways into its essence, Greenberg rewrites the "atmospheric" American play of the 1950s, turning it inside out to set free the Chekhovian rage that's bottled up inside. To see how the story of his young man and young woman might have been treated back then, compare the plays in which lead roles were created by Julie Harris and John Kerr, who embodied the types definitively; only then do you perceive the cunning and delicacy of Greenberg's variation. In what we thought was, he shows us what could have been—and thereby teaches us, rather devastatingly, how we got from the polite evasions of yesteryear to some of the harrowings of today. As Ibsen said, the ghosts that haunt us aren't supernatural, they're the ghosts of dead ideas and worn-out ways of thinking. With what might be described as the last tender sigh of American naturalism, Greenberg lays them to rest.

The American Plan is for Evan Yionoulis.

The author also wishes to thank the following horde: Joan Copeland, Tate Donovan, Yvette Hawkins, Wendy Makkena, Rebecca Miller, D. W. Moffett, Eric Stoltz, Jonathan Walker, Beatrice Winde, Jim Youmans, Jess Goldstein, Don Holder, Thomas Cabaniss, The Manhattan Theatre Club (inclusive); Helen Merrill for the German lessons; and Jonathan Alper, for his patient counsel and quiet wisdom during the development of this play.

PRODUCTION NOTES

The American Plan was first produced by Manhattan Theatre Club Stage II (Lynne Meadow, Artistic Director; Barry Grove, Managing Director) on January 23, 1990, in New York City. It was directed by Evan Yionoulis; the scene design was by James Youmans; the costume design was by Jess Goldstein; the lighting design was by Donald Holder; original music and sound was by Thomas Cabaniss; and the production stage manager was Richard Hester. The cast was as follows.

LILI ADLER: Rebecca Miller
NICK LOCKRIDGE: Tate Donovan
OLIVIA SHAW: Beatrice Winde
EVA ADLER: Joan Copeland
GIL HARBISON: Eric Stoltz

The American Plan was moved to the main stage of the Manhattan Theatre Club on December 4, 1990. The cast was as follows:

LILI ADLER: Wendy Makkena
NICK LOCKRIDGE: D. W. Moffett
OLIVIA SHAW: Yvette Hawkins

EVA ADLER: Joan Copeland
GIL HARBISON: Jonathan Walker

Special note on music used in this play: Permission from copyright owners of songs and recordings specifically mentioned in the play must be obtained before their use. Songs and recordings in the public domain may be substituted.

CHARACTERS

Lili Adler

Nick Lockridge

Olivia Shaw

Eva Adler

Gil Harbison

LILI *lies in hammock, reading a book.* NICK *enters in bathing trunks, from a swim. He lifts a towel from the grass, starts drying himself off, discovers* LILI.

NICK: Oh . . . hi!

LILI: Hi.

NICK: I just took a swim.

LILI: I can see.

NICK: What a pleasure!—I didn't notice you here before.

LILI: I just came out to read a book.

NICK: I won't disturb you, then.

LILI: Please do. It's a horribly tedious book.

NICK: My name's Nicky Lockridge.

LILI: Lili Adler.

NICK: Pleased to meet you.

LILI: Yes . . . I'd been hoping to.

NICK: What?

LILI: I've seen you . . . I've seen you around.

NICK: Oh.

LILI: Is that the wrong sort of thing to say?

NICK: Not at all.

LILI: I sometimes say the wrong sorts of things—

NICK: Not this time.

LILI: Thank you.

NICK: Have you been here long?

LILI: Forever. Mostly, I stay on this side of the lake.

NICK: I can understand the temptation.

LILI: What do you mean?

NICK: Things get a little, well, a little hectic, huh, on the other side?

LILI: As I said, I seldom go.

NICK: Of course you did. Wonderful swimming in this lake, though. I don't know why people don't use it. Everybody's always hopping into the pool at the hotel, but this lake—it's gorgeous!

LILI: It's infested.

NICK: What?

LILI: With snakes, water moccasins.

NICK: Funnily enough, I missed them.

LILI: No, of course I'm making it up. So what brings you to the Catskills?

NICK: It's my vacation. I'm here with some friends.

LILI: Why?

NICK: It's someplace different.

LILI: Yes, it is. And what do you do?

NICK: Um—

LILI: For work.

NICK: Oh, I . . . I'm planning to be an architect.

LILI: Well, everyone has pipe dreams. What do you do at present?

NICK: I more or less write. (*Beat.*) I'm more or less a magazine writer . . . at present.

LILI: Do you more or less write for any more or less specific periodical?

NICK: Yes . . . I write for the *Weekly Cultural Epiphany.*

LILI: Never heard of it.

NICK: Mostly, we spot trends and lionize masterpieces, that sort of

LILI: The *Weekly Cultural Epiphany*—I've never—

NICK: I write for *Time.*

LILI: Oh. (*With recognition.*) Oh! (*Beat.*) You know, I've never in my life known anyone actually to *read Time*—

NICK: Well—

LILI: But everyone I meet these days seems to write for it.

NICK: That's—

LILI: I've begun to believe that *Time* magazine doesn't exist. It's in fact this vast conspiracy designed to lend credibility to the unemployed—

NICK: That may well—

LILI: I see these men on the street—drunk—sleeping—befouled— I think, "Oh, look, they work for *Time!*"—

NICK: Well—

LILI: No, really, I'm sure it's a very worthwhile job.

NICK: I can assure you it isn't. And what do you do?

LILI: I—well—I. (*Beat.*) I'm preoccupational.

NICK: Are you a student?

LILI: I have been.

NICK: Where?

LILI: I attended Sarah Lawrence College.

NICK: Oh. (*With comprehension.*) Oh!

LILI: You're thinking, "That's why she's crazy."

NICK: Not at all.

LILI: Anyway, I didn't stay long.

NICK: Why was that?

LILI (*quietly*): Another day, another day . . . Anyway, feel free to make yourself at home here.

NICK (*puzzled*): I do.

LILI: It's relaxing, don't you find?

NICK: Oh, yes. Especially, after, you know . . . over there.

LILI: Are you getting tired of things?

NICK: Well, the American Plan—*what* Americans live like this? What Americans *eat* like this? The breakfasts and the lunches and the dinners and the coffees and the teas and the snacks and the hardly any exercise in-between . . .

LILI: And are you getting tired at all of Mindy? (*Beat.*)

NICK: I beg your . . . umm . . . Excuse me?

LILI: You're with Mindy Kahkstein, aren't you?

NICK: Well . . .

LILI: I've seen you together.

NICK: We—

LILI: She hangs onto you like you're, I don't know, a Blue Chip stock or something.

NICK: We're together.

LILI: Huh!

NICK: How did you know?

LILI: I go over there sometimes.

NICK: Ah!

LILI: We're not actually with the hotel, but my mother thinks it's good for me to . . . mingle, to observe.

NICK: You're here with your mother?

LILI: Forever. You can see her if you squint.

NICK: Where?

LILI: Across the lake. Right next to—oh look, *quel surprise!* It's Mindy!

NICK: Where's Mindy?

LILI: A little to the left of where you're looking, now. See? The one with the turbulent thighs and the exotic swimsuit—she kind of looks like she came dressed in a Rhonda Fleming movie?

NICK: Oh, yes!

LILI: Well, my mother is the one to her right. That looming, late-Ibsenesque figure with the mah jong tiles. Oh, and right next to my mother—the Negro woman? That's Olivia—she's ours.

NICK: What does Olivia do?

LILI: She endures.

NICK: What?

LILI: She cleans.

NICK: Oh.

LILI: Cooks a little, listens to my mother's tirades. "One of the well-spoken colored," my mother calls her. This is a step up from "schvartzes."

NICK: Your mother's the one they call "the Duchess," isn't she?

LILI: I wouldn't be the least surprised, the way she treats them. People like my mother never come to the Catskills. She's only here because she thinks you should always have a population you can feel superior to—she's really a dreadful woman.

NICK: I'm sure not.

LILI: Why—what do you know?

NICK: Well, if she were so dreadful, it's unlikely she'd have reared such a . . . charming . . . and mercurial daughter. (*Beat.*)

LILI: Protestant!

NICK: Guilty as charged. (*Looks across lake.*) Oh my God, they're playing more Simon Says. What a nightmare.

LILI: Simon Says: A witless unseen despot who derives his authority from God knows where instructs you to deform yourself in truly revolting ways; and if you dare, even accidentally, to act without his permission, you're exterminated. My mother thinks it's a great game for Jews.

NICK: I'm sorry—but I don't find that funny.

LILI: But my mother *is* a Jew—

NICK: All the same. (*Beat.*)

LILI (*vulnerably*)**:** I'm sorry.

NICK: You don't have to apologize—

LILI: I do—

NICK: There's nothing to apologize *for*—

LILI: Please don't lose respect for me so soon—(*Beat. He looks at her—kindly and puzzled.*) So—Mindy's an education major, isn't she?

Nick: Yes, I think so.

Lili: Yes. Those girls are. How did you come to know her?

Nick: She goes to N.Y.U. We met at Washington Square Park. Or the Automat. A museum, I forget. New York is one big mixer.

Lili: Her father, I believe, pioneered broadloom in Central New Jersey.

Nick: Something like that.

Lili: But do you find her *droll*?

Nick: She's—

Lili: Because I've known Mindy for many summers, and, in my experience, I don't believe I've ever heard anyone describe her as *droll*.

Nick: In my experience, I don't believe I've ever heard anyone describe *anyone* as droll.

Lili: Touché.

Nick: She's a very nice girl. I like her a lot.

Lili: She's extremely rich. (*Beat.*)

Nick: And who says I'm not? (*Beat.*)

Lili: Then why do you work?

Nick: What do you mean?

Lili: You hate your job. Why don't you quit?

Nick: Because you have to work.

Lili: Not if you have money, you don't.

Nick: Yes, you do.

Lili: Why?

Nick: Because.

LILI: Why?

NICK: It's not a thing to question. Why do you even question it? (*Beat.*) Why are you looking at me like that?

LILI: I like the way you look.

NICK: I'm flattered.

LILI: Like nothing ever happened to you.

NICK: I don't know if that's such a good thing.

LILI: It's a very good thing, believe me, a *very* good thing. So, is it true that Mindy's a nymphomaniac?

NICK (*pausing, bemused, shocked, and amazed at her effrontery*): Yes.

LILI: *Really?* . . . A *big* one?

NICK: They only come in one size.

LILI: Is that . . . Well, is that *fun?*

NICK: It depends—

LILI: On what—?

NICK: The time of day, the—oh, look, this isn't something I'm really comfortable talking about—

LILI (*quickly*): I'm sorry—

NICK: Maybe I should just go back—

LILI: No—no—absolutely not—

NICK: No, it's been very pleasant talking with you—

LILI (*desperately*): Where do you live? (*Beat.*)

NICK: Where do I live?

LILI: Your New York residence? In New York?

NICK: In the Village. For *now.* This little place in the Village. Where do you live?

Lili: The river Styx. (*Beat.*) This place on Central Park West. Where the rooms are heavy with dark damask and filled with a sabbath light—

Nick: Uh-huh—

Lili: Which is not light at all, but merely darkness visible—

Nick: You live in New York's only Miltonic co-op—

Lili: You recognized . . .

Nick: I went to good schools.

Lili: Anyway, it's a horrible place, and sort of disgraces us. It's the doctors and the intellectuals who got to live on Park Avenue. My father's profession didn't rate.

Nick: Oh, what did he do?

Lili: Before my mother murdered him, he was an inventor of some kind.

Nick: That's not true—

Lili: Oh, yes, he invented—well, I've never actually been sure, but it was very lucrative—

Nick: Your mother did not murder your father.

Lili: Oh, yes. With small doses of cyanide administered in his farina. Cyanide was flavorless so—

Nick: Cyanide tastes like almonds—

Lili: Oh, you've dabbled?

Nick: It's a well-known . . . Dabbled! . . . It's a well-known . . . I read mysteries.

Lili: She killed him, but bribed the law up-and-down . . . she has the scratch for it . . . and now she's holding me captive here.

Nick: Yes. And why is that?

LILI: She's terribly disappointed in me . . . She'd always hoped for an attractive daughter. She thinks I was some sort of genetic mutation.

NICK: That can't be it—

LILI: But it is!

NICK: No one could ever feel shortchanged by *your* looks. (*Beat.*)

LILI (*softly*): Thank you. (*Beat.*) Or yours. You look like—

NICK: Nothing ever happened to me, I know—

LILI: It's your charm! Nicky Tabula rasa, that's what I'll call you!

NICK: Please don't.

LILI: It's a good name!

NICK: It's the wrong name.

LILI: I don't think so.

NICK: Trust me.

LILI (*softly*): I don't think so. (*Pause. They look at each other. Offstage: Eva's voice calls musically: "Lili! . . . Lili! . . ."*) Oh God!

NICK: Who is that?

LILI: Her. She's come back.

NICK: So?

LILI: She's going to send Olivia for me now. Or come herself. She'll take me back to the house.

NICK: The house?

LILI: Yes. Over there.

NICK: Is that—is that yours?

LILI: Yes. Of course.

NICK: Where we are now—is this your property?

LILI: Yes. (*Beat.* NICK *colors, starts foraging for his clothes.*)

NICK: God, I'm sorry—I'm very sorry—I had no idea.

LILI: No—no—it's fine—

NICK: If I had known, I'd never have . . . just sprawled out here like this—

LILI: Don't go—

NICK: It's just . . . that house doesn't even look like a house, really, I thought it was . . . I don't know . . . a boathouse or something . . . and it certainly doesn't seem to go along with this land and so I—I'm very, *very* sorry—

LILI: Stop. Please . . . stop. (*He is dressed by now; he stops, looks at her.*) Look—Please—would you please—come see me sometimes? There's no one—I don't speak to anyone—and they're—they're very stern with me and—oh, please, would you, would you please . . . come see me?

NICK: Lili—

LILI: Just while you're here. Just sometimes. (OLIVIA *enters, stands a little away from them.*)

OLIVIA (*gently*): Lili . . . (LILI *looks at her, looks back at* NICK. *Then she goes to* NICK, *takes his face in her hands, and kisses him. They part and she walks off with* OLIVIA. NICK *stands there.*)

(*Fade out.*)

SCENE 2

LILI, EVA, *and* OLIVIA *are breakfasting outside.*

EVA: . . . and, then, we all repaired to the club where the most mystifying entertainer held forth . . . if only I could remember his name! He was . . . how do you say it . . . *crossed-eyed,* with vast jowls and this idiotic, juvenile voice, and, of course, his language was quite improper, and what he said was simply nonsense, yet those around me *howled,* as though these were the pearls of Oscar Wilde being thrown before them. Unutterably fascinating! I wanted you to be there, Lili, to assure me I had not *lost* my mind.

LILI: Uh-huh,

EVA: Everyone asked after you at dinner—aren't you hungry, why aren't you eating? Olivia has prepared for us a lovely porridge. (LILI *takes a bite.*) That's good. At any rate, I had a pencil with me, my little gold pencil, and I recorded my impressions of the event on a cocktail napkin, lest I forget them. What an extraordinary evening. Yet, not at all . . . untypical . . . for the region. Ve-e-e-ry strange.

OLIVIA: Would you like me to make something else, Lili?

LILI: No.

EVA: That darling Mindy Kahkstein was there. A *m-o-ost* peculiar girl. One of those American girls who can't seem to get used to their bosoms. To show or not to show. To slump or stand erect. You feel these are her sole concerns. She asked after you.

OLIVIA: Would you like milk instead of coffee, Lili? I'll get you some.

LILI: Coffee's fine.

EVA: And, of course, I spent time with Libby Kahkstein—a woman who is *très cher,* but not, I think, intellectually robust. And, once again, she disgraced herself at table. Why, when I tell you what she ate, and in what quantities! The *salad*—served at the beginning— barbaric, anyway, but Libby tore into it like a savage woman. And the Russian dressing—not just a dollop, either, but *gobules*—Gobules?—*Globules.* Then the consommé, then the derma, smothered in gravy and onions, then the filet mignon—a steak the size and shape of a jackboot also smothered in gravy. With a vast baked potato, into which Libby Kahkstein scooped not merely sour cream and chives, but five pats of butter. *Plus* asparagus with hollandaise. *Plus,* infinite numbers of buttered rolls, with seeds popping everywhere. *Plus,* sherbet between courses. *Plus,* barrels of cream soda. *Plus,* coffee with heavy cream and parfait. Then—*then*—after the meal was over, and there was a little desultory dancing—out came this enormous Viennese table. And Libby Kahkstein—using every ounce of energy available to her simply to transport her laden bulk—helped herself not *once,* not *twice,* but *three* times. To Napoleon, sacher torte, and a large plate of little cookies. *Incroyable!* But, my darling, why aren't you eating your breakfast?

LILI: I don't know.

EVA: You must . . . you must keep up your strength. Next time, you will come with me. It will please me to have you by my side, just for your humorous way of looking at things.

LILI: I don't want to go.

OLIVIA: I'll make you some dry toast.

LILI: I'm perfectly all right. Please leave me alone. (*Beat.*)

EVA: Now, Lili, we are only trying our best

OLIVIA: It's all right.

EVA: —our very best to help you, my darling—

OLIVIA: Nobody ever died from missing breakfast.

EVA: And if we misspeak ourselves sometimes, that's—

LILI: I don't need anything. Thank you. And I'd rather not be asked. (*Beat.*)

EVA: Well, then, my darling, you shan't be. (*Beat.*)

LILI: Thank you. (*They sit quietly a moment.* EVA *and* OLIVIA *resume eating.*)

EVA: But . . . you must . . . Lili, you must come *out* a bit—

LILI: Why?

EVA: For your health.

LILI: My health is fine.

EVA: For your *well-being*. (*Beat.*) It is something all the doctors have agreed upon. All we are here for—all we want—Olivia and I—is for our girl to be happy again.

LILI: I am.

EVA: Yes?

LILI (*sullenly*): Drunk with it. (*Beat.*)

EVA: Well, at any rate, I am pleased that you have not entirely confined your circle of acquaintances to us two old ladies—

LILI: What do you mean?

EVA: Nothing, nothing—

LILI: What do you mean?

EVA: Merely that Olivia informs me she has seen you—on more than one occasion, I believe—in the company of a most attractive young man from across the lake.

LILI: Olivia should be shot between the eyes.

EVA: Lili! (OLIVIA *starts laughing.*) What a thing to say! All I meant was I am terribly *pleased*.

LILI: And then her corpse should be thrown to sharks—

EVA: My darling, no!

OLIVIA: She doesn't mean it.

LILI: Every word. (*Pause.* LILI *stares balefully at* OLIVIA; OLIVIA *looks back; her good humor gives way.* EVA *sighs.*)

EVA: Another one of these breakfasts. (*Beat.*) My darling, my sweetheart. (*To* OLIVIA:) My maid. (*Beat.*) I shall leave you to sort yourselves out. Now I must go and lie in the bathtub to soak for two hours in salted water. The price I must pay for the sins of a corrupt and sporting youth. (EVA *exits.* OLIVIA *and* LILI *are left alone, separate and sullen. After a long silence,* LILI *goes over to* OLIVIA *and embraces her.*)

OLIVIA (*yielding gruffly*)**:** Oh, sure, sure, yes, now you want to be friends.

LILI: I don't really think your corpse should be thrown to the sharks.

OLIVIA: Generous of you. Why do you treat your mother like you do?

LILI: How do I treat her?

OLIVIA: Like you do.

LILI: She used to sing, "The Nazis haven't found us, but darling they're around us." I was in my crib.

OLIVIA: You were born difficult. A difficult girl.

LILI: I'm a breeze.

OLIVIA: Ho-ho!

LILI: What?

OLIVIA: You used to run away—

LILI: I was a child—

OLIVIA: We'd find you in the basement with the mailman, sorting letters. We'd find you on Broadway in a coffee shop, drinking coffee black—

LILI: I liked the way it ate my stomach out—

OLIVIA: Or we'd find you not at all, you'd just show up.

LILI: I came back to you—I missed your lap . . . I used to think you were Buddha.

OLIVIA: Hush.

LILI: I'd chant, shantih, shantih, shantih, I want to die!

OLIVIA: Enough of that kind of talk.

LILI: April is the cruelest month.

OLIVIA: This is July. A balmy July.

LILI: This was then . . . when I was a child.

OLIVIA: You were no picnic.

LILI: Wasn't I a picnic?

OLIVIA: Your mother was a woman alone. She gave you nice things. Good schools. She made her way. That was not easy, not easy at all—

LILI: Is she still sick?

OLIVIA: She's climbing her way out.

LILI: I'll be better. I'll be kind.

OLIVIA: She says she doesn't want you to bother—she says you're young—

LILI (*chuckling grimly*): The witch . . .

OLIVIA: Lili!

LILI: Olivia, how old are you when it's too late to start being happy?

OLIVIA: Thirty-five.

LILI: Oh, I have time . . .

OLIVIA (*noting her distraction*): Who are you *looking* for?

LILI: No one.

OLIVIA: That boy?

LILI: He's a man, he has a criminal record.

OLIVIA: He *what*?

LILI: I made that up.

Olivia: Why?

Lili: It came to me.

Olivia: You shouldn't speak off the top of your head.

Lili: I like the top of my head.

Olivia: It will get you into trouble someday.

Lili: I hope so. Did you have a ravenous sex life we know nothing about?

Olivia: Lili . . .

Lili: I'd respect you for it, I wouldn't call you a slut . . .

Olivia: Lili . . .

Lili: Are you a virgin?

Olivia: Lili . . .

Lili: You could be either of these things. I don't know you at all.

Olivia: Being known is not part of my job . . .

Lili: Olivia, does your knitting ever become anything? Or do you unravel it every night? Are you stalling until your husband comes back from the wars?

Olivia: I'm going into town later to buy food. Is there anything special you want for dinner?

Lili: What did my father die of? (*Beat.*)

Olivia: Pneumonia.

Lili: I thought it was malaria.

Olivia: Well, maybe it was.

Lili: Was he in Panama or something? Who dies of malaria on Central Park West?

Olivia: You ask and ask and ask. What are you planning to do with all these answers if you get them?

LILI: Make them into belts.

OLIVIA: Difficult. A difficult girl. (*Looking out.*) There's that young man.

LILI: Where?

OLIVIA: Over there . . . with that girl, that Mindy girl.

LILI: Oh. (*Beat.*) That's a bagatelle. We're best friends already.

OLIVIA: Do you even know him? Who is he?

LILI: His name is Nicky Lockridge.

OLIVIA: Oh, Nicky Lockridge.

LILI: And he's a prince . . . from the east . . .

OLIVIA: A bedtime story.

LILI: Yes. A bedtime story. (*She curls up by Olivia's legs.*) On his piebald steed—I like that word, piebald—

OLIVIA: It's a good word—

LILI: He charges the fields of Greenwich and Darien. His life is a round of jousts and tourneys and tennis matches and he's a mean man with a la crosse stick. His family's heraldic crest is centuries old, and yet this young prince is sore at heart—

OLIVIA: Sore at heart—

LILI: Yes, sore at heart. For to whom can he dedicate his jousts and tourneys? To what fair maiden can he offer the bull's ear? He's a matador, too.

OLIVIA: Right, right—on *weekends.*

LILI: So he's plunged himself into a journey of matrimonial intent. Fearlessly, he's scaled the mighty Catskills. Fearlessly, he's met the natives of darkest Kiamesha, and he has conquered. He has conquered. The pennants shiver in the wind; the maypole drops its streamers. For Nicky has met his match. (*Offstage,* EVA *begins to hum* *the lullaby "Nicht is das gluck."* LILI *reacts to it almost as though physically stricken. She closes her eyes and listens, motionless.* OLIVIA *comes behind her and holds her. They stay this way until* EVA *finishes.*) Olivia, I'm getting married. Nicky's asked me to marry him.

OLIVIA: Lili!

LILI: Don't breathe a word. (*She exits suddenly.*)

(*Fade out.*)

S C E N E 3

LILI *lies in the hammock, listening to Bobby Darin sing "Beyond the Sea" on her transistor radio.* NICK *enters.*

LILI: Bobby Darin.

NICK: I know.

LILI: I am not the praying sort, but if I were I would leave this hammock and genuflect to Bobby Darin. I wait all afternoon for Bobby Darin to come on the radio.

NICK: He's a good singer.

LILI: Are you the praying sort?

NICK: No, can't say that I am, not very much, no. (LILI *flicks off transistor radio.*)

LILI: So, Nick, long time no see. What brings you here?

NICK: You told Mindy I had clap. (*Beat.*)

LILI: No, she got it wrong. What I said was, when I see you pass, you're such a sterling figure, it makes me want to clap. It got lost in translation. From English to Mindy.

NICK: It's like a goddamn whispering gallery over there. Suddenly I'm getting the most incredible looks.

LILI: I have no idea what you're talking about.

NICK: I do not appreciate being associated with a venereal disease. It's not anything I can capitalize on.

LILI: I have no idea what you're talking about . . .

NICK: Lili! (*Beat. She looks at him.*) Stop lying . . . Please, please stop lying. (*Beat.*)

LILI: Why did you stop coming around?

NICK: I got . . . busy.

LILI: Oh, yes? *Time* dispatched you to Southeast Asia, did it?

NICK: Busy here.

LILI: There is no such thing as busy here—

NICK: There was a . . .

LILI: What?

NICK: . . . shuffleboard tournament.

LILI: Ah!

NICK: I won.

LILI: It only adds more luster. (*Beat.*)

NICK: I have obligations, you know. Other . . . obligations. To the people I'm here with. They *brought* me here.

LILI: So?

NICK: So . . . it's . . . it's incumbent upon me to spend time with them.

LILI: Why?

NICK: Why? Why do you keep asking me why? It's practically premoral of you.

LILI: Premoral—does that come by way of Mindy, the psychology major?

NICK: Education.

LILI: Education, yes, I forgot.

NICK: No . . . it doesn't come by way of Mindy. It's . . . it's just the code.

LILI: I'll go across the lake for you now, Nicky. I'll go and apologize to Mindy, and tell her it was all a ghastly mistake. One of my capricious jokes. They all think I'm crazy, anyway.

NICK: She's gone.

LILI: No!

NICK: The whole family—

LILI: When?

NICK: About an hour ago.

LILI: Why?

NICK: Mr. Kahkstein heard the rumor. (*Beat.*)

LILI: I'm sorry.

NICK: It seems you're a very persuasive storyteller. It seems Mindy returned to their cabana in tears.

LILI: Oh God, no . . .

NICK: Mrs. Kahkstein asked her why she was crying—

LILI: She didn't—

NICK: She's not as circumspect as other girls I've known—

LILI: She's a cow—

NICK: Please don't. I am involved, you know that.

LILI: Yes, I'm sorry, again, I'm sorry—

NICK: Mrs. Kahkstein turned out to be more pragmatic than I'd anticipated. She said, "Well, darling, men can be that way. At least you found out in time."

LILI: Oh, no . . .

NICK: Well, at that, Mindy cried even harder and Mrs. Kahkstein said, "Mindy—if this is true—it doesn't affect *you*, does it?"

LILI: She told the truth?

NICK: She said, "Yes, mother it does. We've slept together. Over and over and over again."

LILI: The fool—

NICK: Mr. Kahkstein apparently purpled at this and swore he'd have my scalp—

LILI: I'll tell them, I'll call, I'll alert the Coast Guard—

NICK: He said, something like, "that . . ." *gondiff*?

LILI: Gonniff—it means thief—

NICK: Yes, well, he said, "That gonniff, I'll see him dead for taking my daughter's virtue and giving her a disease."

LILI: He could do it, too. New Jersey is lousy with Cosa Nostra, I'm sure he has connections—

NICK: But then, *Mindy*—who was not at her best—said, "Daddy, don't be ridiculous. He didn't take my virtue. I've slept with hundreds of men. I'm afraid *I* gave it to *him*."

LILI: Even I gave her more credit than—

NICK: Well, he didn't know *what* to do when he heard this, so he punched the wall, yelled at his wife, and ended up giving me a cigar. Would you like it? It's Havana. Before the revolution. Which, I think, must make it more a souvenir than a smoke.

LILI: I'm evil.

NICK: You're . . . effective.

LILI: Well, what should I do, Nick? Should I write a letter?

Nick: Oh, who knows? I don't understand how anyone's mind works anymore. For all I know, everything will be fine in the morning, and we'll still be engaged.

Lili (*startled*): Engaged?

Nick: Yes.

Lili: You never told me that part.

Nick: It's new . . . It's not official, it's . . . understood.

Lili (*softly*): You never told me.

Nick: I know.

Lili: We walked together . . . Well, then, why are you here?

Nick: I want to know why you did it.

Lili: I missed you.

Nick: And this is the simplest way you could think of to deal with that problem?

Lili: My mind doesn't run to simple ways. How is it you've been here so long, anyway? Don't you have a job to do? *Time* magazine must be incredibly liberal with its vacations. They ought to call it, *"Free Time."*

Nick: Lili—

Lili: Mindy has gone; why aren't you going too?

Nick: The room still belongs to me and—

Lili: That's not a reason—

Nick: I want to see you.

Lili: Why?

Nick: I don't know anyone like you.

Lili: Mindy's like me. Mindy's exactly like me. Except stupid and a cow.

NICK: She isn't anything like you.

LILI: and a raving, famous nymphomaniac.

NICK: Granted.

LILI: I'll be a raving, famous nymphomaniac, maybe, someday—

NICK: That's not an ambition.

LILI: Did my mother give you money to stop seeing me? (*Beat.*)

NICK: You shouldn't have said that.

LILI: I'm sorry, I'm sorry—but it's something she'd try—

NICK: The last time I saw you, you ran in the other direction because you were with her.

LILI: You can't meet her.

NICK: God! Why can't you just relax?

LILI: Nick, I'm rich all by myself. Next year I get all this money my father left me. And there's nothing she can do about it.

NICK: Money couldn't have less to do with anything.

LILI: Because sex is the only currency that matters when you're my age.

NICK: I'm sorry, but you're a little . . . *warped* . . . where some things are concerned.

LILI: So I have been repeatedly told. (*Beat.*) Oh, you know too much about me. Why can't we talk about you once in a while instead? Tell me something.

NICK: Like what?

LILI: Anything terrible. (*Beat.*)

NICK: You already said nothing ever happened to me.

LILI: I said that's what you look like.

Nick: Maybe I'm afraid it's true.

Lili: But I want it to be true. I want you to have been spared *everything.* (*Pause. He is brought up short by the sincerity of this.*)

Nick (*concededly*)**:** I stopped seeing you because Mindy asked me to.

Lili: Why?

Nick: Because you're beautiful.

Lili: That can't be pos—

Nick: Accept it. (*Pause.*)

Lili: Oh my God, I can't believe what I said to her. Awful, just awful.

Nick: Yes.

Lili: It's just that you're such a surprise . . . There was no preparing for you . . . If I'd had a year or two, I might have been ready. (*Beat.*)

Nick: Oh . . . look . . . why don't we *swim?*

Lili: What?

Nick: Let's swim. Let's just suit up and swim, okay? And maybe have drinks after? I'm on vacation. I was hoping for a nice time.

Lili: I don't swim.

Nick: What?

Lili: I can't—I don't know how.

Nick: That's terrible—How do you get through the day if you can't throw yourself into water? I'll teach you.

Lili: You have to learn that sort of thing young.

Nick: Listen, I can teach you the butterfly stroke in two weeks. By the end of the month, you'll be entering diving championships.

Lili: I don't think I'd be able to—

NICK: I learned pinochle with Moe Kahkstein: tit-for-tat—

LILI: Of course you did. You're easy in all situations. Because when you're odd man out, everyone else feels uncomfortable. It's the gift of your hegemony.

NICK: All these words! (*Beat.*)

LILI: What are you offering, really? (OLIVIA *enters.*)

OLIVIA: Lili, we're having tea.

LILI: I'm with someone, Olivia.

OLIVIA: I've set four places.

LILI: No.

OLIVIA: Your mother says she's looking forward to meeting the young man, after all this time. Will you join us, Mr. —

NICK: Nick Lockridge.

OLIVIA: Will you join us, Mr. Lockridge?

NICK: I'll be very happy to—

LILI: But—

NICK: Lead the way. (OLIVIA *and* NICK *start off.* LILI *holds back a moment.*)

LILI: To lose you to her so soon. (*She starts off after them.*)

(*Fade out.*)

S C E N E   4

Evening. EVA *and* NICK *at tea table.* OLIVIA *presides.* LILI *idles, paces, leans on the periphery.*

OLIVIA: More tea, Mr. Lockridge?

NICK: Yes, please. It's wonderful tea.

EVA: Another biscuit?

NICK: Thank you.

EVA: Have you spent much time in the mountains?

NICK: Winters, mostly.

EVA: Ah, yes, winters . . . I suspect you of being deeply and confirmedly aquatic.

NICK: Very much so.

EVA: Yes, yes . . . Personally, I don't trust the sea. I do not even, if such a thing is not unutterably foolish, I do not *approve of* the sea—

NICK (*smiling*): Really?

LILI: It's a mania—

EVA: No, I feel that illusion of limitlessness . . . that challenge to embark . . . to sail . . . to immerse oneself in an element for which one is not naturally, not physiologically equipped . . . These things I believe to be seductive and subversive and tragic—

NICK: Huh!

EVA: In the mountains, on the other hand—the borders are visible, tangible, and *everywhere.* Very trustworthy.

NICK: I guess I never looked at it that way before.

EVA: It is for this reason that we come here year after year. Though it means we must suffer proximity to some of this country's most comical misfits. But even *that* is a good thing—it is good to stay in touch with the lower life forms. Olivia tells me you wish to be an architect—

NICK: Olivia?

LILI: Olivia!

EVA: I love architects. Has Lili told you yet of my affair with Mies van der Rohe?

NICK: No—no, she hasn't—

EVA: She will get to it. Of course, it's a preposterous idea, but it's a thing she likes to say.

LILI: It came on the heels of her affair with Himmler.

EVA (*gaily*): Yes, my darling, spin, spin. (*Smiling conspiratorially at* NICK.) Now what kind of architect do you wish to be?

NICK: Every kind.

EVA: Yes, I'd forgotten. There is never any need to ask an American this sort of question; one always receives the same answer. And what do you wish to build?

NICK: A whole city.

EVA: Do you mean, by that, that you wish to build an entire city yourself or that you wish to build a city that is technologically integrated, spiritually complete, and well managed?

NICK: The latter.

LILI: All the cities have already been built.

NICK: Not all of them.

EVA: So . . . As one who is interested in these things, what is your opinion of my little *Nicht Ahin, Nicht Ahier*? (*Beat.*)

NICK: I'm sorry . . . I don't understand the question. Is that German?

EVA: In a manner of speaking. *Nicht Ahin, Nicht Ahier* is my little name for our house—because it belongs neither to the hotel nor to the little rural outposts on this side of the lake. But I am being foolish—the house is humble and not for criticism. A whole city—my, my! Now, tell me, where did you study architecture? Where did you get your degree?

Nick: I haven't . . . actually . . . yet.

Eva: You haven't? . . . But you are not so very young, are you?

Nick: No—not so very young.

Eva: But who am I to talk? I saw Methuselah in his pram—why have you not studied yet?

Nick: I was going to start a couple of years ago . . . but things got in the way—

Eva: Things?

Nick: Personal things—

Eva: Too personal to share, I understand—

Nick: No, no—

Eva: Nothing is required of you—

Nick: Oh, that's really—

Eva: We make a point never to pry

Nick: My father died a while ago and I've been . . . sidetracked.

Eva (*gently*): Oh my dear . . . How did he die? May I ask it?

Nick: Stupidly . . . It was a freak accident. He was cleaning his gun . . . and it went off . . .

Lili: Nicky . . .

Eva: I am so terribly, terribly sorry . . .

Nick: It was tough at first, but I guess I'm used to it, now—

Eva: And your mother?

NICK: My mother died the year before.

EVA: Oh, my dear, random things, random things . . .

NICK: Yes . . . random.

EVA: But it is the people to whom random things happen, and who are then able to survive, flourish . . . it is these people who will see Damascus. My husband and I were in Germany until the last possible moment. We were to discover that the boat we took was the last boat out. What would have happened if we had missed that boat . . . (LILI *has begun to skip rope.*)

OLIVIA: Lili—

EVA: Oh, look, Lili has decided to entertain us with a sporting event. There, my dear, skip, skip, don't mind us . . .

LILI: It's wonderful exercise. Prize fighters do it.

EVA: Just think of the shock for me, Mr. Lockridge—all my background, all my education, and I have given birth to Sonny Liston—

LILI: Nicky and Lili up a tree—

EVA: We are not an eccentric family, Nicky—

LILI: K-I-S-Society—

EVA: Just a little giddy around the circumference—

LILI: First comes love/then comes marriage—

NICK: Lili!

EVA: Have you discussed this scenario, or is Lili improvising?

LILI: Then comes Nicky with the baby carriage—

NICK: That's very embarrassing—

EVA: My daughter is this way because her father indulged her; he found her irresistible—

NICK: What was it Mr. Adler did?

LILI: My father invented Teflon—

EVA: Mr. Adler invented—

LILI: He invented Bakelite—

EVA: He had the patent on—

LILI: He blazed the trail for macaroni and cheese—

EVA: Mr. Adler's work was in—

LILI: He invented the reversible condom—

EVA (*gently*): Lili . . . (*Beat.*)

LILI (*softly; chastened*): Something in lamps. He invented something that's in lamps . . . something that's in lamps. Excuse me, please . . . (*She exits quickly.*)

NICK: Lili— (*But she's gone.*) I should go after her.

EVA: No, please stay with me. Olivia will see to her . . . Will you, please, Olivia?

OLIVIA: Of course.

EVA: Follow at a good distance, remember. (OLIVIA *exits*). Lili has gone through many corrections, but she retains her genius for the inappropriate.

NICK: What upsets her so much?

EVA: Oh, my daughter, my darling daughter . . . Inside her head is a sort of masked ball; you never know with whom you are dancing . . . You seem fond of Lili.

NICK: I am.

Eva: Genuinely fond. . . . Oh, it is always so hard, this part . . . Lili is not charmingly eccentric. She is not your garden variety neurotic. She's been hospitalized.

Nick: Why?

Eva: Who knows, who knows? *This* is better than usual.

Nick: But how long has she been this way? When did it start?

Eva: Oh, it began before it ever began. Has Lili ever told you that I murdered her father?

Nick (*pausing*): No.

Eva: Obviously, that means, yes . . . Yes. Well, I think she half-believes it, you know. And who can blame her? After the thing that happened to Mr. Adler, there was no consoling anyone in that house.

Nick: What happened to him?

Eva: Everything in the world. And nothing you could possibly understand . . . I loved my husband for subtle reasons and he was annihilated for a crude one . . . But that is no kind of story for a summer night . . . Oh, my dear, how can you take the sadness away from a girl who learned it so early in life? It is not possible. It can't be done. Every summer we come here and there's someone. Some sweet boy from across the lake. We hope, we pray, but it's no good. Nothing has worked. It always ends in disaster.

Nick: Are you trying to scare me off?

Eva: Are you scared?

Nick: Not at all. (*Beat.*)

Eva: Oh, no, no, no . . . That is not it at all . . . I simply wonder what kind of effect you might have on her? To pay attention, to flatter her with your presence, when you have, after all, a life you must return to, responsibilities—

Nick: There's nothing that pressing—

Eva: Oh, but surely . . . they require you back at . . . *Time,* is it?

Nick: Not for a while, no. (*Beat.*)

Eva: But, then, in New York and . . . Darien, did you say?

Nick: Yes, Darien.

Eva: Yes, Darien . . . aren't there people who are missing you?

Nick: No one that I care to see. (Eva *looks at him quizzically.*) No one I need to see right away. (*Beat.*)

Eva: Well . . . yes, then . . . yes . . . Perhaps this would be just the thing. Perhaps you are what we have waited for.

Nick: She thinks . . . I shouldn't say this—

Eva: Tell me.

Nick: She thinks you want to keep me away from her.

Eva: She thinks I am the opposite of what I am. Will you tell her, my dear? Will you tell her that I have not discouraged you? That I wish what she does? And will you be good to her? Whatever the cost? (*Beat.*)

Nick: The cost?

Eva: Do you smell rain? I must take off my rings; my joints will swell. (*She removes her rings; they fall to the ground.*) Oh, how clumsy I am!

Nick: Here let me— (Nick *kneels to search for them.*)

Eva: No, don't bother, it's too dark—you'll never find them.

Nick: But they're diamonds!

Eva: They will be there in the morning.

Nick: But what if they're not?

Eva: Then they're not. (*Slowly he rises, faces her.*) Whatever you can do, my dear. That may not be much. After all, we can't expect miracles. (*They look at each other.*)

(*Fade out.*)

Lili *alone.* Nick *enters.*

Lili: The hospital was her idea.

Nick: What?

Lili: I wasn't really sick. I was fine. She didn't think so. On my twenty-first birthday I get the money my father left me. Then I'll be well.

Nick: All right. (*Beat.*)

Lili: So she did tell you?

Nick: Yes.

Lili: Of course. So you'll leave me.

Nick: She doesn't want me to leave; she asked me not to.

Lili: That way when you do she'll seem blameless . . . It's one of her oldest tricks.

Nick: Lili—

Lili: Why did you tell her all those things you never told me?

Nick: She draws it out . . .

Lili: She has you now.

Nick: It's not that complicated.

LILI: This happens all the time. We come here every year: "Please, Lili, play," she says. "Be happy, be free. Please, Lili, find someone and don't frighten him away—" I frighten everyone—

NICK: You don't frighten me—

LILI: She'll do that for me—

NICK: No—

LILI: Oh, trust me—

NICK: Don't—

LILI: Why don't you just go away now? Why don't you just leave me alone?

NICK: Why are you going on like this?

LILI: Because I love you. (*Beat.*) I know that sounds crazy, but I'm not crazy—I know my own name—I don't see things—and I love you . . . I know I can't ever have you, I know I lie . . . I do awful things . . . I don't know why . . . I can't explain it . . . I feel as if everything I've ever done was something that happened *to* me . . . That sounds crazy, too . . . Oh God, this isn't making you think any better of me . . . I'm sorry . . . I haven't meant anything . . . Just go. (*Beat.*)

NICK: Nothing you said sounds crazy—No, *listen* . . . Nothing you said sounds crazy. And I don't believe you've ever done anything so terrible. You have this way of seeing yourself—I think it just comes from living in dark rooms with bad air—Listen—all this stuff about what you've done—even if you *have* done it—pasts are . . . they're nothing . . . Things can be so much simpler . . .

LILI: Look—she'll probably be here soon—It would be better if you just—

NICK: Forget her! The hell with her. There are some people we have to pretend don't exist. We just have to forget about—no matter how it hurts . . . Some people we just have to get away from—

LILI: I can't do that.

NICK: I know you can.

LILI: You don't understand.

NICK: I do.

LILI: She's what I have . . .

(*Pause.*)

NICK: When we met . . . it wasn't the first time I'd seen you . . . I'd been watching you . . . I came here for you . . . I came here to meet you—

LILI: You said—

NICK: I lied.

LILI: But—

NICK: Don't talk! And ever since then, I've been . . . Look, it wasn't because of Mindy that I stopped seeing you. I was scared . . . because I'd never wanted anything so much. (*Beat.*)

LILI: That can't be possible.

NICK: Why not? Because you want it to be?

LILI: Yes.

NICK: Then maybe your luck has changed. (*Beat.*)

LILI: But will you be on my side? Whatever happens . . . will you be on my side? (*He kisses her.*) Nick—?

NICK: What?

LILI: Let's swim. (*They kiss again and lie down. "Beyond the Sea" plays.*)

(*Fade out.*)

NICK *and* EVA *alone.* EVA *is using a cane.*

EVA: It has warmed my heart to see the change in Lili over these last weeks.

NICK: We've been very happy. She's swimming now.

EVA: Swimming, my God, what a wonder you are!

NICK: I don't take credit . . . The cane . . .

EVA: Yes.

NICK: I've never seen it before.

EVA: Ah, well—the body is weak, the body is strong, everything is reversible. Where shall we have the wedding, here do you think, or in town?

NICK: I think that should be up to Lili. I think that would be best.

EVA: What a kind young man you are, how considerate. (*Beat.*) Now, let me tell you what I have discovered about you.

NICK: Excuse me?

EVA: First, you do not work for *Time.*

NICK: What are you talking about?

EVA: One does not find you on their employee roster. Or on any Luce publication—or any publication at all, for that matter.

NICK: I can show you my press card.

EVA: Does it have an expiration date?

NICK: No.

EVA: Too bad. Defunct things should declare themselves defunct. You were fired several months ago . . . You do not remonstrate. Good. This will go smoothly, then.

NICK: I—

EVA: Ah-ah . . . don't interrupt my flow. Second, you have no money whatsoever. I have researched your family—given a certain amount of money, one does have contacts, you know, even against one's will. You come from one of those fine blood edifices that started to crumble virtually upon erection. A fortune with perhaps a crime attached to it. Social registry. Neglect—sudden bankruptcy—a very American story, very boring.

NICK: Eva, listen—

EVA: Third—and most regrettably—your father did not die in a freak accident while cleaning his gun—

NICK: I'm afraid you're wrong there—

EVA: Well, then he must have been licking it clean for the bullet discharged in his mouth. (*Beat.*) Ah. I am sorry for you for this part. (*Beat.*) After that, you lost your job and started to wander. Apparently, you fell quite off the edge of the universe. The rumors had it you were with distant relatives—or friends of friends—here for a week—there for a month—however you people disport yourselves. A mode of existence that must have been unsettling for you—to say nothing of frugal. Then you discovered the girl who brought you here—This part is puzzling . . . Surely, there's some lovely girl of your own kind who would have found in you an excellent candidate for renovation, and drawn you back into the fold—oh, yes, that seems a much more likely scenario than carpet heiresses and the Catskills, no? Well, never mind. Finally, you arrived here and met my daughter, and proceeded to tell not a single true thing about yourself. Yes, I believe that brings us up to date with you. (*Beat.*) Now. Is there anything you'd like to say?

NICK (*very quietly*)**:** I don't think so.

EVA: I think perhaps you should. I think it's an opportunity you shouldn't pass up.

(*Long pause. When* NICK *finally speaks, it's with a simplicity meant to control the difficulty of what he's saying.*)

NICK: After my mother died, my father more or less lost control of things. Not badly—it was more a kind of slip of attention. But, apparently, that's all it took. Things fell apart. It had something to do with a partner, I think, or the board—something shifty—I'm not suppressing the details here, I just never quite learned them. Anyway, just like that, it seemed, we were out of business. Suddenly, as you said. And, yes, broke. I was working in New York then, I'd visit on weekends. Every time I did, he'd have sold off another room of furniture and he'd be sitting in it . . . singing. "I'm a ramblin' wreck from Georgia Tech/And a heck of an engineer . . ." And he wasn't even drinking—that was the funny part, he was stone-cold sober. I'd say, "Dad . . . are you sure you're all right? Can I get you anything?" He'd say, "Oh, no, I'm fine, pal, I'm fine, sport—all I need is a shave and a haircut   that's all I need, sport   a shave and a haircut—just a shave and a haircut—then I'll be ready." (*Beat.*) He didn't understand how everything had happened to him so fast. He wasn't crazy, I don't think . . . just surprised . . . He started singing in the street. He'd forget to *bathe*. The house started looking like a junk heap. One day this group of men—five of them, I think . . . our neighbors . . . came to call on him. They said to him, "Nick, we're sorry to have to say this, but it doesn't look as if you're ever going to be able to take control of things. Wouldn't it be better to go, now, before you have to? Wouldn't it be better just to leave?" (*Beat.*) He called me in the city after. I said, "Oh, look, they're your friends, they'll forget about it." He said, "No . . . I stank up the street. You can do a lot of things, but you don't stink up the street." And he started to laugh. We hung up, he walked into his room . . . and had the unfortunate accident while cleaning his gun. (*Beat.*) I didn't tell any of this to Lili because, well, it isn't the sort of thing you say right at first . . . and because it was so pleasant not to. Those are the only reasons. (*Beat.*) Well. This has been a marvelous party, you've been a perfect hostess, and I've had a splendid time. (*Beat.*) I wish you would let me tell Lili instead of you.

EVA: Oh, but I have no intention of telling her.

NICK: Then what are you going to do?

EVA: After you marry, I will pay for your graduate school in architecture, then give you a start in business.

NICK: What?

EVA: There—you made me give it away—that was meant to be my surprise.

NICK: I can take care of all that myself.

EVA: You mean with Lili's money. No, you see, this is where you are wrong. Has Lili told you she comes into her money on her twenty-first birthday? Yes, this is a thing she says. In truth, she does come into money. On her thirty-fifth birthday. Until then, it is only what she earns or what I give her. Now, tell me, what are your plans for getting through school and life? Go moment by moment. (*Beat.*) Yes, I will pay for you gladly for we will be related.

NICK: That isn't right, somehow . . .

EVA: You have a conscience, excellent! I'll write that down. Oh, look! To deny happiness because it looks like something it is not . . . You have told me everything about yourself—now I understand and pity you. You love my daughter—you are in a condition I can remedy—what stupidity—what *cruelty*—not to let me. (*Beat.*)

Nick: Then I'll tell her about this.

Eva: That I cannot allow.

Nick: What?

Eva: If you will tell her, she will tell me; if she will tell me, I will renege.

Nick: Why?

Eva: Do you know how this will look to her? This lie and that lie. A few swimming lessons do not make one psychologically whole. I'm sorry if you thought that was the case. We don't want to risk your losing her affection, do we?

Nick: But—

Eva: Figure nothing out; look no further; all is well.

Nick: I don't understand. Why don't you just tell her everything and be rid of me?

Eva: Because there isn't very much we can hope for Lili, but at least we can hope for the best.

Nick: And what is the best, do you think?

Eva: An intricately unhappy life, I'm afraid, lived out in compensatory splendor.

Nick: I don't believe that! (*Beat.*)

Eva: And why not?

Nick (*pulling back a little*): I cause happiness; that's what I do. (*Beat.*)

Eva: How nice for you! Well—I believe I must go in—everything aches.

Nick: Eva—!

Eva: What?

Nick: I really do love her, you know.

Eva: That is no longer either here or there.

(*Fade out.*)

EVA *and* OLIVIA. *A table set for tea.*

EVA: Oh, Olivia, this dampness is terrible, every bone in my body aches. (OLIVIA *lights a cigarette.*) That is an awful habit.

OLIVIA (*gleefully*): Yes.

EVA: What do you have for us this afternoon? Is it scrumptious, is it special?

OLIVIA: See for yourself. (*Tilts a cake from the table toward her.*)

EVA (*mildly disdainful*): Yes. Well . . .

OLIVIA: You're in a mood.

EVA: Mmm . . . Have I told you of *shneckens*? And *hörnchen*? With real whipped cream?

OLIVIA: Often.

EVA: Yes. Well, I miss them. It is to be tea, I suppose.

OLIVIA: Always tea.

EVA: I long for demitasse.

OLIVIA: I can do that.

EVA: But the spoons, the spoons, the *macher* spoons—they are somewhere in a basement in Cologne. How can you have demitasse when the spoons are elsewhere?

OLIVIA: Huh!

EVA: Some nights my dreams are filled with tiny spoons . . . and *shnecken* and *hörnchen* . . .

OLIVIA: You come through a war and grieve for the lost whipped cream—I won't figure it out.

EVA: And what do you miss and what do you long for? (OLIVIA *smiles.*) You are a Sphinx, there is no getting it out of you. Aren't there nights when you are lonely and long to tell someone something?

OLIVIA: Yes. But if I did, I think I'd end up lonelier for the information I'd given away.

EVA: Hm. Yes. (*Beat.*) I am hearing him again.

OLIVIA: Mr. Adler . . .

EVA: . . . Walking up and down the hallway, hour after hour . . .

OLIVIA: Those were bad years.

EVA: The years in which someone tries to die always are . . . They killed him. As if with a knife. As if with a gun.

OLIVIA: So you say . . .

EVA: What else can you call it? To do that to a genius . . .

OLIVIA: I never understood all that business; I never knew why they did that to Mr. Adler . . .

EVA: Do you remember the joke, "After the war the Jews were so popular they were trying to get their old noses back?"

OLIVIA: Yes.

EVA: It was a joke. (*Beat.*) Oh, they were so discreet, so tactful. They said to him, "Yes, we will manufacture your invention. Sign the contract and you will have everything in the world." We were so happy, we celebrated. Then—three weeks? A month? They told him, "This can be an enormous thing, a breakthrough! But we must not give way to sentimentality. You must see that Walter Wilson— the partner he had taken on who had done virtually nothing— Walter Wilson with his smooth voice and his smooth history—you must see that he is the better man for all this—for the conventions and the advertisements, for the conferences and the symposia. This is a time of plenty," they said, "not of sad faces with leaky eyes. Oh, but why do you protest? We give you all the money in the world and all you have to do is disappear a little . . ." These men . . . these men who come with their generous offers to take away everything you possess. But why do you stare at me?

OLIVIA: I like that boy, that Nick.

EVA: Do you? And you are such a shrewd judge of character. Tell me—why do you like him?

OLIVIA: Because Lili does.

EVA: And do you think he loves her?

OLIVIA: I have no reason to believe otherwise.

EVA: But does it seem *likely*?

OLIVIA: Anything that's already happened is likely—that's my opinion.

EVA: Yes . . . Oh, but, Olivia, I fully agree—I was *testing* you! Have I been in anyway discouraging?

OLIVIA: Not yet.

EVA: Then relax. (OLIVIA *keeps looking at her.*) Oh, I am stiff again . . . please? I would appreciate it. (OLIVIA *puts out her cigarette, rubs Eva's shoulders.*) You are wonderful at this. I love you dearly.

OLIVIA: Oh, don't.

EVA: Then I won't. See how amenable I am? It is a quality in myself I am surprised is so seldom remarked.

OLIVIA: I don't believe I've ever heard anyone mention it.

EVA: People miss the point, don't you think?

OLIVIA: I don't know any people. (GIL *enters.*)

GIL: Goddamn, would you look at this place!

EVA: And what is this?

GIL: Oh—hi—sorry—I didn't see you. I've been—I tell you it's been quite a time—but *this*—the view and the quiet. There's even furniture! This is great.

EVA. We like it. (*Her look at* OLIVIA *asks, "Who is this person?"*)

GIL: I'll bet . . . I take it you're also fleeing the circus maximus over there?

EVA: *Ah!*—you are with the hotel.

GIL: For *two days.*

EVA: You have my sympathy.

GIL: Thank you . . . It's just . . . well, I don't have to tell you . . . Gals in cha-cha dresses—women in mink stoles in what month is this? These *foods*—

EVA: We mustn't speak of them!

GIL: I came here—I thought I was going to *relax*—All of a sudden, I'm at these events, I'm doing the hokeypokey, I'm winning sets of dishes in bingo games, I'm watching fifty-year-old women in chiffon dresses sing, "My Lord and Master" into a microphone, it's—Oh! There's this one guy, he calls himself a tumbler or something, as far as I can make out he's some type of social director. When I first got here I was allergic to the ragweed or something, every time I sneezed he'd say, *"Stzeszetszt."* What does that mean?

EVA: Drop dead.

GIL: Then I should stop thanking him. This place, though—you can read a book, you can take a nap, this is great. (*He lies down on the bench or somewhere, apparently intending to settle in for the duration.*)

EVA: And who are you, you enthusiastic and attractive young person?

GIL: Sorry. Gil Harbison.

EVA: I am Eva Adler, and this is Olivia Shaw.

GIL (*to* OLIVIA): How do you do?

OLIVIA: Do you have a twin?

GIL: Excuse me?

OLIVIA: I thought maybe you had a brother. Never mind. How do you do?

GIL: Well, I'm just great, just great *now.* (*To* EVA:) Hey, are you the one the gals across the lake call the czarina?

EVA: If there is such a one, I would guess I am she.

GIL: What a sentence—wonderful!—Americans never take grammar to that kind of extreme. I'm in publishing, I know this. They say you stay on this side of the lake a lot.

EVA: This is my place.

GIL: Really? . . . Wait. Am I trespassing?

EVA: Yes.

GIL: God—I'm sorry—I had no idea—This doesn't look like the sort of place someone *owns.*

EVA: No, no, no. So tell me, is this your vacation?

GIL: More or less. I was just looking for a change of scene.

EVA: Was the old scene fatiguing you?

GIL: I thought so—but *this* place—wow! Your little spot here, though—what an amazing relief. (*Notices tea service.*) Oh God, you're having tea—Well, then, I really should leave you alone. I don't want to interfere—by the way, that cake looks wonderful.

OLIVIA: Thank you.

GIL: Well, back to the third circle of Hell—

EVA: Why don't you stay?

GIL: Oh—no—

EVA: Please—we're having a little celebration—the more the merrier—

GIL: Thank you—that would be wonderful—

OLIVIA: I'll bring another cup—or do you take it in a glass?

GIL: Is it iced?

OLIVIA: I'll bring a cup. (*Exits.*)

EVA: Olivia is very witty when she's bored. Pay no attention.

GIL: Whatever.

EVA: Nick and Lili should be back any moment, now; then we'll have our tea.

GIL: Nick and Lili?

EVA: My daughter and her fiancé. They've gone for a walk.

GIL: Oh—oh right!

EVA: What? The ladies by the lake told you about this, too?

GIL: Well, you know . . . blabbety-blabbety . . .

EVA: Are you here with anyone?

GIL: No—I came just for the heck of it—

EVA: I see. And how did you ever choose the Catskills?

GIL: Well, you know, after a while I got so bored with the East End and Nantucket and Fisher's and the Vineyard—I was looking for someplace I'd never been—and here it is—the Catskills.

EVA: Two of you in one summer . . .

GIL: I beg your pardon?

EVA: Nothing, nothing at all. Oh, but here they are. (NICK *and* LILI *enter.*) How are you, my darlings? Look whom I have discovered— a fresh explorer.

LILI: Hello.

GIL: You're Lili, nice to meet you. I'm Gil Harbison.

LILI: Nice to meet you.

NICK (*extending his hand*): Nick Lockridge. How do you do?

GIL: You look familiar; have we met?

NICK: I don't know, it's possible.

EVA: Gil is at the hotel, too. I asked him to have tea with us.

LILI: You *did*?

EVA: Of course. Is that so surprising?

LILI: Yes. (OLIVIA *enters with cup.*)

EVA: My daughter thinks I am a hermit and an ogre—pay no attention. Where did you walk?

LILI: Around the pool. People were asking about you.

EVA: I am missed.

LILI: I didn't say that. (*To* GIL:) Do you really think you've met before? I don't know anyone Nicky knows.

GIL: Maybe. Were you at the Gold and Silver?

NICK: Excuse me?

GIL: The Gold and Silver Ball.

NICK: What year?

GIL: Fifty-five, fifty-six, fifty-seven, or fifty-eight, maybe? I went a lot.

NICK: I don't remember.

LILI: You don't remember fifty-five, fifty-six, fifty-seven, *or* fifty-eight?

NICK: Maybe I was.

LILI: Try to figure it out. I don't know anyone who knew you.

EVA: Gil's in publishing.

LILI: Really? Maybe that's how you know each other—Nicky writes for *Time*.

GIL: No, it's book publishing.

LILI: Really?

GIL: I'm an editor at a small house—we're very sincere.

LILI: How fun. What have you published?

GIL: Nothing you'd have heard of. Right now, though, everybody there is on the lookout for a sexy, suburban novel—you know, "It lifts the lid off a small American town"—oh, I hope I haven't offended Olivia.

OLIVIA: Of course not.

GIL: I just thought you might be religious.

OLIVIA: People think that.

GIL: Anyway, I kind of regret that publishing's going in that direction. I find the older I get the more I respect people who are serious and the less I respect people who aren't.

LILI: Nicky is extremely serious.

NICK: Lili, please—

LILI: He's going to go back to school and become an architect—

GIL: Now architecture is something I can respect, that's a *field*—

LILI: Nicky's going to become great at it—

Gil: I'll bet.

Eva: This is a policy of mine: Never doubt the young. Now, I must tell you all what the special treats are about. Nicky: This morning I called my accountant and he is going to set up that special fund for your education, plus another to start you off professionally, as we have discussed. He says there will be no problem at all.

Nick: Eva—

Lili: *What?* (*Beat.* Nick *stares at* Eva, *horrified.*)

Eva: Oh, have I said something inopportune? Haven't you told her, Nicky? Was I supposed to keep that to myself? I am old and often muddled these days.

(*No one speaks.* Lili *looks to* Nick, *who does nothing.*)

Gil: So, I think that's great that you're helping out, just great.

Eva: Well, you know Nicky is part of the *mischpucha,* now.

Gil: Part of the *what?* That doesn't sound like German.

Eva: It's the only kind of German I speak these days.

(Lili *has picked up the teapot and turned it over; tea trickles slowly onto the ground.*)

Olivia: Lili!

Nick: Lili, I—

Gil (*overlapping*)**:** Is something going on?

(Lili, *for the rest of the scene, is trying to beat back an overwhelming emotion—panic and confusion and hysteria. When she speaks, it's tense, clenched, her breathing shallow.*)

Lili: I don't care—

Eva: My darling, what have you done?

Lili: I don't care if it's the money—it doesn't make any difference to me—

NICK: Lili, please—

LILI: I still want—I still want to be with you—I'll pay! I'll pay for everything!

NICK: That isn't what this is—

LILI: But did you—did you make a *deal* with her?

NICK: Listen to me—

LILI: Are you—are you on her side?

NICK: No, listen—

LILI: I'll pay for anything, but please—please—be on my side—

EVA: My darling—

NICK: Lili, come with me.

LILI: *STOP!* I can't breathe! I can't breathe! (*She clutches herself tightly and her mouth opens as if she's about to scream, but only a strangulated sob comes out.*)

NICK: Lili— (*She collapses.*)

(*Blackout.*)

SCENE 2

NICK *lies in the hammock.* GIL *is looking out at the lake.*

GIL: I sat at the bar through last call. This woman in a gray beehive kept ordering Brandy Alexanders and trying to make me. I was sorely tempted.

NICK: But you resisted.

GIL: I was stalwart.

NICK: You're an admirable young man.

GIL: I think I am. People say so. (*Beat.*) So is tea always such an hysterical occasion here or was this special?

NICK: No. This was special.

GIL: I'm glad . . . Is she okay?

NICK: She's sleeping.

GIL: She seems like a nice girl.

NICK: I love her very much.

GIL: I'm sure you do . . . Why aren't you there?

NICK: I've been banished.

GIL: What?

NICK: Yes. It seems I'm a dangerous influence. It seems I caused all that.

GIL: My god!

NICK: Eva's very clever, she covers her tracks. She said, "Consider where Lili sleeps the castle keep; consider Olivia the sentry."

GIL: And what is she?

NICK (*German accent*): I am the moat.

GIL: What a night!

NICK: Yeah.

GIL (*looking out at lake*): I had a hunch you'd be here. It's where I would be at this time of night. Just sort of swinging and swaying.

NICK: Whatever.

GIL (*moving to behind the hammock*): It's so quiet . . . so dark . . . A real country darkness.

NICK: The hotel's still blazing.

GIL: But behind us it's pitch black. (*Beat.*) No one around. (*Beat.*) No one anywhere. (*Long pause. Then* GIL *leans over the hammock and kisses* NICK *on the mouth.* NICK *allows it, then pulls back.*)

NICK: No.

GIL: What do you mean, "no"?

NICK: It's time to put away childish things.

GIL: Well, I'm sorry, it's a nice quote and all, but that never felt like a childish thing, to me, that never—

NICK (*moving away*): How did you find me here anyway? (*Beat.*)

GIL: Ruth Corbin.

NICK: Ruth Corbin! I don't think I've ever even spoken to Ruth Corbin.

GIL: She heard it from Les O'Hare—they're going out now—he got it from, I think, Jackie de Milne, who works with a guy whose wife is best friends with the cousin of that girl you came here with, what's her name—?

NICK: Mindy.

GIL: Mindy, yes! My research was pretty extensive.

NICK: Nothing's going to happen. Why did you bother?

GIL: Don't you know yet, Nick? I'm here to save you.

NICK (*bursting out laughing*): I'm deeply touched.

GIL: I have spent months looking for you—I've come to these mountains to get you—who else would climb a mountain for you?

NICK: Lili would.

GIL: Yes—but when she got there would it matter?

NICK: I'm marrying her.

GIL: Fine! Wonderful! I have no problems with that—I'm marrying Cinny.

NICK: What?

GIL: At the end of October. It would please me enormously if you'd agree to be my best man.

NICK: You're incredibly perverse.

GIL: I'm not perverse, I'm determined to be happy. I'm inventive.

NICK: Too inventive.

GIL: There can be no such thing. It wasn't even my idea. She kept hinting that she was about to be twenty-four; there was a heavy suggestion that her child-bearing years were drawing to a close. I couldn't let her lie fallow, could I? I think it will be a very good match. She's beautiful, she's smart, and she speaks flawless French.

NICK: She's rich, too.

GIL: Try scoring a point against me with that, see what happens.

NICK: I won't try.

GIL: I like her a lot—and she's crazy about you.

NICK: Is she?

GIL: Asks about you constantly. She keeps saying, "Whatever happened to that nice Nick? I think he's my favorite of all your friends."

NICK: And what do you say?

GIL: I say, "You know what? Mine, too." It's really—it's great.

NICK: It's disgusting.

GIL: Not at all—I have a plan.

NICK: I don't want to know about it.

GIL: You have to—it's yours, too—

NICK: I already know what mine is.

GIL: We marry these women. We become excellent husbands. We prosper. We sire wonderful children. Our families become best friends. And we're . . . us . . . our whole lives. That's my plan.

NICK: And no one ever wonders, no one ever suspects?

GIL: Who *thinks* that way?

NICK: Everyone does.

GIL: Nobody does. (*A light goes out somewhere.*)

NICK: What was that?

GIL: What?

NICK: A light went out.

GIL: It was from the hotel.

NICK: No, it was from the other direction. (*Beat.*)

GIL: It was nothing, it was whatever.

NICK: That means a light was on. (*Beat.*)

GIL: It doesn't matter. Jesus, buddy, this paranoia is no good, it just gets in the way, it just gets in the way of what we want.

NICK: I don't want the same thing as you. Why don't you just believe that and move on?

GIL: I'm sorry, but you lie to the wrong people.

NICK: Look—what happened, happened; it's a fact. It's something I did. Maybe it's what you *are*—whatever that means—but for me, it's only a thing I did. It was . . . who knows? It was like kids in boarding school, it was a *phase*, it was just *something that happened* . . . I'm not marrying Lili the way you're marrying Cinny.

GIL: No—you're having a deep, pure, truthful union.

NICK: Okay, *laugh*, but—

GIL: I'm not laughing . . . I think that's wonderful . . . It's what we all want, isn't it? A deep, pure, truthful union? Oh, so, God, so then you've told her about us. (*Pause.*)

NICK: No.

GIL: You haven't yet? When are you going to? (*Beat.*)

NICK: Gil—

GIL: Would you like me to? Because I will, you know, if that's what you want, if that's easier for you— (*Pause.* NICK *starts off.*)

NICK: Good night.

GIL: No, no, no, you're not going now—

NICK: I think that—

GIL: Your presence at this moment is not a voluntary thing.

NICK: Forget it, I'm—

GIL (*grabbing his arm roughly*): Not yet. (NICK *stops.*) Look, when you took off, I said to myself, "Okay, forget this, cut your losses," because that's how I am, but it didn't work. I'd spent too much time on you, it was too big an effort . . . and you say it was, what, a phase? Yeah, well, I was there, too, buddy, and that's not how I remember it . . . And just because at one sad juncture or another you decided you were a tragic figure, I don't see why my life has to go to pot.

NICK: You should lower your voice.

GIL: I am whispering in the Catskills. (*Pause.*)

NICK (*with difficulty*): I couldn't see you . . . I couldn't see anyone . . . I'm sorry if that hurt you . . . I didn't think it would.

GIL: I could have helped you, Nicky. I could have been your friend. It's very sad to me that that never occurred to you . . . It's very sad to me that your whole life was falling apart all the time we were together and you never thought to mention it. I find that *very* sad.

NICK: I couldn't—

GIL: Why not?

NICK: It was a very strange show that was going on . . . and I was trying to . . .

GIL: What?

NICK: I was trying to dazzle you. (*Pause.*) Oh, look, I've been sort of a mess for a while. I couldn't work. I couldn't think. I've just been running around . . . Somehow I landed here. I think I may be all right now. Please, please go away.

(*Pause.*)

GIL: I'm sorry for everything that's ever happened to you. (*Beat.*) So, plan two: We go someplace where we don't have to lie . . . and nobody cares . . . and people give us money for things we do.

NICK: When was that planet discovered?

GIL: And it never will be . . . but if it were, is that where you'd want to be? (*NICK is silent. Beat.*) Okay, so plan one: We marry these women. And we have our houses and our children . . . and our special friendship. And we have our fine jobs and our fine friends and our fine reputations. And our wives adore us because we're passionate and kind. And our children adore us because we're patient and doting. And we forget about the past—and the world kind of opens wide for us and we laugh like lunatics for the next half-century—because the world thinks it's in love with us . . . the world thinks it's given us everything for free . . . and we know we've stolen the whole damn thing . . . Isn't that a better idea than your idea?

NICK (*quietly*): I think there are some things you don't understand.

GIL: I think there's nothing I don't understand. And nothing I'm willing to give up. I think that's the situation. (*NICK has been staring toward the house.*) Why do you keep looking over there?

NICK: I'm trying to see Lili.

GIL: Why?

NICK: Did you hear her before? It didn't matter what Eva said—she didn't care . . . She's staggering.

GIL: Nick—

NICK: She's under arrest; there is a moat around her—

GIL: Nick, come on—

NICK: You don't exist. (*Beat.*)

GIL: Goddamn you.

NICK: You don't exist. Nothing's ever happened in my life. I'm a man who crosses moats.

(*Fade out.*)

S C E N E   3

Night. NICK *is alone.* LILI *enters.*

LILI: Hi.

NICK: Hi. (*Beat.*) Are you cold—do you want my jacket?

LILI: I'm fine.

NICK (*placing jacket around her shoulders*): You look . . .

LILI: Tell me.

NICK: Sleepy.

LILI: The doctor brings plenty of pills.

NICK: I tried getting to you before, but—

LILI: I know. Olivia told me. My mother's asleep now.

NICK: She kept heading me off at the pass.

LILI: It's one of her best talents; she could teach it . . . This is the first time I've been outside in days. It's . . . *big* out here, isn't it? (*She laughs.*) I *must* be sleepy. (*Beat.*) Talk.

NICK: I'm just . . . looking at you . . .

LILI: A drugged young neurotic in a nightdress; it could set sail the fancy of many a man—

NICK: That's not what I see.

LILI: . . . And that's one of your best talents. (*Beat.*)

NICK: I think we have to get you out of here.

LILI: Yes.

NICK: Do you still want that?

LILI: Oh, yes.

NICK: And with me?

LILI: Why wouldn't I?

NICK: I've lied to you . . . a lot.

LILI: Yes, you have. (*Laughs a little.*) I'm sorry—I had a pill a while ago . . . I'm not my best after . . . Oh God! I'm still hearing her voice, isn't that (*lets the thought trail off*) Nick . . . when you build your whole city . . .

NICK: What?

LILI: Make sure there's a roof and a high fence. And don't give away too many keys. (*Beat.*)

NICK: Has she been talking about me?

LILI: She says things . . .

NICK: I want to explain—

LILI: Oh, don't.

NICK: You have to let me . . . give my version . . .

LILI: I've heard so many versions; I'm sick of them . . . It never happened, okay? Nothing. Just forget it.

NICK: I don't think that's possible.

LILI: Look . . . it doesn't matter that things have happened to you. And I don't care about anything you've ever done. I think you *do* love me. I don't care what it started out to be, we don't ever have to talk about it. Just as long as you're mine now.

(*Pause.*)

NICK: Lili?

LILI: What?

(*Pause.*)

NICK: Nothing.

LILI: What?

NICK: Nothing. (*Beat.*)

LILI: I'm so tired . . . I want to sleep with you holding me. If I have to sleep, I want you to hold me.

NICK: But if your mother—

LILI: Just for a little while.

NICK (*sitting with her*): All right.

LILI: Sing me something!

NICK: I don't sing.

LILI: Yes—a lullaby!

NICK: I don't know any lul— (Beat.) Wait . . . there was one once, it went . . . How did it go? (*Starts to sing in a thin, clear voice.*)

> Hush you 'bye
> Don't you cry
> Go to sleepy little baby . . .

LILI: I've never heard this . . .

NICK: When you *wake*
    You shall have
    All the pretty little horses (*On the brink of sleep,* LILI *laughs.*)

(*Fade out.*)

GIL *and* EVA *are seated.* LILI *and* OLIVIA *are looking out toward the lake.*

EVA: But you can't go! We'll miss you terribly.

GIL: Well, I'll miss all of you, too. You've been awfully nice to me.

EVA: What takes you away so suddenly?

GIL: It isn't all that sudden. I never intended to stay long.

EVA: Has something not worked out for you?

GIL: No, I can't say that—I just have trouble staying at leisure too long.

LILI: I want to swim!

EVA: Out of the question!

LILI: I already have my suit on under these clothes. It's not too cold—

EVA: You cannot go in alone.

OLIVIA: I'll watch her—

EVA: That is not good enough; she is a brand new swimmer—

LILI: I'll stay in the shallow part.

OLIVIA: I promise you—nothing will happen to her.

EVA: I am outnumbered.

LILI: Good!

GIL: Well, I guess I'll say good-bye to you now—in case I'm gone when you get out—

LILI: Good-bye.

GIL: I hope we see each other again some time.

LILI: I hope so, too.

GIL: Good-bye, Olivia.

OLIVIA: Good-bye.

LILI: Beat you there! (*She runs off.*)

OLIVIA: With my blessing. (*She exits.*)

EVA (*calling to* OLIVIA): Keep your eye on her! (*To* GIL:) I hate to see her swim.

GIL: But if she stays in the shallow part—

EVA: She never stays in the shallow part . . . It's always a little further, a little further. I wish she'd never learned. Another of your friend's dubious legacies to us.

GIL: He's not my friend.

EVA: Isn't he? I thought you knew him before.

GIL: I know a lot of people who aren't my friends.

EVA: My mistake, then. Good. He was so disappointing. Even that says too much for him—You know, I didn't trust him from the moment I saw him.

GIL: Is that so?

EVA: Oh, yes. It was clear to me right away that he is the sort who takes what is yours and behaves as if it were his own.

GIL: Then why did you let Lili—?

Eva: Let Lili! Oh, my dear, what a preposterous idea! One does not "let Lili" do anything. If you were to stand with her on the top of the Empire State Building and say, "Please, Lili—do not step over the parapet," she would be a blot on the sidewalk within moments.

Gil: Really?

Eva: Oh, yes. Lili is someone who must be singed by a thing to keep from being incinerated by it. There is really no controlling her . . . I did think Nick might have gone by now, though. What is it, do you suppose, what is it that makes him stay and stay when he knows he won't be allowed to see her?

Gil: He's a nice boy.

Eva: A nice boy?

Gil: Yeah—he has this conscience.

Eva: So a person with a conscience is someone who behaves despicably at all times and, what, feels bad about it after? Spare me people with consciences! They harm my child.

Gil: Well, she looks a lot better today than the first time I met her—

Eva: That night wasn't typical—

Gil: I shouldn't have brought it up—

Eva: The ranting and the crying—

Gil: What a nightmare.

Eva: Awful. Finally she calmed down and fell asleep, but I couldn't sleep. After a while, I went out doors to get some air. I stared out in space to try to calm myself—and do you know what I saw? Down by the lake where nobody but us ever goes?

Gil: What?

Eva: Lovers kissing. (*Pause.*)

Gil: Huh!

Eva: Can you imagine that?

Gil: Well . . .

Eva: At first, I found it curiously . . . revolting. But, after a while, you know . . . what haven't I seen?

Gil: I'd guess . . . not too much. (*Beat.*) Well—

Eva: Gil—

Gil: Yes?

Eva: I was wondering if perhaps you had seen these lovers also.

Gil: I think I may have; I think I may have passed them while I took a walk.

Eva: Did they seem to you deeply in love? Did it seem to you a thing that would endure?

Gil: No. I'd have to say it looked to me like the end of something.

Eva: Really?

Gil: A pretty bitter one, too.

Eva: Well, then it must have been true love!

Gil: Who knows?

Eva: And true love can always be rekindled, can't it? If necessary? (*Pause.* Gil *just looks at her, amazed by her audacity, then considering.*)

Gil: Possibly.

Eva: That's so interesting—but enough about them, let's get back to you. Now, why did you say you were leaving? Can't we persuade you to stay?

Gil: I'd really like to, but . . .

Eva: But . . . ?

Gil: What would it get me? (*Beat.*) Of course, I could always *revise* what I wanted.

EVA: What do you mean?

GIL: Well, you know, an alternative incentive could come along . . . It's like economics—you seek out the situation that brings you the greatest yield.

EVA: Do you?

GIL: Oh, yeah. It's what economists call "rational."

EVA (*taking his hand between hers warmly*): Bless their hearts.

GIL: Isn't this a gorgeous day? I think I might stay after all.

EVA: Really?

GIL: I just wonder if I'll be able to get my old room back at the hotel . . .

EVA: Don't worry. I'll have Olivia call.

GIL: That's very nice, thank you.

EVA: We'll take care of you. (*Looks toward* LILI *swimming.*) Oh, look how she thrashes! How hard every stroke is for her. My heart dies when I see her.

GIL: She's your only child, isn't she?

EVA: Yes. My only child.

GIL: I'm sorry.

EVA: Why?

GIL: Just that things haven't turned out the way you wished.

EVA: Oh, my dear, you wish for so many things . . . isn't that so? And you really don't get any of them, do you? Because the world has a wish of its own for you . . . and it's never good . . . You try to shelter those you love from this wish, you become something you never dreamed. But no . . . All you may do, really, is stand by, in a kind of horror, until the world has finished and you can collect whatever remains.

GIL: It must be awful to believe that. (*Beat. She turns to him.*)

EVA: Gil . . . You revise and revise and revise the thing you want . . . and what are you left with?

GIL: Other things you want. The trick is wanting a lot of things. (*He smiles. He starts off.*)

(*Fade out.*)

NICK *and* GIL. *Night.*

GIL: You're shivering.

NICK: Yes.

GIL: Are you sick?

NICK: Yes.

GIL: When did you get sick?

NICK: I've been getting sick; I've been . . . coming down with something. I can't move. Sometimes I just . . . stay in place.

GIL. You're talking to me.

NICK: Yes.

GIL: That's an improvement . . . Where does it hurt—here? (*He massages Nick's temples.*)

NICK: Yes. There. (*Beat.* GIL *continues, then moves to his neck.*)

GIL: So when are you leaving this place?

NICK: We're going tonight.

GIL: But you're sick—how can you go when you're sick?

NICK: I have to—I've wasted too much time.

GIL: Just staring. Just staring across the lake.

NICK: Yes.

GIL: I've been staring at you staring across the lake. (*Beat.* GIL *takes his hands off* NICK. NICK *grabs them and replaces them on his neck.* GIL *starts off again.*)

NICK: I think you hate me.

GIL: Why would I hate you?

NICK: Because I think . . . Because I guess you would be right to.

GIL: Does it feel like I hate you?

NICK: How can I tell?

GIL: I'm not strangling you. (*Beat.*)

NICK: I think, I think the problem is . . . we never said good-bye, we never really got a chance to say good-bye, I cheated you out of that, I think that's, I think that's the problem.

GIL: Could be.

NICK: What if . . . we did?

GIL: Did what?

NICK: Said good-bye . . . What if we said good-bye? Would you . . . would you go away then, would you leave me alone, then? (*Beat.*)

GIL: So how do we do that, say good-bye? How do we arrange it, when? (*Pause.*)

NICK: Now. (*Pause.*)

GIL: Where else does it hurt? (*Slips his hand inside Nick's shirt.*) Here? (NICK *takes Gil's arm, draws him down, kisses his neck.*)

(*Fade out.*)

Night. LILI *kneels, staring out.* EVA *enters behind her.*

EVA: It's time to go in my darling. He won't be coming for you tonight.

LILI: Did Olivia tell you I was here? (*Silence.*) Of course she did . . .

EVA: Oh, my darling, my darling . . . The spell is broken—the enchantment is over.

LILI: I want to leave here. I want to go tomorrow.

EVA: Of course, my darling. First thing in the morning. I'll have Olivia pack the bags and then we'll—

LILI: Not home! Anyplace . . . anyplace else . . . But I won't go home with you. (*Still kneeling, she reaches her arms out to her mother, who embraces her.*) Not home . . . not home.

EVA: But you are my home, *mein kind.* (*The lullaby "Nicht ist das gluck" plays.*)

(*Lights fade.*)

In the darkness another music takes over—driving late sixties rock into next scene.

Ten years later. The den of Eva's apartment. Dark with two heavy chairs. NICK *stands looking out a window, downstage.* OLIVIA *is there with him.*

NICK: I guess it's quite a task, dealing with tradesmen.

OLIVIA: Well, you know *her*—first you have to inspect the *goods*— say it's ham—is it Boar's Head ham or Virginia ham or plain boiled ham? And how much does each kind cost and how much is there of it and is there tax on that? Then how much does she tip or has the boy been rude or what other complaints does she have with the world.

NICK: Does this happen all the time?

OLIVIA: We have a lot of delivery people. I can't get her to go out much. Are they still making noise on that street?

NICK: It's getting closer.

OLIVIA: Closer? Wasn't it right out the window a few minutes ago?

NICK: No, that was at least five blocks away.

OLIVIA: What lungs they have!

NICK: I suppose they're . . .

OLIVIA: What?

NICK: . . . fueled by righteous indignation.

OLIVIA: Well, who ever wasn't?

NICK: Yes. You look exactly the same.

OLIVIA: I've become a very old woman.

NICK: Never.

OLIVIA: If that's how you want it, I won't say no . . . Have you been well? (*Beat.*)

NICK: Yes.

OLIVIA: What brings you to New York?

NICK: I don't know . . . Compulsion.

OLIVIA: What?

NICK: Accident.

OLIVIA: Yes?

NICK: Vacation.

OLIVIA: Oh! Maybe I'll have one of those one of these days.

NICK: When I heard the news—

OLIVIA: How did you hear it?

NICK: I'm on a lot of grapevines . . . That's a lie; I've been keeping up.

OLIVIA: Oh.

NICK: When I heard, I thought, "God, now it's just the two of them."

OLIVIA: Two old maids playing Jewish card games—you don't have to worry about us. Life . . .

NICK: Yes?

OLIVIA: I don't have anything to say on the subject. (*Beat.*) I'll get the tea, now. (*She exits.* NICK *looks out the window again. A long moment, then* LILI *enters. She is much more grandly dressed than we've ever seen her before—but somehow more severely, as well. She seems older and more studied, harder and more appraising than she used to be.*)

LILI: What do you see out my window?

NICK: Oh! God, I didn't hear you—

LILI: What's going on?

NICK: There's a guy with a bullhorn, and a lot of people with signs, and some construction workers, I guess, and I think some Canadian mounties or something.

LILI: The usual crew.

NICK: You see this sort of thing a lot?

LILI: It goes on a lot. Mostly, I draw the shades.

NICK: We don't get this much out where I am.

LILI: I don't suppose you do—where is that again?

NICK: Twenty miles outside of Cincinnati—

LILI: My God! And what are you doing?

NICK: I'm teaching math at the Dunn-Bradford School.

LILI: I've never heard of it . . . Do you know math?

NICK: A little. Enough.

LILI: Huh!

NICK: I was sorry to hear about your mother.

LILI (*a little distantly*): Yes . . . we're both orphans now.

NICK (*taken aback*): Yes.

LILI: Olivia's getting us tea, why don't we sit? You don't hear the noise so much when you're sitting. (*They do.*)

NICK: Does it bother you, all of them out there?

LILI: Yes.

NICK: Just the other day, I was waylaid by a group.

LILI: Were you?

NICK: Around Columbia. This big hippie parade. God, it was amazing! This . . . smelly, screaming mob! Things flying out of their hair, babies in papooses, flowers everywhere, everybody linking arms, some of them were ripping their clothes off, it was . . . unbelievable, wonderful. I thought, a few years ago I wouldn't even have been able to hallucinate this! (LILI *is staring at him.*) I'm sorry if I'm going on . . . I . . . Why are you looking at me?

LILI: I suppose you never built a whole city.

NICK: What? What do you mean?

LILI: Once you said that's what you wanted to do. Do you remember? You were asked, what do you want to build? And you said, a whole city. But I guess you never did.

Nick: No. I never built anything. (*Beat.*) This room looks exactly the way I always pictured it. Exactly the way you described it to me the first time we met. "Heavy with dark damask," you said.

Lili: Did I?

Nick: Yes. I remember it exactly. I remember a lot of things exactly, I . . . Well. I guess now that the place is yours, you'll put new furniture in, won't you? Do it up the way you want it to look.

Lili: But this is new furniture.

Nick: What?

Lili: Every piece. I did it all over myself last year. Don't you like it?

Nick: Oh. Yes. Of course. I just didn't . . .

Lili: What?

Nick: I just didn't think this was your taste, that's all.

Lili (*looks around, as if genuinely wondering*): Isn't it? (*Beat.*)

Nick: Lili . . .

Lili: I wonder what's taking Olivia so long. I'd say she was slowing down, but she's always been slow.

Nick: I'm sorry. (*Beat.*)

Lili: For what?

Nick: For what I did to you.

Lili: But what an egomaniac you are! Do you really think something you did ten years ago could possibly be of the least consequence?

Nick: It's been . . . of consequence to me. (Lili *rises, goes to window.*) Lili—I didn't just run out. It wasn't something I did lightly. I meant to talk to you . . . I always intended to tell you why.

Lili: Then why didn't you?

Nick: Too much time passed and I didn't know what to say. I wasn't lying to you when I told you I loved you.

LILI: This really couldn't matter in the least—

NICK: Somebody I'd been in love with came back to me . . . There are some people you can't get rid of. This was one.

LILI (*quietly*): And did you end up together?

NICK: Only for a little while.

LILI: Why?

NICK (*quietly*): Things didn't work out the way we'd planned.

LILI: Oh. (*Beat.*) But you haven't told me who it was. Please tell me. I'd like to know, it will make it feel finished. (*Long pause.*)

NICK: Her name was Cinny. (*Beat.*)

LILI: Cinny?

NICK: Yes. She was a girl I knew back home. (*Beat.*) Well, I'm . . . I . . .

LILI: Don't feel awkward, it's fine. You're a guest in my home, I'd hate for you to be uncomfortable in any way. We've settled our accounts, now we can be friends.

NICK: I'd like that. (OLIVIA *enters with tea tray.*) Let me help you with that.

OLIVIA: No, that's fine—I'm just setting it down.

LILI: Are you going to join us, Olivia?

OLIVIA: I might in just a minute—I want to get my knitting first.

LILI: Go do that—we'll help ourselves.

OLIVIA: All right, I will. (*She exits.* LILI *wanders over to the window.*)

NICK: What's happening now?

LILI: It's still going on—this one will make the papers, for sure.

NICK: It makes me feel about a thousand years old.

LILI (*her veneer dropping suddenly; during the next beat, it's as if the decade hasn't happened—she's as vulnerable and passionate as she used to be*): Cinny! My God!

NICK: What?

LILI: Do you really think I didn't know? My mother found out—I didn't care! I wanted you anyway—I would have gone with you anyway—anything to get out of this place! Anything to get out of this *place*! I would have let you have your life—I would have let you have your story, too. You could have built a whole city and I would have lived in it!

NICK: Lili . . .

LILI (*thrusting out her hand to quiet him. A moment passes. She composes herself, draws herself up. The ten years have returned. She's almost regal, perfectly philosophical*): But that is *nicht ahin, nicht ahier* . . . I haven't poured you any tea. How rude!

NICK: I'll go.

LILI: You have to stay. You have to stay for tea. Do you take sugar? Oh no, I remember, now. No sugar. (*She pours.*) How is it teaching math? Do you enjoy it?

NICK: It's . . . all right.

LILI: I'm glad. It's such a relief to find your place in life, don't you think? (*She hands him tea; he takes it and looks at her.*) You look tired. Maybe I'll sing you a lullaby. You sang me one, once . . . remember? I thought it was hilarious!

NICK (*remembering*): Then you sang one back to me . . .

LILI: No. Did I?

NICK: Yes. It was something your mother used to sing to you . . . some German song . . . "Nicht ist . . ." "Nicht ist . . ."

LILI (*singing sweetly*): *Nicht ist das gluck fur mich*
    Es ist fur andre menchen.

NICK: You told me what the words meant . . . something like, "There's no such thing as happiness—"

LILI: No, wrong again!

NICK: What, then?

(LILI *drifts toward the window, finds herself looking out, almost against her will.*)

LILI: Happiness exists . . .

NICK: Happiness exists . . .

LILI: . . . but it's for other people.

NICK: That's right . . . that's right. (*She stares out the window; he also looks straight out.*)

(*Fade out.*)

karen finley

THE THEORY OF TOTAL BLAME

Domestic disharmony reaches the surface: MOTHER (Karen Finley, *far right*) tries to dull her feelings of guilt at the family's holiday gathering, while JAN (Carol McDowell), JACK (Tom Murrin), and BUZZ (Chazz Dean) search for some insight into the blame.

This play is a feast of normality. Finley may be best known for her solo performances, but it doesn't stop her from having an utterly shrewd and complete sense of group dynamics. The American family, the aesthetic center of our theater just as it's the spiritual center of our culture, gets a sort of definitive deep analysis here, not a debunking. Finley's cubist version of a family, its alternative versions all interpenetrating, is a loving and thriving unit at the same time that it's a record of endless disasters. It's just that the loving side isn't the most immediately visible, since the characters openly speak their subtexts, their places in the social scheme, their Gestalts, in lieu of the usual platitudes. Far from attacking the notion of family, Finley simply implodes the naturalistic treatment of it, thereby getting rid of all the unhealthy ways in which a hackneyed image reinforces hackneyed social attitudes. Every line and gesture that demolishes the conventional view of family life, with outrageous humor or even more outrageous horror tales, is really a cry in the dark, a plea for family life—and the social organism of which families are the cells—to be put on a sane, humane basis.

Here as elsewhere, compassion is the root of Finley's art. The hostility that's hounded her work in recent years can only be explained as coming from people who haven't seen it: To watch her performances or read her texts is to perceive instantly that the violence, shock, and profanity she employs as artistic tactics are defensive measures, cries of protest against analogous tactics being employed, on a giant scale, in ways that are all too real. The role she writes for herself here is a perfect instance: the mother as tragic archfiend, the ultimate victim and perpetrator of the family as societal trap. It's probably as close as American playwriting can get to a work of the stature of *Medea*. Finley has no inhibitions about writing and playing such a monster, because she knows that monsters are not of their own making: Her intention is to help the audience start identifying the many Dr. Frankensteins involved.

The private rituals that punctuate and conclude the play are another sign of Finley's purity of heart: What her family doesn't have, as a family, is a religion they can all believe in humanely. The world as a whole doesn't have one either, using religion mainly as a way to prove the separateness of each human group from its neighbors—just as Finley's family uses its blood ties to demonstrate, ferociously, its individual apartness. We're members of one another, but we only use that knowledge to wreak havoc on each other's egos; that's the total blame at the core of her theory. But giving each member of the family at least a private, personally evolved, religion gives them the moments of absurd, transcendent grace without which human life in any form isn't bearable. Rather than posturing in shock at Finley's work, we ought to ask ourselves what we've done to make an artist with such a generous soul so angry. Or maybe, even, ask what we can do to change that . . .

PRODUCTION NOTES

The Theory of Total Blame premiered at Pyramid Arts Center, Rochester, New York, on October 20, 1989. It was directed and designed by Karen Finley; lighting by Carol McDowell; costumes by Finley and the following cast:

IRENE: Karen Finley
JACK: Tom Murrin
JAN: Carol McDowell
ERNIE: Gary Ray
BUZZ: Chazz Dean
TIM: Michael Overn

I am especially grateful to this cast, who contributed much to the overall production of TTOTB.

—Karen Finley

CHARACTERS

IRENE, the matriarch. She's had a hard life and alcohol is her self-prescribed reward for making it through the day.

JAN, the daughter of IRENE. She wears outdated clothes. One of her characteristics is that she always eats food that is color coordinated with her outfit.

JACK, the husband of JAN. He comes from a well-to-do family. He could almost be called a yuppie but it should be obvious that he is the "black sheep" of his family.

ERNIE, a son of IRENE. He still lives at home and is very self-conscious about it. He has a fixation with being in the army and seems to have combat-fatigue syndrome, although he's never seen battle.

BUZZ, another son of IRENE. He has just returned home from ten years of spiritual soul-searching. He wears sixties-style meditation clothing. He likes to keep to himself a lot.

TIM, a third son of IRENE. He is either depressed, comatose, or dead—whatever the scene calls for. Sometimes this character also becomes the father. He remains on the sofa throughout the entire piece. He wears a bathrobe.

AUTHOR'S NOTE

This play is always to be presented in a realistic setting. It is my intent that this play shall never be deconstructed or placed in a black hole, no-props set. The physical setting of a Home is important to all of our memories and is integral to the play. It is important that the actors can be transgressive with the roles rather than distanced. It is thus better to audition an actor on her or his real life, not on how s/he can pretend to act.

Setting: The family is home together for the holidays. The setting is a room that is a combined kitchen, living room, dining room, and bar. The kitchen table and chairs are directly center stage; a sofa and chair are positioned stage right; bar and stools are upstage; a refrigerator with a green light is upstage left. The decor is an example of a collection of bad taste and colors from the past several decades. The sandhill, where the religious experiences will occur, is outside the Home, stage right. It should be between four and seven square feet and be set with glitter and candles; a purple curtain hangs behind it. Everyone is constantly smoking and drinking throughout the play.

ERNIE *is seated at the table, reading a book of war stories;* TIM *is stretched out on the sofa;* IRENE *is preparing the dinner table while* JACK *and* JAN *prepare some cocktails at the bar. It is obvious that everyone, except for* TIM, *is drinking heavily.* JACK *finishes making the drinks and begins to serve them to the family.* IRENE *takes Jell-o molds from refrigerator and removes contents onto plate.*

IRENE: It's so nice to finally have the entire family together. (IRENE *and* JACK *toast.*)

JACK (*pointing to* TIM): Well, Tim, he's so depressed he'll never get up. Is he still a scientologist? Here's to a roomful of emotional derelicts that look like me.

IRENE: I can't keep up anymore. I make it a rule never to call my children if I can help it.

(JAN *starts setting the table, and with* IRENE *begins to prepare appetizers.*)

IRENE (*to* JAN): It is so nice that you were able to come home for the holiday.

JAN: Nice? Yes, it is nice. Cut the crap. Cut the crap right this minute, Mother! Why don't you ever call me? Why don't you ever call me?

IRENE: Jan, isn't it obvious to you? I don't love you. You're my daughter, but I've never loved you.

JAN (*shocked*): You, you don't love me? But I'm the only daughter of yours that is still talking to you! I've comforted you, consoled you.

IRENE: Jan, you've always been an embarrassment to me. Why can't you accept the fact that your only opportunity is a biological opportunity and produce me a grandchild.

JAN: Are all of you listening? Are you? Everyone knows that I was raped when I was eleven and birthed a baby that YOU took away from me, Mom!

IRENE: That's what the family is here for! You made a mistake and we took care of it. I only wish that it had happened now so that we could have sold the little brat. There's a gold mine in surrogacy. If I was a little younger I'd round up all the homeless women and young girls — keep 'em in a stall with a TV, Cap'n Crunch, and keep 'em knocked up. I'd especially take the emotionally disturbed, the retarded girls, girls without limbs, and I'd take them off the social service's hands and just keep 'em knocked up. I'd sell those babies to the rich folk. Sell 'em to the lawyers. 'Cause this country is so cruel to women having children — the ability to have a child is the end of a career. The men planned it that way. You never see a Kennedy or a Rockefeller being a surrogate mom. The sooner you realize that women are second-class citizens, the better off you'll be. (*Pause.*) Jan, you're bright but you're dreadfully dull. Do you remember when I tried to drive the family car into a brick wall and tried to kill us both?

JAN: How could I forget?

IRENE: Good. Then you know what I'm capable of—that I've always intended to make your life as miserable as possible.

JAN: Mom, I wasn't expecting this from you. Well, maybe I should go home. (*Turns to* JACK.) Jack?

IRENE: If you'd like— (*Pause. Mad.*) But I've been sweating here for days making your favorite marinated vegetables. Go on, get out of here! I have plenty of other children to torture.

JACK (*to* ERNIE)**:** So, how's everything at the National Guard?

ERNIE: Knock it off, pinhead!

JACK: I just asked you a simple question.

JAN: So, even though we're all grown up, I still feel as depressed as ever.

JACK: It's a lot better to be depressed and rich than to be poor and optimistic.

JAN: You know what your problem is Jack? Your problem is that you're a poor fuck. Rich, depressed or, shit Jack, JACK-OFF! (*Pause.*) Don't you think it's a little weird that Buzz hasn't been out of the house since he returned home last week from his ten-year tour of meditation?

IRENE: Is he hurting anyone?

JACK: It is a little weird. All he really does is sit in his room in front of his mirror and jerk-off.

ERNIE: What's wrong with that?

(*Enter* BUZZ.)

BUZZ: You're always comparing me to you! I was away from home for ten years and you never wrote me once!

JACK: Face it, Buzz, you've never accomplished anything in your life—you're an escapist.

IRENE: That's enough, prettyboy!

BUZZ: Yeah, I escape. I escape. I escape into the basement with my sludge, my rats, my music, my wanking, my chanting . . .

JAN: Don't forget the crystals!!

IRENE: All my son needs is a good fuck. (*To* BUZZ:) Go with your brother down to the Greyhound bus station and pick up a "toastie," "a dude-rancher," or "a fiesty piece of ass."

JAN: It's funny, we're all related but none of us knows how to talk.

BUZZ: Yeah, 'cause you always cause such a scene.

(ERNIE *starts eating before* IRENE *sits down at the table.*)

JAN: Ernie! Why don't you wait for Mom to sit down.

ERNIE: Because I'm a chauvinistic pig, that's why.

IRENE: And I like it.

BUZZ: Ma, get me some milk.

JAN: Ugh! DAIRY! Didn't living in Tibet teach you anything? I hate the way you treat Mom like a slave.

IRENE: But I like it. A mother stops being a mother once she stops being needed.

JACK: Shit! The Bears are on!

MEN: We're going to watch TV, Mom!

JAN (*moving to front of television*): Wait, I never get a chance to see you. (*She turns the television off.*)

ERNIE: You don't want to talk to us!

JACK: We're boring ignorant slobs and we don't want to talk to you either.

ERNIE: Get your hands off that TV or we'll break your arm!

JACK: I'm a white middle-class slob. I design menus for micro-waves—that's the limit to my life.

ERNIE: That reminds me of a story when I was young where I got beaten up by the nuns 'cause my adenoids were too big for my body and I couldn't talk and—

JACK (*interrupting* ERNIE): Hey Jan, get me a brewski!

ERNIE: Everyone always interrupts me.

BUZZ: That's because you're a boring storyteller just like your mother. You're nothing but a stupid mama's boy.

ERNIE: Everyone's always hinting at the idea that I want to sleep with Mom and I'm sick of it!

JACK (*hugging* IRENE): You said it—incest is best! Ernie, it's a joke. Okay, attention everybody, who wants to play father?

BUZZ: Why don't you play father? You diminish people the best.

IRENE: This is my house and I say Jack gets to play Dad.

JAN: Well, I'm pissed. Why do men always get to play Dad? Just because I don't have a dick doesn't mean that I shouldn't be able to play Dad!

IRENE: I have an idea. Why don't you play the hurt wife?

JAN (*to* JACK): Tell your son that he is the smelliest slob that I've ever met!

IRENE (*to* JACK): No, his father was the smelliest slob I ever met—but Wally was even smellier.

JACK: Who the hell is Wally?

BUZZ (*walking downstage; to audience*): Wally came to our house in the sixties and just never left. He was a Fuller Brush salesman and we kept him underground because he worked with the Black Panthers or Patty Hearst—anyway, he was some kind of political activist. Everyone was an activist back then. (BUZZ *starts to get starry-eyed.*) Ah, 1968, it just seems like yesterday—the riots, the meaning of life, the meaning of dissent, the hair, the paisley—paisley just isn't paisley anymore.

JAN: You know, everything has gone downhill since then.

JACK: Yeah, like your butt. (*Gooses her.*)

JAN (*turning to* JACK): And look what happened to you—Mr. Anthropology-Berkeley-Brain-Parapsychology-Save-the-World-Make-Love-Not-War-White-Mystical-Hippie-Revolutionary! You're nothing but a drag! A drag. Tell your son that all he does is sit around the house and drink beer and smoke pot!

JACK: And it's a hell of a lot of fun, too!

JAN: You're a bum!

JACK (*hurt and getting angry*): Don't you ever call me a bum.

JAN: BUM!

JACK (*menacingly*): Jan?!!!

ERNIE: HE'S A BUM!

BUZZ: NOTHIN' BUT A BUM!

ENTIRE FAMILY: BUM! BUM! BUM!

JACK (*sitting at table*): Yeah, you just want to keep me down all the time. You think I'm stupid. Well, why should I look intelligent when my entire culture is based on the mall, the video rental counter—it's an imperialist culture, Carl Jung isn't our hero, James Joyce isn't our mentor—no. No, people in our society look up to Alan Thicke*! It makes me sick!

JAN (*to* IRENE): Mom, tell him to tell us what really happened.

IRENE: Tell us what really happened in the sixties Jack.

JACK (*quiet and profound*): Well, I was on Grant Street in San Francisco and I had just caught one of those topless shows. I went into the Saloon and some guys cornered us—they forced us to take a drug and then they kidnapped us for weeks.

---

*Or any other bland, popular, forgettable man.

JAN: I wish it was forever.

JACK: They gave us LSD and they were from the CIA, just casually giving us LSD to experiment with our minds. After that I realized that the whole sixties movement was an entire invention. An entire experiment by some bureaucratic creeps, and then the inflation of the seventies was designed to stop the bohemia that they created!

JAN: You've always been so naive. Everyone in this world is a liar and a cheat. My own mother sold me as a whore.

IRENE: Yeah, I did.

JACK: You don't understand! I believed in the spirit of the sixties!

ERNIE: Yeah, you sold out! Now you just have those Chem-Grass companies.

JACK: That's a front!

FAMILY (*in total disbelief*): WHAT???

JACK (*proudly*): Chem-Grass is a hoax! I'm nothing but a grass deal-er—I sell POT! We deliver the grass to all the lawns we spray. Do you think I'd risk my neck with herbicides? That's dangerous stuff. We spray only water! Then we drop off the goods in the garage or wherever.

IRENE (*stunned*): Well, if you're a drug dealer why do my daughter and I live like this? I want a new Trans Am! I want a new Jeep Cherokee! I want Cannon towels, swimming pools, appliances made by Braun—I want DESIGNER EVERYTHING! I want a drug dealer's life-style! I don't want anymore of this chicken feed. And for starters, you can start paying me rent!

JACK: I knew this was going to happen. You'd hound me for every-thing I was worth. I just sell pot, Irene. I'm small-time! There isn't that kind of a profit—I'm just your neighborhood pot delivery boy service. You know, nine to five. Anyway, I give most of my money away.

JAN: AWAY?!?!

ERNIE: WHAT? ARE YOU CRAZY??

JACK: I give it to the drug rehab centers.

IRENE: Well, there should still be more money. I want you to expand your hours to twenty-four hours a day.

ERNIE: We want a drug dealer life-style! We want all the problems that money can bring!

IRENE (*to herself*): I wonder if my brownies would make good hash brownies?

BUZZ: Will you guys peep down? We're trying to watch the game!

(*Black. Lights come up on sandhill.* JACK *crosses to sandhill.*)

JACK'S RELIGIOUS EXPERIENCE

JACK *becomes a kachina doll. He is dressed and masked in a ceremonial costume and lights candles and places them in the sand. It is night; stars shine upon him and his altar. He performs rituals, scattering fairy dust and chanting to invoke the gods and godesses.*

(*Black.*)

Later that same day. Lights up. IRENE *is alone, sitting on bar, drinking and talking to herself.* BUZZ *and* JAN *sit at the table in the dark, drinking and listening to* IRENE.

IRENE: Why should I pretend to stop drinking? For the children? Shit, they're the reason I drink! My so-called daughter hasn't called me in years for my so-called intoxicated life-style—who cares if my decisions are intoxicated, liquor motivated, no one cares, no one listens. No one cares about me. Why should I care about me? Let's see how low they'll let me fall before they'll let me up—besides, I can stop whenever I want to. And you know children, as soon as they're in trouble they call on you to bail them out.

I know everything, that's my problem. I'm too smart for this world. My analysis can be so deliberate that I'm known for my psychic pain. Clever, smart, driven pain. I'm always right.

I feel your shiver when you suspect me drinking, but you'll never find my vodka behind the kitty litter box! 'Cause I'm the only one who works around here. No matter how much I drink I always make it to work on time! I'd like for you to feel pain, to feel my pain of raising a family alone. I don't get any widow benefits. People and family members are scared of me. They don't know what to do with a widow. Everyone blames his death on me. Everyone blames his life on me. Even though he pulled the trigger. The only consoling words I ever received are, "You're so lucky he didn't kill you and the children too," or, "You're so lucky he blew his brains out in the garage and not in the living room." I hate people who have to rationalize suffering, to know a reason to blame on everything. They just can't accept that bad things happen to good people. Because if they did they'd be out of control. They'd be like me—out of control. Yeah, I admit it, I'm out of control. (*Acts out of control.*)

(*Pause. Quieter, accepting.*) Soon my words will slur—my muscles and facial expressions will drop and change. My head will bob and my sentences will run on and on and on till you want me to stop but I won't. I'm a living hell and I let my devil come out, to prove my point.

(*Enter* JACK.)

JACK: Oh, Irene, it looks like another night of drunken passion. You know we all hate it when you drink! You're nothing but a sloppy drunk.

IRENE (*getting off bar, walking drunkedly and trying to make point*): I can drink whenever I want to. I deserve the right to drink. No one else rewards me for going to work every day. No one else goes to work like I do. I clean this damn house. I had five kids, three miscarriages, and one abortion. I've been a mother, a whore, and a slave. I've been needed, rejected, and desired but never valued by any of you.

JACK: Oh, Irene, we all know how much you sacrificed to have all the kids.

IRENE (*holding table for balance*): And I'd do it all again, because it was my destiny, to be your mother. You know why I had all of you kids sleep in one bed? 'Cause I didn't want you to masturbate. And I let you all go to sleep when you wanted to—'cause if you send a child to bed when they aren't sleepy they get bored and masturbate, not that jerking off is bad, but jerking off when you're bored—that's what is bad.

JACK: What the FUCK are you talking about?!

IRENE: I'M TALKING ABOUT HOW YOUR FATHER IS DEAD AND I HAVE NOTHING TO LIVE FOR!!

BUZZ: START LIVING FOR YOURSELF! I hate seeing someone I love killing themself like this!! That's why I left, Mom! To get away from your life!

IRENE (*in Buzz's face*): I can destroy you in one minute, Buster!

BUZZ: You already have.

IRENE: Get me another drink!

BUZZ (*handing her a bottle*): Why don't you just end it now?

JACK: I think you've had enough. (*Takes bottle from* IRENE.) Sleep it off. Sleep it off.

IRENE: Don't you ever tell me what to do! I just want to die! I want the pain to go away! Do you know why I drink? Because your father and I got married thirty-five years ago today.

(IRENE *exits*.)

BUZZ: I hate this. I hate you. I hate this ENTIRE FAMILY!

JAN: Leave her there. Just let her bottom out. Just as long as I don't have to hear her damn stories over and over again. If I hear the story of how her water bag broke or breast feeding in the fifties I think I'll scream.

JACK: Watch what you say, Jan.

(IRENE *reenters wearing a nightgown and falls on* TIM.)

JAN: I'm sick and tired of watching what I say in front of my drunken slob mother. We all love her and we all try not to say the wrong thing in front of her, well how about saying the right thing for a change.

BUZZ: Yeah, like get straight and stop blaming your fucked up life on us.

IRENE: I'm going to sleep now. I don't want to be a bother to anyone.

EVERYONE: Go to sleep. Sweet dreams.

(*Lights fade as* JACK *leads* BUZZ *and* JAN *in a chorus of "Goodnight Irene."*)

Next morning. IRENE *wakes on sofa with hangover.* ERNIE *makes breakfast, goes to fridge.* ERNIE *and* IRENE *talk and drink.*

ERNIE: This greenhouse effect is all man-made. And you know who is responsible? McDonalds. See, they all went into Mexico and made beef the big paying demand. All the farmers and politicians bought up all the land, rain forest—cut down the rain forest and raised cattle. Then the land became desert. So no crops, no cattle. That's why there is no food in this world. And the less rain forest the less absorption of CO_2. I wish Teddy Roosevelt was alive today. Now, there was a man. Here's to Teddy!

(IRENE *and* ERNIE *toast.*)

IRENE: What's that spot on your face? (*Begins to examine Ernie's body.*)

ERNIE: Nothing.

IRENE: Do you have herpes?

ERNIE: No. (*Looks up at* IRENE.)

IRENE: Stop looking at my tits. (*Begins whacking* ERNIE *on the head.*)

ERNIE: I'm not!

IRENE: Don't you look at my tits—

ERNIE: Mom, I'm not.

IRENE: You better not.

ERNIE: I'm not.

IRENE: You haven't been looking too good lately. Do you still hang out at the Greyhound bus station looking for chicks?

ERNIE: You know I can only have sex with strangers!

IRENE: Thank God, 'cause I didn't think you could have sex at all. But you should really protect yourself.

ERNIE: I can have sex just as long as it's a stranger and I never see their face or know their personality.

IRENE: Penises and pussies have faces too! And personality!

ERNIE: Stop giving me your Jungian symbolism jargon!

IRENE: You think you are the only one entitled to psychosexual liaisons? My father was fucking me without guilt before you were even born. The rest of my life I wished I was ugly—so I slashed my face with razor blades and I drugged myself so I couldn't feel. Don't you ever look at my tits.

ERNIE: What happened to your father?

IRENE: He became your father. He lived. I lived. So don't tell me about problems—I've had 'em all. You'll be fine. You feel guilt and guilt cures all crimes. I think I'm going to start dinner. I bet Buzz hasn't had meat loaf in a decade.

Buzz (*enters, hung over, wearing his mother's robe cinched with a belt*): I feel like I've been run over. I feel like dog meat.

Ernie: That's what ten years of the lotus position will do to you.

Buzz: Shut up, puss butt.

Irene: If you feel like dog meat so much, why don't you just fit yourself in old Scrappy's bowl?

Buzz: Scrappy's still alive???

Irene: He's died twice since you've left home, this is Scrappy the third.

Buzz: Why didn't you tell me? Why didn't you write me and tell me Scrappy died?

Irene: I thought that that was something to tell you in person. I just didn't realize that it would take you ten years to return home from your cop out spiritual journey. (*Goes to refrigerator for ingredients to meat loaf. Moves to table where she begins preparing it.*)

Buzz: And there I was in Pago Pago, the Taj Mahal, at the Valley of the Kings, and my little Scrappy was dead. Everything else looks pretty much the same.

Irene: Remember your old girlfriend Sally?

Buzz: The one I got pregnant?

Irene: That pregnant is now nine years old.

Buzz: Boy, am I glad I skipped town on her.

Irene: Don't worry, she's already married. She married your father after we got a divorce.

Buzz: Divorce! My parents can't get divorced! Well, this is really going to screw up my holidays. By the way, where is Dad?

Irene: On the couch in a coma.

Buzz: Oh, he was always getting himself into things.

IRENE: He tried to kill himself but he didn't succeed. He never succeeded in anything.

BUZZ: Where's Sally?

IRENE (*kneading the meat mixture*)**:** Exhausted—from all the multiple orgasms I gave her last night—HOW THE HELL SHOULD I KNOW WHERE SALLY IS!! But, of course, I'm stuck with the little mistake. But what do you care? For all you know I could have farmed out the little "mistake" for a little kiddie-porn action or have her on the street. Get her on some grocery bag or milk carton and get some recognition for this family like it deserves.

BUZZ: I don't appreciate your jokes that you and Sally are lesbian lovers and that my daughter is some kiddie-porn star. (*He is shaking, potentially violent.*)

IRENE: For a guy who's been around the world you're pretty square. You're a loser, Buzz. You walked out on your responsibilities. You've always gotten uptight around gay issues and you deny your sensitivity. I think that your problem is that you're a queer and you won't admit it. That's why you spent so much time in that monastery with all those perverted monks who HATE WOMEN.

BUZZ: Mom, things are completely different for me now. For one thing, I don't eat red meat.

IRENE: That's a safe way to get out of eating live, bleeding pussy. (*Smashes meat loaf in Buzz's face.*)

BUZZ: I eat seaweed—and I'm macrobiotic. All I wear is cotton, so Mom, if you want to buy me something make it one hundred percent cotton.

IRENE: I wouldn't buy you horseshit! Remember how I had to teach you to wank off—you wouldn't even touch yourself? And you give blow jobs don't you?

BUZZ: You know I learned that from you too.

IRENE: Well, in every ounce of cum there is the potential for a half million babies to be born, so don't give me any of your save-the-whales, tortured-animal bullshit cause my philosophy is LET THE ENTIRE WORLD COLLAPSE!!

Buzz: WHAT THE HELL ARE YOU TALKING ABOUT MOM? I'm not trying to have an argument, I'm just trying to say that you should wear cotton crotch panties 'cause your pussy stinks! Your birth canal wakes me up!

Irene: Yeah? Well your asshole tastes like a leather donut! So I'm going through my change and I smell a little. What, does it turn you on?

Buzz: Mom, all I'm saying is that I'm macrobiotic and rice is fine with me.

Irene: That rice, macrobiotic bullshit makes me think of someone. Yeah, your real father. I've got to tell you the truth, Buzz, your real father was Japanese. (*Moves behind* Buzz *and begins to massage his shoulders.*)

Buzz: That's funny, I don't look Japanese.

Irene: That's funny, my father was an asshole and I don't look like an asshole! Your father was a famous Sumi wrestler until they put him in an American concentration camp during World War Two and there he died.

Buzz: America had concentration camps? Why didn't you tell me this sooner?

Irene: Because being Japanese was a disgrace forty years ago, but now it's chic.

Buzz (*pointing to the sofa*): How long has this dad been in a coma?

Irene: Years.

Buzz: I was hoping he'd be dead by the time I got back. Why didn't you tell me?

Irene: I didn't want to upset your trip. Besides, you know I'm not much for writing.

Buzz (*looks at Dad lying on the sofa*)**:** Shit, I was hoping he'd be dead by the time I'd get back. How many Dads are there anyway?

Irene (*standing over* Tim)**:** As many as you need. (*Shouting.*) Why don't you go over to your father and tell him how much you hate him? Tell him you've hated him for years because he was insipid and boring. I'll do it for you, you weakling. (*To comatose father:*) I hate you! I hate you, Dad! I hate you because you had money and you never spent it on me, your son! I hate you because you always voted for losers like Goldwater and Mondale! I hate you because you lost all your money on the stock exchange and spent the rest on orphans. And I hate you because you never said "I love you." (*Turns back to* Buzz.) He never said "I love you baby Buzz, I love you little Buzzy!" You know what, Buzz, you're a disgusting, selfish person. You're no son of mine. Every day that man worked for your ass—(*puts* Buzz *in neck hold*).

Buzz (*screaming*)**:** I don't want a confrontation! I don't want a scene! I don't want an argument!

Irene: Look who's raising their voice. You've run away your entire life. No Tibetan monastery changed your little honky heart.

Buzz: You don't know me. You never knew me.

Irene: Yeah? Well I know plenty. You're a vegetarian who walks out on pregnant women. You cry more for a dog than your own father. Get out of my home! Get out of my home! Yeah, go back to the pyramids, to Tibet, to the jungles of Peru. You're nothing but a parasite! (Irene *walks out.*)

Buzz (*shaking, upset*)**:** Why do I feel this way whenever I come home? It's always like this. It never changes. I'm either running away or I'm totally depressed. Where are my feelings, my chances, my opportunities? I've always been totally disregarded by my family. I've never shared my love with my family. I've traveled everywhere, I've made love to many but I still don't know the meaning of life because I can't get past my father beating me everyday. BEATING ME EVERY DAY! I'm afraid of touching 'cause I'm afraid I might kill it. I still feel scared of the night—not for what might happen to me but that I might hurt somebody. I left home because I wanted to kill him! I don't want to feel anymore! I don't want to feel anymore! I don't feel—that is how I survive.

(*Black. Lights up on sandhill.* Buzz *crosses to sandhill.*)

BUZZ'S RELIGIOUS EXPERIENCE

Buzz, *shaking, carries a flowering plant to the bottom of the sandhill. He takes off his belt and beats the plant until it is beheaded. He beats the plant like he was beaten.*

(*Black.*)

Lights come up. IRENE *is on stage; enter* JAN.

JAN (*looking in the refrigerator*): Every time I wake up in this house I wake up feeling dead.

IRENE: What you need is a good full day of housework. Clean the toilet! Take out the garbage!

JAN (*sitting at table with* IRENE): Will you quit fucking analyzing me? I'm trying to politely say, I DON'T TRUST ANYONE! And do you know why? It's because you never trusted me and I never trusted you, mother. It's all your fault!

IRENE: You know that you've been a problem since the time you were born. Your labor was twenty-eight hours and I almost died. You've been trying to kill me since you were in the fetal position.

JAN: I never asked to be born! It's all your fault!

IRENE: If you think that I was going to carry you in my belly for thirty years until you were fucking ready to be born you've got to be kidding! I accept the fact that your life was my fault, all my fault. It's a mother's profession to take the blame for her children's psyche—even Jesus blamed the Virgin Mary, Prince Charles blames Queen Elizabeth. It's in the mother's contract—the unwritten, unspoken contract—generation after generation. And it's your job as a child to blame me, your mother, for your successes, your faults, and your problems. Just accept the game plan since I blame you. Yes, I blame you for the fact that having children is the reason why I never accomplished anything in my life. It's a nice trade-off. (*She breaks down.*)

JAN (*comforting* IRENE): Mother, Mother, you have accomplished so much. You, you gave life to me, to all of us. But I guess we just weren't enough for you. My entire life is dedicated to winning approval from you!

IRENE (*sobbing to herself*): I know I'm no good. I'm no good, I'm no good.

JAN: You never held me. You never gave me confidence.

IRENE (*shouting*): No one loves a smart woman! Why give you confidence when the only real opportunities for women are biological opportunities? Who are we? Our father's last name? Our husband's last name? And if we change it we're asked "why?" If we don't assume our husband's last name we're considered arrogant and dogmatic. The Chinese had it right—KILL ALL GIRL BABIES! Then when there are no more girl babies left maybe the men will miss us—but probably not—all they'll miss is raping us and dinner on the table. As soon as they learn how to make babies in test tubes, we're a goner!

JAN: Mom, can't you ever look on the bright side? Do you have to be such a pessimist? Women HAVE advanced!

IRENE: You've got it all wrong! Women are already advanced. It's just that men have to advance to accept this fact and treat us equally and stop punishing us because we can have children and they can't.

JAN (*screaming*): Everything is a crisis for you! Everything is a crisis situation! (*Gets more and more upset.*) I'm nothing! I'm worthless! You don't love people, you only love their problems. You don't love me, you only love my inadequacies! (*She gets so upset she starts to have trouble breathing.*)

(*Enter* JACK *and* ERNIE *with a six-pack as* JAN *breaks down.*)

JACK (*rushing to* JAN, *who is now having a severe asthma attack*): What the hell is going on here? I told you not to talk to your mother. She only upsets you. (*To* IRENE:) Irene, what the hell did you do to her? She's going to stop breathing again, I know it!

IRENE: That asthma bullshit is all psychological. She just won't face her problem.

JACK: Yeah, and that problem is YOU!

JAN (*trying to suck in air*): I, I, I can't breathe!

JACK: Come on Jan! Breathe in deeply and slowly. (*To* IRENE:) What have you done to her? What did you say? (*Back to* JAN, *soothingly:*) Slowly, baby. Just breathe in. You don't want to have another episode, do you? Just think about cool distant lakes and clear blue skies. We can beat this together. I don't want to have to tranquilize you like the last time, remember?

JAN (*confusedly*): But I'm hearing voices. I'm seeing auras. I'm seeing halos.

(ERNIE, *wearing military fatigues, begins to exercise.* BUZZ *enters, dressed in a caftan, sits at bar, and begins smoking.*)

JACK: Don't go away from me now, Jan! (*To family:*) Irene, all of you! Look at yourselves. You've ruined her! Every time she comes here you have to upset her. I don't have a wife, I have a child. I'm nothing but a babysitter! Jan won't grow up—and I can't let a child have children. All I wanted out of life was to be a father so I could undo what my father did to me. I'd be such a good father too. (*Shaking and grabbing* JAN.) Come on Jan, let's have a baby! Let's have a child! I don't care if it's ugly, retarded or even if it's born dead! (*Jan's asthma gets worse again.*) Irene! The rest of you! Do you see what you've done to her? She can't feel—she can't feel. She's numb inside. When I make love to my own wife she doesn't even feel me!

(ERNIE, *now bored with exercise, goes to table and begins to read.*)

JAN (*shouting between gulps of air*): I can feel! I can feel! That's where I'm different from all of you! My body stopped feeling but my heart took over. My insides were ripped open with a beer bottle by three Catholic priests on a pool table—

ERNIE (*looking up from his book*): So the night belongs to Michelob? So what else is new? All women go through that rape stuff.

IRENE (*upset to* ERNIE): Do you hear yourself? Lots of women get raped so get used to it, huh?

BUZZ: You know what, Jack? I was thinking and I think that your problem is that your family was rich and famous. Your family had everything—books, beauty, charm, and money. They had brains, power, and health. Your family had everything except PROBLEMS, except CONFLICT, except CRISIS. Now our family has problems. We are very creative problem-making people, we've worked on it for generations.

IRENE (*to* JACK): Yeah, and you sit there on your ass in my house, with your trust fund, married to my daughter, and you're addicted to us! Our dynamics make you feel alive! Why don't you take your white-collar ass and do what you're supposed to—give your money away to charity, give your time to the sick, the suffering, the homeless?

JACK: And why don't you take that boring, blue-collar work ethic and shove it right up your rosy-red ass! You're the kind of person who believes that you've got to work for it, you've got to pay your dues, you've got to suffer. Well I hate that Puritanical garbage! I hate that fucking crap! I hate people like you who believe that poverty, disease, and racism is deserved! You can take your intellectual sarcasm, your books, your biting analysis, and lay those on the graves of the hungry! (*Clears items from table with an angry sweep of his arm.*)

IRENE: Cut the crap! I don't need your pity. It's so convenient for the rich to be progressive.

JACK: I'm not rich. You know my family gave me nothing. They disowned me—I'm the black sheep of my family. The only thing they gave me was an attitude.

(JAN *is having problems breathing again.*)

I don't know what to do for her anymore, Irene. What have I done to deserve this?

BUZZ: Here, I'll help show her how to breathe. It's an ancient yogi technique I once learned from a busboy at the Yaffa Cafe. (*To* JAN:) Put your thumbs under your cheekbones and breathe deeply while cramping your right foot. (BUZZ *looks into Jan's eyes as she begins to breathe again.*) Boy, are you psychically out of wack! Your chakras are disorganized, your pupils are dilated. You've got problems, girl, big problems.

JACK: She doesn't have any problems, Buzz. I take care of all her problems. She's just sick (*pointing to his head)* just like everyone else in this family: manic attacks, depressed, paranoid, and schizoid. Now I have the real problems around here. The IRS is after me for inheritance taxes, my bleeding ulcer, and I don't know if I should stay in options or futures. I have problems you can see. Jan has problems that you can't see—they're invisible.

JAN (*becoming coherent again*): That's why I don't want a baby! I don't want to have another generation of hate and discontent. If I had a baby I'd kill it as soon as it cried. You can't trust anyone Jack—you or me. All YOU want to do is control! You want a perfect little baby and a perfect little wife and a perfect little life. Loving is controlling for you. WELL, I WANT OUT OF CONTROL! (*She goes crazy.*)

JACK (*putting his arms around* JAN; *she becomes calmer*): Gee, honey, I don't know what to say. I'm doing the best I can, really I am. I look at life more simply—go to a few games, pitch a few balls, retire, picnics. But I love you, Jan. Please don't let your family come between us. Please! (*Tenderly to* JAN:) I wish I was crazy. Sometimes I stay up nights thinking that maybe if I was crazy you'd want me more, need me more. Maybe you'd want to take care of me. Sometimes I fantasize that I'm sick and everyone is around my bed as I'm sweating and wheezing and they're all telling me to get better. They're asking God to make me better—

(JAN *suddenly shoves* JACK *to the ground.*)

JAN (*screaming*): Don't you ever talk about committing suicide! Don't you ever say that again! (*The breathing problem starts again.*) I married my father! Oh God, I've married my father!

IRENE: Yes, you did.

JAN: I've got to get out of here! (*Runs out of the room.*)

IRENE (*waiting until* JAN *is out of the room*): Jan! No, wait!

(*Black. Lights up on* JAN, *who moves to sandhill.*)

JAN'S RELIGIOUS EXPERIENCE

JAN *hurries to the refrigerator, opens the icebox, and pulls out a pair of high heels and a wool scarf and hat. She throws off her robe to reveal her girdle-bra armor. She puts on the scarf, hat, and heels and carries a gallon of milk to the sandhill.* JAN *pours the milk in a straight line in front of sandhill and quickly shovels the milk and throws the shovel offstage.*

(*Black.*)

Lights up. Enter ERNIE; *the room is dark.* IRENE *and* JACK *are at the table,* BUZZ *is sitting on a chair; they have all been drinking heavily.*

ERNIE: So, ahhh, who cut one? Hey (*looking around*) why are the lights turned down in here? What's going on?

JACK: Can't you see that we're having an emotional dialogue? But then again, you just like to talk to hear yourself talk.

IRENE (*to* JACK): He can't help it. Don't worry, they'll be dead by age fifty-five from high blood pressure, a heart attack, stress, or my favorite, spoiled balls.

MEN: SPOILED BALLS?!?!

IRENE: Prostate cancer.

ERNIE: Ma, don't say that around here. You know it makes my balls itch. And what's that smell? Mom, you're smelling again. Can't you take a bath?

JACK (*to* IRENE): Irene, aren't you wearing any underwear? All the neighbors are going to see you.

IRENE: So I like to air out! (*Jumps on a chair and pulls her housecoat over her waist to expose her pubic area.*) So I like to get some air up there! I'm at my change of life and I like to keep my oils where I can find 'em —on me! The problem with this country is that there are no smells left. No life, no death, only plastic. Plastic-wrapped fruit. Plastic-wrapped crotch. Do you know the poisons that they put in deodorants?

ERNIE (*jumping at the chance to lecture the family*): That's right—the poisons that they put in deodorants and antiperspirants, it's ruining our planet. DuPont, I know it, Saatchi & Saatchi, Folgers Coffee in Brazil, they're all out to poison us! They're all behind the war of the world. They are all behind the drugs coming into this country. That's who we have to fight! Jesus, would I love to bomb Chase Manhattan Bank! I want to fight capitalism. GOD, GIVE ME A WAR! I want a war. My problem is that I've been taught to kill and I don't want to. I know how to kill with my bare hands. I know how to blow up an entire village. I know how to shoot from so far away that I can't even hear a man's last dying cry. I'm a soldier. I'm not a man, I'm just a soldier—totally depersonalized. And YOU let me go into the army! My family let me go into the army. You never had the time for me. You don't know how hard being a "grunt" in the army is.

(JAN *enters wearing an exercise outfit; moves to bar.*)

BUZZ: This is a pacifist family. We don't believe in fighting. None of us wanted you to go.

ERNIE: You all made fun of me my entire life! You called me retarded! (*In a singsong voice.*) Retarded, Cootie-boy, Booger-eater!

JACK (*drunk*): Ernie, that was a long time ago. Here, have a beer with your booger. (JACK *falls out of chair.*)

ERNIE (*to* JACK): You are so bourgeois! You're so putrid! Your La Costa look makes me sick! You know nothing. You might have found the dying, dead body but I buried it! I was the oldest male. I was the oldest male. I AM the oldest male! And when Dad killed himself I wanted to kill someone back.

JACK: So by going into the army you ran away from your pain.

ERNIE (*extremely upset*): I want to blow something up now! Let's fight! Put 'em up! Let's fight!

(JACK *and* ERNIE *pick up chairs to fight.*)

IRENE: Settle down. Ernie, make me a drink.

ERNIE: All right, Mom. (*They cease fighting.*)

(ERNIE *goes to the bar and pours* IRENE *a drink.*)

ERNIE (*lecturing again*): You know what the problem with this country is? The Yalta Agreement. Yeah, we got the wrong end of that shit stick! Roosevelt was dying and MacArthur wanted to take over Japan, Russia, and Eastern Europe. We had our chance and blew it. We were the first nation to build countries up and let them have their freedom after we blew them apart.

BUZZ: Will you please stop lecturing us? We're on your side. Maybe you should go to therapy. You seem to be having flashbacks without ever having fought in a war.

ERNIE (*shouting, with knife in hand, pointing it while talking*): No one can talk to me 'cause they haven't been through what I've been through! You haven't been in the army! You haven't been ignored! No one ever needed me. No one ever needed me. No one ever loved me!

IRENE (*hugging* ERNIE): I love you, Ernie.

(*Everyone puts their arms around* ERNIE.)

FAMILY: We love you Ernie! We love you Ernie!

ERNIE (*pushing away from family and screaming*): Don't touch me! Don't touch me! No! No!

(*Black. Lights come up on* ERNIE *at kitchen table.*)

ERNIE'S RELIGIOUS EXPERIENCE

ERNIE *brings one of the kitchen chairs to the sandhill. He puts a drop cloth under chair. He stands behind the chair, takes down his pants, opens a bottle of hand lotion and sensually massages the chair. He continues massaging the chair, moaning, embracing and holding the chair until he attains ecstasy.*

(*Black.*)

Lights up; IRENE *and* JACK *at table.* JAN *at bar.* BUZZ *sits in chair by couch.*

ERNIE (*in his normal, paranoid voice again*): You know what I do? Every day I ride my bicycle back to the old house on Maple Avenue. I ride my bicycle around and around the block remembering what it was like before everything happened. I go around and around the block and then stop in front of the garage where he killed himself. Sometimes I peep through the window and imagine my father's body on the bloody cement. Once I found the door open and I went inside and I acted out his ritual. And I just think to myself, he wasn't a man. He couldn't stand up to life and make decisions for his family. He couldn't think about anyone else but himself. I wasn't good enough for him. I'm not good enough for anyone to live. No one ever loved me. No one ever loved me. You wonder why I'm not involved with life? Have joy in life? It's because no one ever loved me. How can I love anyone if I don't know how to love? (*Coming to a realization.*) I don't know how to love! Oh, help me! Help me! (*Everyone tries to put their arms around* ERNIE.) DON'T TOUCH ME! DON'T TOUCH ME!

JACK (*drunkenly to* IRENE): 'Cause it turns him on!

ERNIE: The only way to survive in this family is to make fun of yourself. The only way to survive is to make fun of everyone else. The only way to survive is to move, to get the hell out of here. The only way to survive is to display your damaged goods. All right, I admit it! I'm a pervert! I'm insane! I'm no good! I'm ugly, I'm retarded—I'M A BOOGER-EATER!

BUZZ: Why don't you visit the booger buffet. Stop acting like the martyr. You aren't so sick. Dad was the one that was sick. But psychologically speaking, it was Mom who was really sick. Look at us—one brother overdosed, another likes to bring trash in from the street and never bathe—and makes a meal out of his nose.

ERNIE: I don't do that anymore!

JACK: Everyone is a damn shrink! Everyone is a damn shrink in this house. Face it, maybe your father was a child molester and liked to finger little girl's pussies and then no wonder he killed himself. This family is nothing special. You're just the average American family!

JAN: That's my problem, I can only love sick people. My parents were insane. My mother was crazy. My mother IS crazy. They never fit in. My father was crazy. Mental illness runs in this family. Alcoholism runs in this family. Addiction is a talent for this family.

JACK: You are so unaware of other's needs. You think you'd be so different if you were brought up by a dancing mother in a toga?

Buzz: Low blow, Jack. So she fantasized about being Isadora Duncan a little too much. So what's the big deal? So she's a little delusional at times.

Jan (*confronting* Buzz): You know what your problem is little baby brother Buzzy? You won't face Dad's death. Face it—Dad is dead and you were the last one to see him alive!

Buzz (*uncomfortably*): Stop it! Shut up, She-Ra.

Family (*taunting*): Come on, Buzz, tell us your story!

Buzz: No, No. No. No. No. (*Pause.*) All right.

Irene: I already hate you.

Family (*yelling*): Come on, Buzz. Yeah, come on, Buzz!! (*Builds to a crescendo.*)

(*Pause.*)

Buzz: Well okay. It's all my fault! We had an argument—I told him to get out of his depression and then I told him to drop dead. And then he just turned up the music real loud while I was in my room, went out into the garage, and shot himself. And he was lying in his frozen blood while I was upstairs masturbating and listening to the Grateful Dead. I told him to drop dead and he did! My wish came true! It's all my fault. I can't get away from that memory. I just can't shake it.

Jan: What a fucking asshole! Do you know what that fucker did to me? He was supposed to meet me at 3:00 P.M. and he never showed up. He shot himself instead. I guess I just wasn't worth staying around for. And for weeks he'd said that he felt like dying and I'd laugh at him. I told him to grow up. We were just kids. We were just kids.

Ernie: You never told me that, Jan. I could have saved him. I should have saved him but I left home instead!

Buzz: You know why I don't get involved? You know why I left home? Because I was afraid that I'd be next—that I'd take my life next.

ERNIE: Yeah, I know what you mean—I get those thoughts too.

JAN: Well, you know, everyone always blames Mom for having those affairs. That's what really tore him apart.

IRENE (*exploding*): All right, the party is over! I knew one day it would come to this! You'd all blame me! I've been waiting for this moment for years! Get out of my house! Get out of my house!

EVERYONE: No! No!

IRENE: Well I was his wife! I was his wife! He was perverted. He was sick. You're all like Hitler blaming the Jews! Get out of my house! GET OUT!

BUZZ: Why can't we ever have some superficial conversation around here? Why does everything have to be so analyzed all the time? (*To* ERNIE:) So what do you think about the lights at Wrigley Field? (*To* JACK:) Great weather today, huh? (*To* JAN:) Hey Jan, nice shoes! (*To* IRENE:) Hey Mom, what's for dinner?

IRENE (*screaming*): DON'T "WHAT'S FOR DINNER" ME! Don't "what's for dinner" me. I see it in all your faces. You blame me. ME the widow, the wicked witch! Well, get out of my house. All of you!

BUZZ: I hate you! I hate this! I hate this entire family!

IRENE (*turning to* ERNIE): You—get out of here, you've been hanging around for years!

ERNIE (*rushing off stage yelling*): THIS IS PROOF THAT YOU NEVER LOVED ME!

IRENE (*to* JAN *and* JACK): And you two, too! Get out of my house right now!

JACK (*leaving*): I'm doing the best I can—

JAN (*following* JACK): This is it, Mother—GOOD-BYE! (*Both stomp off stage.*)

IRENE (*to* BUZZ): Get out!

Buzz: I hate you! (*Storms off stage.*)

Irene (*looking around the room and spotting* Tim): AND YOU TOO! GET OFF THAT COUCH AND GET THE HELL OUT OF HERE!

(Tim *looks up in surprise and horror and runs out of the room.*)

Irene: Yeah, you can all get out of my house. Don't you realize that the reason why I keep you all emotionally tied to your father is to keep him alive? Keep his memory alive? Sure you come into this house and act like a child but then I'm a mother and I'm not a widow for a few moments. I don't want to be in physical time. I don't want to be in real time. I WANT TO STAY IN EMOTIONAL TIME! I want to keep him alive! I want to keep him alive! I want to keep him alive.

(*Black. Lights up on* Irene.)

IRENE'S RELIGIOUS EXPERIENCE

Irene *leaves the home and walks to sandhill with chair. She takes off her robe and is wearing a black slip. Her hair is down. She experiences a younger self, a new self, a different self. She reads her prayer, "The Black Sheep."*

> After a funeral someone said to me
> You know I only see you at funerals
> It's been three since June
> Been five since June for me
> He said I've made a vow
> I only go to death parties if I know someone before they
> were sick
> Why?
> 'Cause—'cause—'cause I feel I feel so
> sad 'cause I never knew their life
> and now I only know their death
> And because we are members of the
> Black Sheep family

We are sheep with no shepherd
We are sheep with no straight and narrow
We are sheep with no meadow
We are sheep who take the dangerous
pathway through the mountain range
to get to the other side of our soul.
We are the black sheep of the family
called Black Sheep folk.
We always speak our mind.
    appreciate differences in culture
    believe in sexual preferences
    believe in no racism
    no sexism
    no religionism
and we'll fight for what we believe
But usually we're pagans,
There's always one in every family
Even when we're surrounded by bodies
we're always alone
You're born alone
and you die alone
written by a black sheep.
You can't take it with you
written by a former black sheep.
Black Sheep folk look different from their family
The way they look at the world
We're a quirk of nature
We're a quirk of fate
Usually our family, our city, our country
never understand us
We knew this from when we were very young
that we weren't meant to be understood.
That's right. That's our job.
Usually we're not appreciated
until the next generation.
That's our life. That's our story.

Usually we're outcasts, outsiders
in our own family.
Don't worry—get used to it.
My sister says I don't understand you!
But I have hundreds of sisters with me tonight.
My brother says I don't want you!
But I have hundreds of brothers with me here tonight!
My mother says I don't know how to love someone like you!
You're so different from the rest!
But I have hundreds of mamas with me here tonight!
My father says I don't know how to hold you!
But I have hundreds of daddies with me here tonight!

We're related to people we love who can't say
I love you Black Sheep daughter
I love you Black Sheep son
I love you outcast, I love you outsider
But tonight we love each other
That's why we're here
to be around others like ourselves
So it doesn't hurt quite so much
In our world our temple of difference
I am at my loneliest when I have
something to celebrate and try
to share it with those I love but
who don't love me back.
There's always silence at the end
of the phone
There's always silence at the end
of the phone
Sister—Congratulate me!
NO I CAN'T YOU'RE TOO LOUD
GRANDMA LOVE ME
NO I DON'T KNOW HOW TO LOVE
SOMEONE LIKE YOU
Sometimes the Black Sheep is a soothsayer,

a psychic, a magician of sorts
Black Sheep see the invisible
We know each other's thoughts.
We feel fear and hatred.

Sometimes, some sheep are chosen to be sick,
to finally have average, flat, boring
people say I love you.
Sometimes, Black Sheep are chosen to be sick
so families can finally come together
and say I love you.
Sometimes, some Black Sheep are chosen to die
so loved ones and families can finally say:
Your life was worth living
Your life meant something to me!
Black Sheeps' destinies are not in
necessarily having families,
having prescribed existences
like the American Dream.
Black Sheep's Destinies are to give
meaning in life—to be angels,
to be conscience, to be nightmares
to be actors in dreams.

Black Sheep can be family to strangers
We can love each other like MOTHER
FATHER SISTER BROTHER CHILD
We understand universal love
We understand unconditional love.
We feel a unique responsibility
a human responsibility for feelings for others
We can be all things to all people
We are there at 3:30 A.M. when you call
We are here tonight 'cause I just can't
go to sleep. I have nowhere else to go
I'm a creature of the night
I travel in your dreams

I feel your nightmares
We are your holding hand
We are your pillow, your receiver,
your cuddly toy.
I feel your pain.
I wish I could relieve you of your suffering.
I wish I could relieve you of your pain.
I wish I could relieve you of your death.
Silence at the end of the phone.
Silence at the end of the phone.
Silence at the end of the phone.

(*Black.*)

ethyl eichelberger

DASVEDANYA MAMA

THE THREE SISTERS (all played by Black-Eyed Susan) bid *do svidanija* to OLGA (Ethyl Eichelberger).

A printed text gives only the barest sense of a performance art like Ethyl Eichelberger's, but the wide-ranging, free-flowing richness of this one conveys, I think, how powerful and strongly woven his seemingly artless performances were. *Dasvedanya Mama* does not "add up" in any conventional sense: It is tragic and bawdy, trashily melodramatic and delicately capricious, endlessly local in its topical allusions and eternal in its awareness of how comedy works and how the theater stays alive. The deep distaste—in some cases close to loathing—that reviewers with a middlebrow mindset always showed for Eichelberger's work used to cause me endless perplexity; I saw him as a living presence in the theater, whose approach would have seemed like unsurprising—though delightful—business as usual from Aristophanes' time to that of Bobby Clark.

When Ethyl appeared on Broadway as the Streetsinger in my translation of *The Threepenny Opera* (alluded to in *Dasvedanya Mama*, produced six months later), he performed with total professionalism, brought down the house every night, and won the admiration of leading Brechtians for the admirable way he conveyed the spirit of the work. His reward for this in the daily press, astonishingly, was to be greeted with almost universal execration, though there was nothing either "wrong" or "embarrassing" about the performance, nor anything that could be objected to on technical grounds; the reviewers were reviewing their awareness that he appeared in drag in other pieces (he did not do so in *Threepenny*), their objection to his rapport with the audience, their distaste for theater that breaks the bounds of a tidy frame, categorical or visual—almost anything *but* his performance. To Ethyl their remarks, though disheartening, were nothing new; to me they brought home, with violent force, the extent to which puritans, who in other centuries would have called for the banning of the theater, shape its definition in ours.

And yet the theater lives on, in venues however eccentric. *Dasvedanya Mama,* its burlesque luridness undercut by perfectly genuine tragic pathos, is a slice of theater as it has always lived, tossing off gems of wit and high poetry almost in the same breath as the lowest grossness and absurdity. Thanks to P.S. 122 and its archivists, performance videotapes survive (as they do, thankfully, for much of Ethyl's work), on which the writer-performer's artistry can be seen and felt. The evolution of a script in performance, and improvised interchange with the audience, were essential parts of Ethyl's approach; the task of transcribing these sections from the videotape and interweaving them with the typescript was an object lesson as well as a pleasure; it redoubled my admiration for his humor, his skill, his theatrical and musical knowingness, his breadth of passion mixed with an unerring drive for precision of detail. *Dasvedanya Mama* may or may not be performable by others; it may or may not "mean" something in the largest literary sense. It certainly does mean something in the context of our time, and the climate of disapproval that makes every step into the imagination a step toward danger. One we should all take bravely, as Ethyl did, head held mockingly high, to a tangy accordion tune.

For making the script and tape accessible to me, and helping to elucidate many points, I am enormously grateful to Joe E. Jeffreys.

PRODUCTION NOTES

Dasvedanya Mama was first presented at P.S. 122 in New York City, July 19, 1990. The set was designed by Ethyl Eichelberger. The lighting was designed by David Ferri. The costumes were designed by Mr. Fashion (Gerard Little). The author composed the score and directed. The cast was as follows:

FIERZ: Helen Shumaker
OLGA: Ethyl Eichelberger
MASHA, IRINA, AND MAUDE: Black-Eyed Susan
NINA: Joan Marie Moossy
VASLAV: Gerard Little

CHARACTERS

FIERZ, an old servant

OLGA, a retired actress

MASHA, IRINA, and MAUDE, the three sisters*

NINA, the ward

VASLAV, the prodigal son

*Played by one actress with wig forms on her shoulders.

The set is simple, stark, ceremonial. There are two chairs and a bench, each on its own platform. As the lights come on, FIERZ *is doing his daily work, and we see Olga's back as she listens to the old servant.*

FIERZ: You live with your dreams, Olga, you don't know what is real anymore . . . You've been eating couscous from an aluminum cooker too long, too long! And where does that leave me, Fierz, the faithful retainer who has lived in this mansion with the sisters for how many hundreds, how many hundreds? You must control yourself as I do . . . You must fight for your sanity, Olga, struggle to see what is going on around you. Too long have you listened to the bad advice of your quarreling sisters . . . but I listen, I clean the samovar, I empty the ashtrays, I keep my eyes and ears open, and say little . . . But *now* you've gone too far, Olga Oglalaovich, to plan for your son Vaslav's return. You've gone too far . . . men in little white jackets, Olga . . . But it is not faithful Fierz's place to say anything. Do you hear your alert guardian? I will not taunt you, I tell you the truth . . . Do not ignore me—I warn you by all the fruit in the orchard that you must not challenge the gods!

OLGA (*turning front*): Oh, shut up! Fierz, Fierz, you see me to my very soul . . . I wish you didn't! You know too much . . . yours is the wisdom of the wily woodland peasant from Chernobyl . . . but be gentle with your advice. You speak too painfully to me. Remember who I am, Fierz, not the little girl you bounced on your knee and diddled. I am Olga Pluchinskaya, who was the greatest actress of the

'60s. And the '70s. I was the foremost actress of the Bull Shahoy Conservatorium of Mensk. No one remembers anymore, I know . . . but what care I? I was the star, and that's all that matters . . . I was the best . . . Well, of course I had my rivals, and they were good, but no one could top my Ekaterina the Great, my dying swan, my Rapunzel, my Nina, my Pinta, my Santa Cecilia . . .

FIERZ: All in the past, long ago even to me, who have seen generations come and go in this house . . .

OLGA: Do you remember the command performance in gay Paree? Ah, those were the days.

FIERZ: It snowed and Her Imperial Majesty canceled at the last minute . . . You were crushed! I had to console you.

OLGA: And the award ceremony where I got the purple sash of success . . . Where is it, Fierz? I should wear it for Vaslav's return.

FIERZ: You are cruising for a bruising, my mistress . . . You should live and let live, and live one day at a time.

OLGA: You should cut down your intake of goat curds, Fierz, then maybe you'd be more like the rest of us . . . Does it not matter to you that all your friends are gone, that you alone are still here rubbing the walls with patchouli oil on Sunday, and mopping the stairs? We are both relics, Fierz, you and I. But you make me look like a babe in the woods . . . You should have departed when the geniuses of your generation swooped off to the Great Unknown. But no, you must stay here to make my days miserable with your whining and ka-vetching about everything and nothing.

(*Gong.*)

FIERZ: Hark! The sound of sobbing emanates from the upper rooms . . . Could it be young ward Nina has begun her nightly wanderings about the hallowed halls?

(NINA *enters sobbing, pulling three intravenous bottles on a stand. She then attempts feebly and with little success to do herself in by pulling I.V.s out of her arm.*)

OLGA: Fierz, take those away from her before she hurts herself. Where are Masha, Irina, and Maude? All they have to do in this world is to guard Nina from her baser inclinations . . . but they fail. They shirk their duties . . . They are good for nothing anymore if they cannot even stop arguing long enough to baby-sit the ward!

FIERZ: Do not rouse your ire, Olga Pluchinskayavich, or your temper will flare and you will regret . . .

OLGA (*coming down off her platform and going to* NINA): Hush, little Nina, don't cry. Oh, you are so innocent. *Io innocente.* Look at that lovely face. Why should anyone have to suffer like that? Oh, Nina, Nina . . . Sometimes I think the whole world should just up and drop dead. Yes I do. Why do we have to eternally struggle like this? I've got no bones to pick. I just tend to think that there are two kinds of people in this world, people like myself and assholes.

(FIERZ *gasps.*)

Well, Fierz, don't look so shocked—I've got one, you've got one, too, whether you want to admit it or not. Let me remind you that your lovely pink mouth tinted from the fermented juice of tender beebleberries is a sphincter muscle too. So you can do more than eat with it, I do assure you!

FIERZ: Madame, I'm shocked. Nice women don't say such things.

OLGA: Nice women don't go on the stage. Oh, forgive me, my nerves are strained, I am impatient even with the little bunny rabbits leaping to and fro in their hutches in the back, hippy-hop, hippy-hop, I hear them, the little buggers, all night long.

FIERZ: Pah, it is Vaslav's return that makes you nervous, and well it should . . .

OLGA: What are you saying, Fierz? Do you dare to remind me once again of your sordid opinions? Vaslav is my son, my joy, the light of my life, my reason for living.

FIERZ: You would do well never to think of him again. I will pray to the Holy Imperial Virgin, Her Majesty Mary of Barnnisshycough, the Immaculate Conceiver, who intercedes for us with the Lord, and hope to hear only that he is gone, never to return again.

OLGA: Well, pray all you want, peasant, and still he will return. Medical school in Ivanovichville is difficult and time-consuming, that is why I have received no letters, no word to ease my mind of its wanderings and sufferings . . .

FIERZ: He has forgotten you, this son of yours.

OLGA: No, no, how can you stab a mother in the heart? He is coming back, I know it. He loves me . . . He needs me . . .

(*Gong.* THE THREE SISTERS *enter in a huff and a snit. They kneel in prayer.*)

MASHA: Saint Francis of Assisi, have mercy.

IRINA: Father died just a year ago today, think of it, and I dreaded his funeral—it rained.

MAUDE: Olga did not cry, did you dear . . . I cried . . .

MASHA: We three devoted sisters did cry our eyes out.

IRINA: My shoes were ruined. It was a miserable affair.

MASHA: Why think of such things, Irina?

MAUDE: I leapt out of bed this morning early, saw the sunlight, saw that summer was finally here, my heart fluttered with joy, and I longed so to return to Petersburg again.

MASHA: Why think of such things, Maude?

IRINA: Oh, how I long to return to the past, everything as it was, and no sorrow, no remorse to drown in here in this empty mansion in the Chechenko Woods.

OLGA: Stop this incessant chattering, ye sisters three. Let us busy ourselves with finer things. Today Vaslav will return and we must make him welcome.

IRINA: Vaslav is coming back? Oh, no . . .

MAUDE: Vaslav will return to take us to Petersburg. Oh, yes . . .

MASHA: Vaslav will never return, Olga. Do not get your hopes up too high. He was never a good son, and he has not written in the ten years he has been gone.

IRINA: Vaslav, oh woe.

MAUDE: Vaslav, oh huzzah.

MASHA: Vaslav is a fig newton of Olga's imagination. No one is coming to help us out of our financial straights . . . We'll soon lose this house and the orchard and the tidy rabbit hutches in the rear . . .

(IRINA *moans.*)

Quiet, Irina.

(MAUDE *shrieks.*)

Hush, Maude; do not try to write the future before it happens. Vaslav will come back or not and no one can tell which it will be . . .

OLGA: Vaslav is a good son, I know he's coming back, back to comfort his mother, and to save our estate. Oh, ye of little faith, do not doubt my premonition. A son needs his mother. Vaslaviloffsky, do not forsake me, little will-'o'-the-wisp, keep on the pathway you have chosen here to your mother's arms.

FIERZ: Foolish woman, dreamer of barren dreams, where is your husband first, and then your son . . .

OLGA: Do not taunt me, old one.

FIERZ (*sneering*): No husband!

OLGA (*threatening*): No job!

IRINA: I'm getting a headache. Masha, make Olga stop her sad dreaming.

MAUDE: Oh, how exciting, Olga and Fierz are at it again.

MASHA: Hush, hush, sweet sisters, let Olga have her dreams.

OLGA: My dreams are real.

MASHA: Of course they are, boobala.

OLGA: Do not condescend to me, Masha.

MASHA: Of course your dreams are real, Olga, and pigs have wings to fly, the leaping porkers.

IRINA: Oh, Masha, you are so cruel.

MAUDE: Give it to the old girl good, Mashinski.

MASHA: Hush, both of you, Olga and I understand each other.

FIERZ: Idle arguing in a house of unfulfilled dreams and desires.

(*Gong.*)

ALL: Who comes this way, clutching her rosary and muttering?

(NINA *enters with a hangman's noose.*)

NINA (*as in Ponchielli's* La Gioconda): *Suicidio! . . . In questi fieri momenti . . . Tu sol mi resti . . .*

ALL: Russ-i-an, in Russ-i-an, please!

NINA: Vaslav, my love, in this traumatic moment of your return, you alone mean anything to me . . . You alone tempt me to fulfill my destiny, the slit wrist, the arteries torn, my arteries, my last will and testament, the stations of the cross . . . oh . . . Once upon a time . . .

ALL: IN THE BEGINNING . . .

NINA: The hours flew gaily by, and I was happy just to be at Vaslav's side. Lost now my love. He is gone to someone else, methinks. I sink demented in the darkness . . . I am reaching the end . . . I ask only of the Orthodox Russian heavens to let me sleep quietly in the grave, deep within our Russian soil . . . so brown and filled with slimy Russian slugs . . . Vaslav has forsaken me . . . He will never return.

OLGA: Hush, quiet, desist, Nina! Keep your paranoias to yourself, girl. I know that Vaslav will return. I know it, I know it, I know it! Wanna know how I know? . . . I sit in this house and I listen, I listen for the sound of Vaslav's return; clop, clop, I hear his horse; clip, clip, I hear the hedges being readied for Vaslav's return; drip, drip, I hear Fierz sniffling in the hall—I wish he'd retire and go off to Uranil to live with his aunt—she needs him more than ever now that she's a hundred years old and the chickens refuse to lay—

ALL: Auntie needs him now that the chickens refuse to lay—fowl situation . . .

OLGA: Prick, prick, I hear the key turning in the lock, could it be Vasilli Vasillievvich at last? Click, clack, the footsteps move away— it was naught but the slithering loony from the mottled woods who wishes to come in.

ALL:

Lock the door and hide the key
The loony comes a-looking for thee.

(NINA *exits.*)

OLGA: Oh, why did Vaslav set out that fine morning so long ago never to return? Masha says it was my fault, that I drove him out the massive iron door, carved in the Bledermeier style my mother loved so well. But she is wrong, it can't be—I have lived for Vaslav, I have tickled his little piggies off to market and made him smile, I have wiped his little snout after a blow, I have sung to him tales of the burnished woods of Stolichnaya. Why does he not come home, home to the room in blue he clutched to his bosom so fondly in his youth, home to the grandfather clock that Aunt Minnie Vex-alayavich wound so faithfully to remind us all that tomorrow was another day—and now it is another day and Minnie Vexalayavich is gone—yet still the clock is wound. Why? Why? Yet now the clock is wound for Vaslav—come home, come home.

ALL: Or stay where you are, far away.

(*Gong.*)

FIERZ: What, now our young ward has a bird on her tail. A lifeless, inert, smelly corpse. A putrid, pungent appendage to her bustle, pursuant poultry. She cannot escape it, it follows her everywhere, avian rigor mortis has set in. What could it portend?

NINA (*entering with prop bird on a string*): The erne, the erne, the wilde erne is dead—I gathered it in my embrace when the neap tide was abed—my grief is as the essne's of yore, so fecund, so moribund, as was Queen Ana's of Spain—

MASHA: Petrovich Petrushka, get that carcass out of here.

IRINA: Lice it carries and filthy disease.

MAUDE: Oh, but it's beautiful, it would make such a great hat.

IRINA: Boo hoo, how do you suppose it died? Was it Aloysius the cat who lives under the stoop that did tear out the erne's throat?

MAUDE: It's the way of the wild . . . but save the tail feathers for me.

MASHA: Sisters, have you no shame? Let us question Nina and find out why she got the bird, and why she wears it so proudly.

NINA: Is it not death that gives meaning to life? This erne gives me meaning in its demise.

(*Gong.*)

FIERZ: Listen, oh, listen to the carriage pulling to a stop outside the front door. Could it be Olga's son, the prodigal student returned to fill his mother's heart with gladness?

ALL: Let us put out the caviar, the champagne, and the samovar. Vaslav is returned and life can begin again . . .

OLGA: Let us make him welcome, wait on him and entertain him, massage him, soak his feet, and fan his brow . . .

Masha: Vaslav is coming! Vaslav is coming!

Fierz: Pamper him like a pasha! It's the kind of service you get in a whorehouse.

Olga (*singing*):

> Keep the door open
> E'en though storms rage without
> Good luck may be passing
> And to the throng she'll shout
> Don't batten the hatches
> Don't nail tight the door
> Don't secure the latches
> Don't pull the rugs from the floor
>
> But keep the door open to your heart
> Keep the door open
> Yes, keep the door open
> Good fortune is coming
> So smile and start humming
> And keep the door open to your heart
>
> Throw open the curtains
> Shake out the welcome mat
> Just smile, and be certain
> You're wearing your favorite hat
> Don't batten the hatches
> Don't nail tight the door
> Don't secure the latches
> Don't pull the rugs from the floor
>
> But keep the door open to your heart
> Keep the door open
> Yes, keep the door open
> Good fortune is coming
> So smile and start humming
> And keep the door open to your heart.

(NINA, *who has been seated during song, gets up nervously and runs around looking for a place to hide, bumping into* OLGA, *who shoos her out. Gong.* VASLAV *enters, crosses downstage center.*)

VASLAV: When is dinner? (*No answer.*) Are you all deef? I have traveled far and the road was rough. My horses I pushed beyond their limit, and old Vanyatchi had to be *eliminated* between Sgorsk and Petrograd.

FIERZ: No, oh no, my favorite nag that depended on me for life. I raised him from a foal, and presented the creature to you at your bar mitzvah to be your very own.

VASLAV: I know. Fierz, I know you well, and you have not changed—so I have brought *you* a present—(*Throws horse hide on the floor.*) Now Fierz and his Vanyatchi can sleep together and keep each other warm.

(FIERZ *throws himself on the skin and carries on;* VASLAV *eats a banana.*)

FIERZ: No, no, Vanyatchi, my little papooshka. No! . . . (*etc., ad lib*)

MASHA: He has not changed, we see, this errant knave. The Vaslav we knew as children has returned, the very same. Oh, why, oh, why couldn't he have gone to the gold rush in America and been trampled by the greedy hordes . . .

IRINA: Masha, dear Masha, he will put spiders in our beds and snakes in the apple-bin—we will have no peace now, I'm afraid . . .

MAUDE: Vaslav's back, Vaslav's back! Never a dull moment will greet us now, I dare say . . . Life is on the upswing here in the orchards of Belattaslava!

MASHA: Vaslav does not worry me, Nina will keep him occupied. It is Olga who will be made to suffer, the prodigal needs his mother's attention now that he has seen the world and tasted bitter fruit.

VASLAV (*carefully placing banana peel center stage*)**:** But where is Nina, my intended? Has she waited faithfully for me? I should think so—ha ha. (*Holds up large key.*) I have the key—the key . . . here, clutched in my left hand, that will open the gateway to her garden of delights. Gee, I hope that chastity belt hasn't given her an unappealing rash!

MASHA: Ward Nina, do not hide. Vaslav is here, he calls to you—

IRINA: Come from the shadows where you hide.

MAUDE: Leap into his waiting arms, fulfill your divine destiny. (*Calls in all three voices.*) Nina, Nina . . . Yo, Nina! (*Begins chanting "Nina" over and over again, as if in an Actors Studio "private moment."*)

OLGA (*coming down from platform, dropping character, and trying to stop her*): Susan, what are you doing? This is *not* what you said you were going to do in rehearsal. Now stop! Listen, just because you work with the Mabou Mines does not mean everything is avant-garde!

MASHA (*glaring at her, hands on hips*): This happens to be Robert Wilson and Anne Bogart. (*Goes into disco dance movement.*)

OLGA: What's that?

MASHA: Television dancing.

OLGA: Television dancing! Not on my stage, you don't. Susan, Susan, Susan! (*Going to her and making her stop.*) For God's sake, H. M. Koutoukas is here. An expert in the art of acting!

MASHA: Well, he would understand this.

OLGA: He would not. You agreed! I told you! You said you could do heavy Method acting . . . like I'm doing. You examine your navel, you get very heavy, very serious, very serious.

MASHA: I beg your pardon, that is exactly what I'm doing.

OLGA: Oh, it is not! That is not Actors Studio acting. I know Actors Studio acting and that isn't it. (*Imitating Brando.*) "Stella, Stella!" I have never seen Marlon Brando jump about and go "Nina, Nina, Nina."

MASHA: And you have never seen Marlon Brando do Masha from *The Three Sisters.*

OLGA: No, but I've worked with Lois Smith, one of the founders of the Actors Studio. She worked with James Dean, she's up on Broadway now in *Grapes of Wrath,* I worked with her. She *never* acted crazy like— (*Thinks about it.*) Actually, she did.

MASHA: Listen, I am playing my intention. I want Nina to come out here. She has been pining, yearning, she's slitting her wrists, she's carrying on, like this demented, depressed woman, because she's yearning for Vaslav. Now he's finally here, and where is she? Hiding! Well, she'll be content to hide there for the next twenty-five years—you know how Russian plays go! But I and my two sisters, Irina and Maude, would like to see her come out here, get into her beloved—he has a smashing figure, I have to admit that. And then life can return to normal.

OLGA: Normal, normal, now you're talkin'!

MASHA: Yes. She even went to our dressmaker, and what does she have done? She doesn't have a morning dress, or an afternoon dress, or a dinner dress, or an evening dress. She has a wedding dress! Doesn't that tell you something?

OLGA: Well . . .

MASHA: Listen, this is based on Chapter Twenty-two of *An Actor Prepares.*

OLGA (*encouraging*)**:** I read a book once by Robert Q. Lewis.

MASHA (*sternly*)**:** Robert Lewis wrote *Method or Madness.*

OLGA: *Method or Madness!* I read it in high school, that's the one! I read the very book.

MASHA: Well, this is Stanislavsky, *An Actor Prepares.*

OLGA (*impressed*)**:** Oh.

MASHA: In Chapter Twenty-two, he discusses the subconscious. "After an actor has done his basic preparation, asking himself the very vital questions "Who am I? What do I want? What do I get? How do I get it?—"

OLGA (*repeating quickly for memory*): "Who am I? What do I want? What do I get? How do I get it?" Okay.

MASHA: "then it is time to tap into the subconscious, so that you lose your self-consciousness, you lose your alter ego, you are able to concentrate purely on the role and live it, as in real life, for the brief few moments you are on stage." Heaven. Yes. Now that is what I am trying to do. I am trying to get Nina to come out. She does not respond to just calling her name, she's so frightened. So I figured that if I just actually went all around the room, and just created some kind of turmoil out here, she would be curious, she wouldn't be able to stand back. Suddenly her curiosity would overcome her fright and she would run out—and see Vaslav!

OLGA: Doesn't Stanislavsky talk about how pretty you are on stage, and how you should worry about your looks, and wear lovely costumes?

MASHA: Actually, yes, he talks about that . . . saying that you shouldn't ask yourself stupid questions, like "How do I look?" (OLGA *gasps.*) You should be in your part. "How do I look? How am I doing? Is my timing right?" You know, you have to live your part.

OLGA (*to audience*): I'm impressed. She knows what she's doing. (*To* MASHA:) Miss Black-Eyed Susan, can you ever forgive me?

MASHA: Shall we get on with it, huh?

OLGA (*chastened, scurrying back to her place and into her character*): Oh, yes!

MASHA (*"preparing" like a Method actress, then calling as before*): Ward Nina, do not pine! Vaslav is here! He calls for you.

IRINA: Come from the shadows where you hide.

MAUDE: Leap into his waiting arms. Fulfill your divine destiny, Nina. Nina? Nii-naa.

IRINA: Nina, get out here! Greet your beloved!

(*Dramatic music.* NINA *runs to Vaslav's arms, but hits the banana peel center stage and lands in the wings.*)

VASLAV: Ah, how good it is to be back. (*Follows* NINA *off. Gong.*)

OLGA (*turning to audience*): What is this son of mine? A thing caught between heaven and hell. A reminder of my age and my failings. A tiny babe wrapped in wee swaddling clothes . . . me bonny bairn . . . the perfect part of my best nature . . . my son! (*Comes downstage.*) I was told when he was born to throw him back into the Ural from whence he came. I consulted mystic after mystic 'cause he never cried, and when he spoke he never called me Mama. What could I do? Finally Fierz brought me the family Ouija board, and I found the answer, and Vaslav left our home. Oh, would that I had never listened to Fierz . . . Oh, would that Masha, Irina, and Maude had never urged me on . . . Oh, would that Nina and Vaslav were happily married with nine children they couldn't afford. . . . Fierz, bring the family Ouija board; it is time we question the spirits that surround us and find out what we must do to keep Vaslav here in the bosom of our home.

(*Gong.* FIERZ *brings Ouija board on a small table.*)

It comes. It approaches. We demand our query.

(FIERZ *sets table down on Olga's foot.*)

OLGA: Ow, oh, ow! Please, these shoes hurt. Back to the scullery, get off, get off. Ow, oh, ooh la la.

(FIERZ *exits. Testing foot:*)

I'll live, I'll live. Dear sisters, draw near, do not be afraid. We will question the spirits. Kind spirits, lovely spirits that surround us. We must ask the kind spirits what we must do to keep Vaslav by our side—

IRINA: No, no, nyet, nyet, not the Ouija!—Remember Uncle Veselka who burned his board after being told an evil tale by the spirits he petitioned.

MAUDE: Yes, yes, da, da, ask many questions—I promise not to cheat and guide the pointer. Who will I marry? Which is the prettiest sister? Should I go to the plumbers' ball on Saturday night with Vesshitz?

MASHA: Be wary of the inanimate object guiding your life and giving you advice . . . Do not trust to a toy to be rational— Better we should invite the old bishop to dinner and plague *him* with our questions.

OLGA: Hesh up, Masha . . . Dim the lights. Now, prepare yourselves for some serious doings. Irina, Maude, concentrate! (*Over Ouija board.*) Oooooohhhh, faint spirits from beyond the grave, oh, ghosts of Christmas past, oh, elfins of the burnished woods, hear our plea—

ALL: How shall we keep Vaslav here?

(*They begin moving the planchette across the Ouija board, with* OLGA *in charge, and they spell out* SACRIFICE. OLGA *screams.* MASHA *begins to shake.*)

OLGA: No, don't! Too late—she is possessed!

(MASHA *begins to flip out and run about the room, then goes back to the board, pointing to letters and running away from the board after each one; this time the board spells out* WARD.)

OLGA: Ward! Sacrifice the ward?

MASHA (*still possessed*): Bring the sacrificial fowl!

OLGA: No, no, not the sacrificial fowl.

(*Voodoo drums.* MASHA, *with prop chicken, does a voodoo-possession dance, then falls to the floor.*)

(*If audience applauds:*) Don't encourage her! She just played Maya Deren for Stuart Sherman and she just can't get over it!

(*Back in character:*) The spell is cast. It says we must sacrifice Nina, but how, but how?

MASHA: It says we must sacrifice Nina, but why, but why? . . .

ALL: We'll let the future take care of itself!

(*Gong.*)

FIERZ (*entering*): Lord, Lord, Lord!!! I went to the back to feed the rabbits their daily gruel and shovel out their smelly droppings from beneath their cages, when—lo and behold, what did I see?—a stranger sight than ere I had ever seen before, from the day that I was born.—The rabbits!

OLGA: The rabbits?

FIERZ: The rabbits!

OLGA: What about the rabbits?

FIERZ: They were lying all, all about the hutch, they were maimed and a-bleeding.

OLGA AND MASHA: Ooooh!

FIERZ: All of their little feets had been mysteriously removed, cut off, I tell you. Ooooyyy! Someone or some-THING had stolen all their little feets! SORDID! SORDID!!!!!!

(*Gong. All exit in consternation.* VASLAV *meets* NINA *in the woods.*)

VASLAV: Is that you, Nina, my little scared rabbit? Have you come to me here in the dank, darkened woods where we are so alone, so all alone?

NINA: Welcome home, Vaslav Pluchinskaya, we have missed you and longed for your return. All is not well here in the estate of your ancestors. You must take up the familial banner of your Crimean kiosk and save our home.

VASLAV: A pretty welcome home speech, Nina, my pet. Come closer. Do not be afraid of your Vaslav. I'm here now and your destiny will surely be fulfilled. Keep still, my pretty.

NINA: Vaslav, please stop.

VASLAV: Stop what, Ninainska?

NINA: Stop pinching me. Every time you move near me you grind my tender flesh between your mighty fingers. My bottom begins to resemble a quilt made from old army fatigues—green and blue and yellow . . . Ouch, stop it.

VASLAV: It is only your poor imagination pinches you. I am not hurting you. Vaslav is your obedient servant, and will only do what you bid your lover to do. . . . (*Twists her nose.*)

NINA: OUCH!!

VASLAV: What is this on your wrists—an imperfection! Take it from my sight or it must be removed. (*Takes a large knife from his pocket.*)

NINA: No, no, it's just a scratch that will heal . . . Put that thing, that huge tool, back in your pocket.

VASLAV (*weeping*): Forgive me, my Ninotchka. Here, have a token from your master to show how sorry I am to have scared you . . . unnecessarily. (*Pulls string of bloody rabbits' feet from his pocket and drapes them around Nina's neck like a necklace. They embrace violently.*)

NINA: I love you, do you hear me, I love you, I love you, I love you! Take me, here in the Tolkienovich woods! Oh, oh!

VASLAV (*putting head under Nina's skirt*): Ohh, moan moan, slurp slurp, lickety lick, clang clang. (*Brings head back out from under.*) Clang clang? This damn chastity belt is all rusted! I told you to cut down your salt intake during my absence! Really! (*Burrows under Nina's dress, bringing out rope, chains, etc.*) It's a long way home! (*Brings out a large metal tongs.*) Finally, success!

NINA: NOW! Do it now! I'm yours!

VASLAV: You'll regret it, little furry nose-twitcher!

NINA: What did you speak, my love? I understand you not . . .

VASLAV: Enough talk. Prepare yourself for a ramming!

NINA: No, no.

VASLAV: Yes yes!

NINA: No no!

VASLAV: Yes yes!

NINA: No no!

VASLAV: Yes yes!

NINA: All right!

VASLAV: Too late. Ha, ha! Come with me to the hidden glen where we played doctor and nursie as children.

NINA: I'll follow you to the tundras of sodden Siberia . . . You understand me, Vaslav. You know my needs and respond . . .

VASLAV: I've learned, ward Nina . . . I've been around. I've acquired skills . . . I'm listed in the *Guinness Book of Records* as a world-class lover now.

NINA: Off to the woods!

VASLAV: Yes . . . Wait—now CRAWL . . . (NINA *crawls offstage.*) Oh, baby. And now I have a request to make to Mother!

(*They exit. Gong.* OLGA *sweeps in.*)

OLGA: The secrets of the wooded glen will never be known. What has happened there now is to be shunned and never questioned . . . Let it be, Olga—what goes around comes around and will resolve itself! The young will meet in the woods—it has always been, it will always be, till the forests are gone from the world and every monkey lives in a zoo . . . You are old, Olga, the woody ardens hold no intrigue for you now . . .

The passing of your youth is over—so comfort yourself with the whir of hummingbirds in their solarium in the West Wing—Fierz takes pride in his breeding of the blue-green hummers—and they are my delight. (*Looks around.*) But something is amiss here.—Now that Vaslav is returned, I wonder what it was that I had missed so.—Sometimes the longing pleases more than the final fruition— Vaslav is here . . . He has come home . . . and he will stay this time. . . . But he disturbs the house. . . .

VASLAV (*entering*): As a child I was shunted from nursemaid to nursemaid! Fierz was my only playmate, and I was told "Children should be seen and not heard!" You acted on the stage and danced and sang. I was denied the pleasure of witnessing your triumphs. You traveled the world while I stayed at home, not knowing who my father was . . .

OLGA: He was a second-rate Italian poet with pretensions!

VASLAV: Not knowing where you were!

OLGA: I was on the road!

VASLAV: Not knowing, not knowing . . .

OLGA: Well, now you know!

VASLAV: But I will witness your gaudy triumphs now—all that was denied me as a child will be given to me now! Even the film you made for Eisenstadt will be shown to me now—

OLGA: No, no!

VASLAV: —for I am the master now and will be given my own way—

OLGA: You want to see me dance? You want to hear me sing? You want to see the film Eisenstadt made? But that was years ago, I was young and beautiful. (*Squaring her shoulders.*) Well, I just happen to have the projector set up! Come on, play some music. Let's go with it!

(*Film: A flickering, Eisensteinish silent with 1920s dance music as accompaniment, extensive closeups, and heavy posturing, featuring* OLGA *as a glamorous beauty in white.*)

VASLAV (*after film*): And now you must dance! Let the graceful swan die once again!

OLGA (*putting on toe shoes as she speaks*): I won't dance for you! I'll show you what I looked like when I danced, but I won't dance. I never dance without a full orchestra. I was a star, you understand. Besides, my great teacher, Ekatherina Sobechanskaya, would never forgive me. She doesn't dance any more; she got too fat. All right, she let out her tutus and she works in clubs, what can I say? God bless her, she taught me all I know. She taught me when to run. No, no, I won't dance without a full orchestra, I need a full orch—Oh, by George! Right there in the wings, a three-piece ensemble! Masha! Irina! Maude!

(THREE SISTERS *enter.*)

Do something, Vaslav, clean up the floor. If I'm going to dance for you, I want a clean floor. These shoes hurt enough, I don't want to dance on Nina's rosary. Now get it out of here.

(VASLAV *clears the floor;* MASHA *goes to the piano.*)

Play, play, be inspired!—Get that rosary outa here.—I feel inspiration pouring. Play, gypsy, play! I feel a dance! I feel like the dying swan! Now I am inspired! I will dance. The Dying Swan!

(MASHA *pounds violent chords on piano. Dance.* FIERZ *appears as beautiful as Helen Shumaker. As dance is building to a climax,* NINA *appears with her hands cut off.* OLGA *sees her.*)

What is it? What's happened? Aaahhh!

(OLGA, FIERZ, *and* NINA *run off.* MASHA *finishes playing, gets up from piano, screams, and runs off.*)

VASLAV (*sitting in front row*): Come back! Let me see you in your GREAT role, for which you won the OBIElatsky for Sincerity! I demand to see the great Empress Ekatherina as she really was!

OLGA (*trudging back on, half out of costume*): Oh, please, leave me alone! Well, all right. Wait till I get my good shoes back on. Now I want to warn you, no holds barred now, Vaslav—I *will* show you Ekatherina. It got the Bull Shahoy's funding taken away by the Committee for the Tsar, and I had to leave town till the locals forgot . . . This piece is X-rated. I used to do it down at 8 B.C. That club's gone now—I didn't close it. Phoebe Legere and I used to work there together, until she pissed on the audience one night. I didn't mind, she can pee on the audience anytime she wants—it was 3:30 in the morning, they were all Eurotrash. But she did it on *my* line. I never forgive things like that. Ah, yes, those were the days. We used to have to work hard. I did this piece for a living. I did it at the Chandelier, I even did it at the Pyramid. It's filth. But I thought I'd do it for you again. (*To sound man:*) David Ferryinsky, play the tape!

(*Balalaika music.* OLGA *mimes to an audio tape of Ethyl Eichelberger's* Catherine the Great.)

ETHYL AS CATHERINE (*on tape*): Those revolting peasants make me wanna puke!—I burn, I burn. For some noogie I yearn. Where's my stud, where's my stallion?—Where's some pig meat for my roll?—Where's a hot poker for my furnace and a match to light my coal?—Where's old Dobbin when I need him to soothe my undulating hole?—I itch—ooh, ah, ooh—I itch—This bitch needs some action—Gad, these nights are long in olden Russia—It garates on my nerves to be Catherine the Second, Ekaterina Alekseevna, when I'm locked here in my castle and my ass longs to get pummeled by a hot rod from the fields of yon Ukrania—Bring on that mule—Where is Francis to talk to me? I want to hear some smut—I can take it no longer—I'm in a rut—I'm bored, I'm high, I want to get laid—Bring on my horse!

(NINA *and* MASHA *enter leading* FIERZ, *with three large pink pillows pinned to the front of his costume, as the horse.*)

Oh, dance for me, prance for me—Shake that big thing all around—Pour me a drink—Make it a stiff one—Let me swallow it down—I've got some nice sugar, Dobbin, wanna smell it, wanta see, wanna lick of my sweet sugar?—Get down on your bended knee—Suck my pussy, Pegasus, my ponderous, palpitating, pert, protruding pussy—Eat my smoldering smooze—Taste my tantalizing cooze—*chicha me, Papi; mas fuerte*—Lick my oozing honeypot—I've hid some sugar up my snatch, Dobbin, come and get it, big boy—come and get it! Find Mama's sugar!—Come on, get it, Trigger—get a-crackin'!—Try a-nibblin' on my cupcakes; they'll raise a hardy appetite—Fuck, shit, piss, cunt; sock it to me, you smelly runt—Wait—Not yet—Kiss me first—Ram that throbbing wedge-shaped hammer down my waiting love canal—Come on, Dobbin, come on, boy—don't be afeard of my glistening red beard—Look at the size of that thing!—Goddam, that sucker's big —Egad, he's gonna do it, here it comes—This is a dream come true —Oh, oh,—I don't believe it's actually happening, I'm finally doing it—I've watched Dobbin in the fields so many times and wet my thighs—I'm gonna take it all—I want to feel it—I can live on the memory tomorrow—I'm a pig, I'm a sow, what would my Austrian mother think?—Yeck, look at that thing—It's putrid pink and wet and shiny, fat and long and full of veins—Arg!!—It's gonna hurt —Oooeee!—Stick a popper under my nose, I'll be split from stem to stern—My salts, my salts—No, no, no artificial stimuli—Here we go—Ouch, eeytch, ouch *(etc., ad lib)*——Is it in?—

(Tries to put plastic bag, as condom, over pillow, then puts it over her head; NINA *and* MASHA *throw glitter over lovers to symbolize orgasm.)*

I wonder, can a stallion stud have herpes? Oh, paranoia, fear, and shame! Harder, deeper, faster—Talk dirty to me, Dobbin! Ouch, don't!!! Stop!! *(etc., ad lib)* Fuck my quivering slit—Rub against my shivering clit—Rock that old man in the boat—Ooohh, Mr. Ed, Mr. Ed, I think I love you!!!—Pull out, pull out! I don't want to get pregnant!!! AAAH—I'm coming—I see fireworks! I smell smoke!—Get off me, get off!—Ooh, what a gooey mess! Go with it, Kate, go with it!!! *(Looking at horse in disgust.)* Now get out!

VASLAV: Filth, filth! You're offending the good people.

OLGA: Whaddaya mean, filth? That was my great role! That role made me the actress I am today!

VASLAV: Made? Actors aren't made. Actors and idiots are born.

OLGA: Uh-huh. Actors and idiots have children like you, too.

VASLAV: How could you do this piece when you know what the National Endowment for the Arts thinks—

OLGA: Oh, honey, that's exactly why I did it! I can't smear myself with chocolate, I'm not beautiful like Karen Finley. I saw her make a tit sandwich once, but these ain't real, and I don't want to tell you anything.—I bought 'em. They come in different sizes.—And I wasn't lucky enough to be born a lesbian, like Holly Hughes. I have to do what I do, and you know what I'm talkin' about. I mean, that was a heterosexual act—that horse had genitalia, it was male, and I am *obviously* a woman—so it's gotta be all right! Listen, you want to see gay art, you go over to the Public Theater. There you will see living, in the flesh heterosexual men playing faggots, and they'll make ya cry and feel sorry for them. You come over here and you'll see a real live, living, nonheterosexual faggot play a woman, and all I can do is make ya laugh. I'd rather make ya laugh. That's the difference. This is my kind of theater. You don't see homoerotic art in my dramas ever, do you? That's why I did it! Now ask me another stupid question.

VASLAV: Who wants to see that garbage?

OLGA: Whaddaya mean, who wants to see it? Your mother's still here. Hello, Mrs. Fashion. (*Waves to actor's mother in audience.*) She coulda left.

VASLAV: Come on, show me something nice.

OLGA: Nice? Nice art? My son the rightwing lunatic! Where have I gone wrong? (*Begins to stalk offstage, muttering.*) Nice art, you want nice art, all right, here we go. Nice? You want nice? I'll give you nice. (*Shouts into wings.*) LA-DIES!

(*Picks up accordion as* NINA, MASHA, *and* FIERZ *come on wearing large cardboard-cutout flower costumes.* NINA *gives* OLGA *one.*)

Why, that's *nice*! Thank you. (*Puts it on as others line up.*) They're all graduates of the school of gardening.

OLGA, NINA, MASHA, FIERZ (*singing*):

We're four little flowers
Growing in the wood

We wave in the breezes
And we are so very good

To all and sundry
We nod our little heads
We flirt with bees and butterflies
Who kiss us in our beds

NINA:

I'm a little sunflower
Basking in the rays
Of Sol's great life-dipper
I face him all the days
I give him my attention
He smiles straight back to me
He tells me that I'm lovely
Till I giggle and tee-hee

(*They dance.*)

MASHA:

I'm a wax begonia
I spread out and I'm wild
When others see me coming
They cry, "Mothers, hide your child!
"The waxy creeper's coming.
"She'll take all your flowerbed.
"She'll choke your little plantlings.
"And fill the woods with dread!"

(*They dance.*)

FIERZ:

I'm a little yucca
I love to kick my heels

Up o'er my ears and elbows
And make the other flowers squeal
I come from warmer climates
But I can thrive in Russia too
I'm hot-blooded and cold-hearted
And if you like, I'll grow on you.

(*They dance.*)

OLGA:

I'm some poison ivy
At home in every clime
I'll give you such an itch
If near my leaves and stems you climb
Oh, I'm a woody tuber
And I'll tube you if you should
Come strolling near my members
You'll remember me but good!

OLGA, NINA, MASHA, FIERZ:

So when you go a-walking
Within the nether woods
You just might hear us singing
And you'll smell our fragrance good

OLGA (*to stage manager*): Pedro, fragrance, fragrance! (*Air freshener is sprayed on audience.*) That's Roman de l'amour. It brings you love.

(*They repeat last stanza while audience is sprayed.*)

OLGA, NINA, MASHA, FIERZ:

But if you stop and pick us
And take us home to tea
We'll droop and wilt
Our heads will tilt
You'll get nothing for free
Oh, four little flowers are we!

OLGA (*to* VASLAV, *as others, after song, clear props and move to their ritual places onstage*): There! You wanted nice, you got nice!

VASLAV: Oh, I can't take it! I'm beginning to regret my birth.

OLGA: Oh, give him some insulin!

VASLAV: My heritage!

OLGA: Give him some more insulin!

VASLAV: How embarrassing being your son.

OLGA: And vice versa.

VASLAV: You are trash, Olga. Your parents were pig farmers in Putsch! Then you married below your station—

OLGA: I never married him!

VASLAV: No easy task finding that trashy poet with political pretensions—

OLGA: That's your daddy you're talkin' about!

VASLAV: And it's been all downhill from there, girlfriend . . . Besides, you couldn't act your way out of a paper babushka, you old bag!

OLGA: I resemble that remark!

VASLAV: You are fatuous and avuncular.

OLGA: I got words for you, petunia.

VASLAV (*getting up*): Petunia! I'm leaving once again, this time for good!

OLGA: Wait a minute! Shut up and sit down! Get that chair out from in front of those lovely people and go sit up where you belong, up where Mama put that chair!

(VASLAV *takes Olga's chair, which he has been using, from front row of audience, brings it back to upstage platform where it was originally placed, and sits.*)

What kind of son is that? You asked to see my great roles. This is all your fault. I have another one, you know. This isn't the end.— Fierz, Masha, quick, restrain my wayward son! Hold him down!

(MASHA *goes to* VASLAV, *sits on his lap.*)

Restrain him, that's it!

(MASHA *lifts her skirt and begins to wriggle.*)

No, no, no, restrain him, don't entertain him.—Look the other way, Nina!—Hold him down!

(FIERZ *brings rope, which he and* MASHA *drape around* Vaslav's *neck.*)

OLGA: Got him tied? That's it, make him lovely. Now, Vaslav, my beloved son, you demanded that I relive the past . . . I didn't want to do it. You made me do it . . . But I know I can *still* do it—I'm not too old, I tell you . . . Why, if called upon, I could still play a twelve-year-old. (VASLAV *laughs mockingly.*) And I will! Now I'm gonna act for you once again! You'll be sorry. You'll fall right outa your chair, you'll be so impressed. (*Mounts platform at side, throwing shawl over her head. Plays Juliet.*)

"Oh, Romeo, Romeo, wherefore art thou Romeo?
"Deny thy father and refuse thy name
"Or if thou wilt not, be but sworn my love
"And I'll no longer be a Capulet."

MASHA (*as all applaud*): Wonderful! Younger than springtime!

OLGA: "Oh, a rose by any other name would smell . . ."

(*Begins to lose focus.*)

"The mask of night is on my face . . ."
The warmth of night is on my ass—No, no!
"Romeo, Romeo, wherefore—art—"

VASLAV: Get the hook!

OLGA (*delirious*): What play is this? Where am I?

FIERZ (*beginning to leave*): I'm not going to stand here and watch you destroy the remains of your career!

OLGA: What remains? Ask the *New York Times* what my career's worth! After *Threepenny Opera* I might as well give it up.

(FIERZ *exits.*)

Oh, well. Some critics liked me. Michael Feingold was nice to me. But then Ross Whetstone, or whatever his name is, in the *Voice* called me "an eye-averting embarrassment." (*Striking flamboyant pose.*) I'm just trying to live up to my press! "Oh, that this too, too solid—" No, that's the wrong play. Cordelia! Ophelia! (*Begins to stagger around the stage.*)

MASHA: She's dissembling.

OLGA: Dissemble, dissemble, dissemble. Where am I? It's the actor's nightmare! What is going on around me. Oh, Vaslav, I know your mother will die young. She was born under the sign of the burning Hesperides, and her Mercury has been in retrograde too long. Besides, she has the diva's craving for red meat—not conducive to long life. Oh, I die, I die—(*Turns upstage and sees* VASLAV.) Aaahh! Who are you? Who are you? Aaahh, turn the other way, you're scaring me. (*Turns around.*) What play is this? Who am I? I die, I die.—I forgive everyone. But I doubt that everyone's going to forgive me. (OLGA *dies, violently and acrobatically. Gong.*)

MASHA: I told her not to read her own reviews. She is gone for good this time, she who has carried heavy Russian burdens to the grave! May she sit beside the banks of the Lena River and be happy!

IRINA: Evil, it is evil what Olga perpetrated in the many theatrical seasons before she died!

MAUDE: Oh, pish-tosh, Irina! Olga was a camp! The old girl knew how to live!

MASHA: The truth! It is time to speak the truth!—Yes, Vaslav is Olga's cherished son . . . but *too* cherished! And what is more

. . . oh, shame upon shame! . . . ward Nina is Olga's child too, gotten 'tween the sheets by Olga with— (*turns and points at* VASLAV *accusingly*) Vaslav, her own son! Nina is cursed! She bears the vile stigmata of incest and shame—inbred half-witted child who mutilates herself to atone for others' crimes! Oh, woe. . . .

IRINA: Oh, sad sister dearest!

MAUDE: I wouldn't have believed it if I read it in *Pravda!*

MASHA: You won't read it in the newspaper. You won't hear it on the street. You must go to the library, for it is a gothic tale!

(*Gong.*)

FIERZ (*reentering in horror*): The birds, my babies, the sweetest little nectar-licking hummers this side of the Volga! Someone or some THING has cut out all their little tongues!—Why, why? Sweet innocents have suffered once again in this damned house of shame—But what is this? Olga, Olga! Olga has died! *Esta muerta-inska!* Nooooo! I can bear it no longer! Good-bye, cruel Mother Russia! (*Shoots himself.*)

MASHA: The plot sickens. What next, what next?

NINA (*rising from stage floor, shows that her tongue has been cut out*): Ooaslaw, ooaslaaw!

(*All stay motionless as music begins for final song, excepting "dead"* OLGA, *who plays accordion from her prone position.*)

VASLAV (*gradually rising from chair, sings to "dead"* OLGA):

> Dasvedanya, Mama
> My lover and my friend
> I'll cherish your sweet memory
> Until I reach the end
> Of this strange life I'm leading
> I know I've been a beast
> But when I'm gone it's famine
> And when I'm here it's feast.

You nursed me as a baby
You cursed me as a child
Now I'm all grown up
No more a pup
So of course I turned out wild

Dasvedanya, Mama
Good-bye, good-bye, good-bye
If I think of you by accident
Well, maybe then I'll cry

You were such a good mama, Mama
You answered my every request
You taught me all I know, it's so
You taught me incest is best

Dasvedanya, Mama
My lover and my friend
I'll cherish your sweet memory
Until I reach the end
Of this strange life I'm leading
I know I've been a beast
But when I'm gone it's famine
And when I'm here it's feast.

(*End.*)

david greenspan

DEAD MOTHER, OR SHIRLEY NOT ALL IN VAIN

Maxine (Mary Shultz) is delighted to meet her fiancé Daniel's ''Mother'' (David Greenspan), an introduction that creates much anxiety for Daniel (Ben Bodé) and his father, Melvin (Steve Mellor).

We don't think of family drama as being epic; it's too small. And when we see it as farcical, we regard it as a separate genre, something not as serious as drama, related to that degrading word "sitcom." But by rights, in this post-Freudian era, the gigantic presence of the unconscious should make every family drama an epic, and the perception of absurdity in our daily life should make every family epic a farce. By a stroke of genius that, like many such strokes, is merely a logical extension of common sense, *Dead Mother* acts on these assumptions; it's a work of modern art. It takes life and the underpinnings of life as it finds them, without bothering itself about what kind of work it will turn into. Yet its sense of form, like its sense of comedy when it chooses to be comic, is unerring: Its life, like any daily life, is infused with the memory of other works of art, structures and parameters shoved in to shore up an emotional turmoil—brought on by a family's forced "togetherness"—that would otherwise make no sense. It doesn't anyway, for its unfortunate hero, who at the end has vanished into an inexplicable twilight, like the hero of a Greek myth turned into a constellation by the gods.

The matrix of Greenspan's American family farce is that non-American, not very familial play *Charley's Aunt;* his epic vision is shaped by Dante's *Inferno*—Catholic and versified where the play's family is Jewish and prosy—and by the Charles Laughton stagings of Shaw's *Don Juan in Hell*—sparkling, yearning Edwardian socialism in the face of this post-Holocaust family's affluent California crassness. Though the script seems to sprawl like urban Los Angeles itself, these antinomies support it from underneath with the rigid strength of steel girders; nothing's unplanned, superfluous, or wasted in Greenspan's profusion. The breadth of an epic simply calls for an epic flow, connecting every part of life to every other: A trip to the dentist is the cue for a rhapsody on the entire evolution of biological life (and man's minuscule place in it); likewise—in an ideal world, or in *Dead Mother*—a trip to the theater can be a voyage through the whole range of human possibility. It's no accident that when Greenspan's characters go to "the Iliad Theatre," they talk about having seen an adaptation of *The Odyssey* there. But the play they see now is also the one we're seeing, a different odyssey, and one of them will subsequently write the letter of complaint that serves as its prologue, objecting to the theater's emphasis on plays with homosexual protagonists.

Should homosexuality have a prominent place in the theater? For that matter, should it have one in life, which survives and evolves by reproduction? The complicated and topsy-turvy perspective given by the unconscious is Greenspan's answer: Homosexuality must have some relevance to human survival because it exists; certainly a lot of the awfulness human beings have created for themselves to live in comes from pretending it doesn't. Equally certain is that it has something to do with liberating the imaginative capacity, just as Harold's ability—and desire—to impersonate his dead mother liberates his brother to marry, his father to purge the unresolved guilt that leads him to mistake Harold for Shirley's ghost. The moral metaphysics of the farce feed directly into the vision of Hell, where Virgil's stand-in is Alice B. Toklas, spokeswoman for forthright same-sex love, and those most terribly punished are the false heirs of Freud, psychiatrists who in life confused natural tendencies with illnesses and inflicted suffering on thousands with the ostensible aim of "curing" them. An ominous new disease, we're told, will continue the evil work they started . . .

And so the web of dream and farce, fantasy and prophecy winds us back to where we started, sitting in the theater, for Greenspan's writing, like his production, has no illusions: The audience was seated facing the EXIT sign, which glowed over center stage all evening long. The author played Harold-as-Shirley in men's clothes, with only the addition of a pearl necklace and a grand manner to mark the change from Harold-as-himself. This anti-illusionism, of course, nurtures imagination rather than stifling it, if one isn't literal-minded; it goes without saying that New York's daily reviewers mostly are. (*Newsday*'s Linda Winer, here as in many other cases, has been a gratifying exception.) In other cities, where critics and audiences have a greater breadth of mind, *Dead Mother* is likely to prove more rewarding, its mixture of sheer playfulness with grandeur of scale something to marvel at, not to disdain. The underlying connections that shape and justify the grandeur are all there, waiting to be found.

PRODUCTION NOTES

Dead Mother, or Shirley Not All in Vain was first presented by Joseph Papp at the New York Shakespeare Festival/Public Theater, January 1991. The set was designed by William Kennon. The lighting was designed by David Bergstein. The costumes were designed by Elsa Ward. The author directed. The cast was as follows:

CHARACTER 1: David Greenspan
CHARACTER 2: Ben Bodé
CHARACTER 3: Terra Vandergaw
CHARACTER 4: Mary Shultz
CHARACTER 5: Ron Bagden
CHARACTER 6: Steve Mellor

CHARACTERS

Acts 1 and 5

Character 1—Harold ⎫
Character 2—Daniel ⎬ sons of Melvin
           ⎭

Character 3—Sylvia, Harold's wife

Character 4—Maxine, engaged to Daniel

Character 5—Uncle Saul, granduncle of Maxine

Character 6—Melvin

Act 2

Character 1—Eris

Character 2—Peleus, Paris

Character 3—Thetis

Character 4—Aphrodite, Athena, Hera

Character 5—Prometheus

Character 6—Zeus

Act 3

Character 1—Harold

Character 5—Uncle Saul, Lynn

Act 4

Character 1—Harold

Character 2—Daniel, Narrator

Character 3—The Whale

Character 4—Maxine

Character 5—Uncle Saul, Alice B. Toklas

Character 6—A Ferryman

AUTHOR'S NOTE

Aside from the few props called for, the only "set" is a couch. It should remain—center—immobile—until the moment in Sylvia's epilogue when Character 3 pushes it away.

Character 1 never dresses as a woman! Aside from any costuming of the Greek section, he should remain in his own clothing throughout the entire escapade. A single strand of pearls may be added when he disguises himself as his mother, but no more. The mythological characters in Act 2 can be costumed fancifully. In the production at the Public, we used cartoony bodysuits with attached anatomical parts—genitals, etc.

Light illuminates a couch, center. Seated on the couch, left, is CHARACTER 3. *Seated on the couch, right, is* CHARACTER 1. *Seated on the back of the couch, center, is* CHARACTER 2. *Standing off to the side, right, is* CHARACTER 4.

INTRODUCTION

4: I would just like to say that I've come to this theater now for many years—since the early seventies. I'm a subscriber—and I really . . . I'm a big supporter of the work that goes on here—I really love it—I love this theater. But lately I've . . . I'm beginning to feel a little . . . alienated because . . . well, the last three—I think—plays we've seen here the leading characters have been . . . gay people and I'm just beginning to feel a little on the outside, I don't know. Now I don't feel—my—you know my son is gay, and I don't have a problem with that. I think it's great—it's important that that kind of thing is seen on stage, etcetera. It's just—and I say this with the greatest appreciation for what you do here—it's just that I'm feeling a little left out. I guess I would like to see a play—more plays—with heterosexual characters. And . . . well, that's all. I think that's all I wanted to say. (*Pause.*) I hope I haven't offended anybody.

(*Light changes.*)

3: Yes; yes, I remember, Daniel—I remember that night you arranged for Harold to come to me you did. It was dark the night air rushed in about me I left open my window. I regard the moon out my window—it is there—full circle in the sky is the white blot beyond the open window it hangs there bright moon hanging there I look to the moon is there. The breeze gently blown—I feel it on my legs—it blows against my ankles I rub together from the chill of the breeze blown in through the open window out which I regard the distant white moon bright—stop.

Heartbeat. Stop. Heart beating faster now heartbeat I hear sound of I here still gazing at the moon out the window I hear steps—nearing below the wind oh, steps—feet—meaning some thing/one climbing up the—"Oh, the trellis"—oh, legs quivering now heart stopping breath stop moon human silhouette climbing in the sky—someone covering the moon as Daniel said it would it be it "Harold?"—climbing up the trellis?—blotting out the moon out the window I look out now against the sky standing there man's figure standing there I look out.

I there now. It there. Figure. The. The figure of—It climb out the sky into room standing there. Long solid shadow it step aside and the moon is there.

Man in the room. It/he in the room. It/he move in my room towards my bed I oh, my ankles quivering. The breeze I—oh, it speak—it say something. What I can't remember; something, it say. I just say "Shhh," softly, "shhh." My voice just say. I say, "It so dark." Face dark. I cannot see face; it must be "Harold?"—as you said, Daniel, it would be "Harold?"—through the window would come to me to love it must be "Harold?" I say. "Harold, who is it?" It say It is I. I. I, I see eyes green eyes that I see all I see that's all I see I see his . . . his . . . his eyes I see his. . . . I whisper "Why Harold, is that you?" Voice say, It is I. I. I. I then I look to the moon still white I look to the moon. And he bends down to me.

Hands on my legs reaching down grab my feet with palms of

hands cold hands warm it tickles soles of my feet I giggle giggle he it I giggle we hands grab my ankles. Pressure feels—oh god against my cheek his cheek against my lips his hands travel traveling up my legs into my gown I oh my tongue to my my lips his tongue it tongues my tongue slips out two tongues together in my—my—my mouth his mouth I "Oh, I—Harold, mouth my mouth my" hands now moving his—"Harold, Harold, I love you, Harold."—pressing down—him down hard against me it—it—it—it tongues to that his mouth my mouth's lips wet bitten "Ouch, I—Harold! I"—I hand his he hands it's pulling at my "Oh my my my my" down my "oh, my" his fingers pressing in my hair down there his hands palm of his near thumb of his hand it's . . . It's . . . "It's there, yes—press" I pressing him down—down his rump I hands on his rump it— it—It—it—"It dark—" I say, "Harold," I say, "True Love— I've—I've—I—I've always loved you" my voice saying, "Shhh. Shhh, shhh, shhh, shhh, shhh, shhh, shhh, shhh."

(*Light changes.*)

DANIEL REMINDS HAROLD

2: You do owe me one, Harold. Harold, you owe me one. You owe me a favor. Harold, you owe me a favor. You owe me a favor, Harold, I'm your brother.

1: Daniel

2: Harold, if it wasn't for me Sylvia would never be your wife. If it wasn't for me.

1: Daniel, I know and I'm—I'll

2: Harold

1: I know, Daniel. In her room. You in her room that night with the moon shining white bright. You for me. You did for me. You said for me you would woo, and you you did. You for me did for me woo my wife Sylvia in my place.

2: Yes I did for you woo for you I did for you were less than confident, Harold.

1: It's true, Daniel, I was less than confident. And you

2: What's more, and this I think a sign of true brotherly devotion I display for you I did at that time display my brotherly devotion to you—whose i—whose ideas—idea was it to you—for you—to dress up as Mommy—to convince—to fool Daddy—to convince Daddy to let you marry Sylvia? My idea. I told you that you could masquerade as Mommy and fool Daddy that you were Mommy. And as Mommy you convinced Daddy to let you marry Sylvia. That was my idea. I convinced you you could do it and you did do it. And you did marry Sylvia, didn't you?

1: Yes, yes, it's true. I . . . I had no id—

2: Yes. I knew you could pull it off. If anyone knew I knew if anyone you knew Mommy. It was you look like her, Harold

1: But

2: Harold

1: Daniel

2: If anyone, you could.

1: But it was dark. And I was there was only a moment I was there in the dark with Daddy was sleeping when—as I woke him you kept Mommy downstairs talking I crept into their bedroom as you kept Mommy occupied downstairs I crept into their bedroom dressed in one of Mommy's old muumuus I sprayed with her perfume on my neck and arms—I rolled into bed and wrapped my arms around Daddy's back and stirred him out of his sleep and whispered, "Melvin, wake up, I wanna talk to you a second, darling." "What," he said. I said, "Melvin." He said, "It's—Shirley—it's late." I said, "I know it's" (and all this time you kept Mommy occupied downstairs with some—what was the story you were going to tell about a problem you were having with—what was the problem you made up a to keep Mommy downstairs with you she was I'm surprised in hindsight she took time to listen to your problems—for that matter when did she ever have time for anyone's problems but her own she did have) "Melvin, I know it's late and this'll—but this'll only take a minute, so wake up and listen, I want to talk to you about Harold and this girl." And Daddy said, "Shirley, I don't want to talk about it now, I don't like the girl has no family, she wants Harold for his money, and Shirley,"—"For Christ sake will you listen to me, Melvin, listen to me when," I interrupted. And I spoke like Mommy. And I badgered him and I kept him awake the way Mommy would do when she wanted something really bad she'd just keep him awake until he was too weak and tired to refuse that time in the night with my arms wrapped around his paunch, stroking his face and chest I said, "Melvin," I said, "he's going to marry Sylvia whether we like it or not and if he doesn't get your—our—blessing, he'll leave us for that girl—Melvin, who are you—who are you going to leave the business to run the business to Melvin, for Christ sake, Danny is an idiot in the business," I said you were an idiot.

2: You

1: That sounded like Mommy would say something like that.

2: Yes it does; she would.

1: "You worked your entire life," I said like Mommy, "to leave this business that you worked your entire life for to a son of bitch like that with no brains for business. And I swear" (I swore as Mommy) "he'll never speak with you again—Melvin, he'll never speak with you. Harold won't speak with you—with us—if you don't give permission. This I know because he's said"—as much as I thought this was stretching it as Mommy I was in the mood to stretch it. And with the hour late, and my hands stroking him he agreed—he was so tired. So tired. And he fell off to sleep. And as he fell off to sleep, I fell out of the bed and as quickly moved out of the room I saw Mommy's shadow coming up the stair—the clump, clump of her white feet in fuzzy slippers she clumped up the carpeted stairs, burping the last bits of whatever it was she'd eaten while talking to you about a problem that never existed. And I ran to my room, ripped off the old muummuu, I washed off the fragrance. I leapt into bed and I fell to sleep.

2: And whose idea was that Harold? Whose idea was it my idea? Can't you help me out for just this once Harold do something for me for once be a brother to me for once. Brothers are supposed to help each other.

1: But Daniel, what you ask me!

2: Harold, after all I've done for you, this small

1: Small?!

2: favor I ask of you.

1: You're asking me to dress up as my dead mother.

2: Our dead mother, Harold. After all I've done for you.

1: But Daniel

(*Light brings* CHARACTER 4 *into focus.*)

4: Daniel, I can't—I can't marry you without Uncle Saul's permission. And I'm telling you, Uncle Saul refuses to even consider our marriage until he's met your mother—after all I've told him that you've told me about

(*Light brings* CHARACTER 3 *into focus.*)

3: Your mother? What did you tell her about your mother?

2: I—

4: It's such a small

1: Small?

4: thing I'm asking for— Danny. I don't under—	**2:** Maxine; I—I— no; you don't understand; it's

Danny; Danny, she's your
    mother—

          Right, but Max—
She's your—   Max—
          All right; wait.

Sweetheart, she's your
    mother—   Wait.
Danny—how is it—tell me
how is it possible she can't
make the time to—make the
    —your own   It's not a question
                of time; it's—

How is it possible
    your own mother can't
    make the . . . This has nothing
              to do with—
So, if it's not a question of with . . .
    time—   It's just that—
            Maxine, darling—
If it's not a question of time— Baby, listen—baby—
No. I want to meet your
    mother.

1: So, you told her . . .

2: I told her that . . . well, I really didn't tell her that . . . I just

3: You told her your mother was alive?

2: I—yes, I no, Sylvia, no I didn't—didn't tell her . . . I just . . .
Yes; I told her . . . I told her that . . . that Mommy was

1: Alive? Why?

4: Because; I can't; I cannot—I will not; I will not marry you until
I meet your mother. After

2: Maxine

4: After all you've told me about her. And besides

3: Have you talked to Harold about any of this?

2: No.

4: Daniel, I can't—I can't marry you without Uncle Saul's permission. And Uncle Saul, I'm telling you, refuses to even consider our marriage until he's met your mother—after all that I've told him that you've told me about her,

1: So Maxine thinks that
    Mommy is

3: Maxine thinks your
    mother is

2: Sylvia thought I should
    speak with you, Harold.
    You see

4: Well, frankly Danny,
I don't see
why your—
why your mother—
your own mother can't
attend—can't

3: But Daniel,

2: Sylvia, what am I going
3: Why did you . . .
. . . Why didn't you just tell
    her the truth—your

1: Mommy's Dead.

3: What?

1: She swallowed a bottle of muscle relaxers. Half a bottle of muscle relaxers.

3: Oh my god.

1: My father just called from the hospital.

3: A suicide. Oh my god.

2: I couldn't tell her that, Harold. I don't know; I just couldn't tell Maxine that Mommy had swallowed

3: Daniel

1: But Daniel,

4: Danny

2: Sylvia,

1: So . . . so who is this Uncle Saul?

2: What am I going to do?

3: Just—tell her your mother is out of town.

4: I don't believe you.

2: She didn't believe me.

1: See—this is getting so complicated I can hardly follow it.

2: Oh, Harold, come on—

1: Yea, but what about

3: Your father;

4: Your father;

1: What about Daddy? Does Daddy

2: No, I haven't mentioned anything to

4: Your father; what about your father? Will he be able to

2: No; Uncle Saul is staying in a hotel in Westwood. Daddy doesn't know anything.

1: You're promising me, Daniel, Daddy doesn't know a thing about

2: Harold, I promise you, Daddy won't be there. Come on—as soon as Sylvia and I—and I mean Maxine and I are married, Harold, I'm going to tell Maxine the truth; I'm going to tell her everything. Believe me, Harold. Harold please believe me; I love Maxine like you love Sylvia. I love her, Harold. (*Gently.*) Harold.

3: I don't know. Maybe you should talk to Harold.

4: Well, after my parents were killed—in the hijacking—I was placed in the care of my great great uncle—Uncle Saul.

2: That's what I'll do; I'll talk to Harold.

(*Light changes.*)

ARRIVING IN THE HOTEL

2: Sweetheart, we're here. Maxine?

4: I'm coming, I'm coming—Hi! Come in, come in; come on in.

2: Hi.

4: Hi.

1: Hello, is this her? Maxine?

4: Hello, hi.

2: Oh yea, Max, this is my mother. Ma, this is

1: What do you call her? What does he call you, Max? Like a man? What do you . . . She's a girl. Maxine.

2: I know, Ma.

1: Never mind. Hello.

4: Hi.

1: I'm Danny's mother.

4: Of course you are. It's so nice to meet you. Come in, come in, make yourself comfortable.

1: Right, listen, darling, you'll excuse me I can only stay a minute; I'm sick with a cold, and

4: I know, Danny told me you're not feeling well; I want you to sit right down and be a good girl; I'm going to pour you a nice hot cup of tea; we have lemon and honey . . . (*Rolls in a tea cart. On the cart, a tea setting. On the lower rack of the cart, a large bowl of fruit and a bowl of ice with cans of soda in it.*)

1: Oh, I love her. Oh god, I love her, is she a doll or what? Oh, look at this; that's great. You're great. Let me look at you. Let me look at you look great. I'm sold; we could go; we could leave right now. (*Hold. 2 shakes his head.*) I love her. I love you. You do I love you in that dress you look swell, really swell I'll always love her. How are you—excited—getting married to my . . . ? Come on, we'll sit and where's your uncle?—what's his name—Saul? I'd love to meet him.

4: Oh, right, let me—yes, he's in the other room; I think he fell asleep in the other

1: How'm I doing?   **4:** room I'll—
4: What?

2 (*hold*): Nothing sweetheart nothing; why don't you go on, get Uncle Saul. (*Hold until 4 exits.*) You're fine, you're fine. Just relax, don't talk so much, calm down.

1: What?

2: Yea.

4 (*from offstage*): Here we come.

1: Oh my god.

4 (*from offstage*): What?

2: Nothing honey, nothing. Mommy's just—a little—you know, nervous—meeting Uncle Saul.

4 (*from offstage*): Oh, don't be silly.

1: I'm not—what are you talking about—like—nervous. It's just that I can't stay long I'd love to stay but I'm sick with cold and my friend, Dorothy, I'm a friend of Dorothy, I've got to visit is crazy in the hospital. She's

2 (*aghast*): What?

1: It's true. I'm a friend of Dorothy. What can I do?

4 (*from offstage*): Oh, no.

1: It breaks your heart, I know; she lost her mind—so sad to say—I hate to say it's true—they locked her up!

4 (*from offstage*): That's terrible.

2 (*hushed*): Harold, are you crazy?!

1 (*to 2*): Crazy? I'm not crazy. (*To 4:*) She's crazy, but not dangerous. Or at least not as dangerous as

4: Okay, here we come.

(CHARACTER 4 *enters with* CHARACTER 5 *as* UNCLE SAUL—*as old as the hills—older. He's in a wheelchair and, except where indicated, he never gets up.*)

2: Hey, here they are.

1: Oh look, look! Here's the—here's your uncle—what's his name, Paul?—is he in pain? That he's with that—I don't—didn't know you were a cripple—hello—I would have brought something for you if I knew my name is Shirley. Hello. I'm Danny's mother of course I am in pain aren't you with that chair is he's deaf isn't he? Can't hear me the poor thing he must be blind. Can he read my lips? If I bend down to him close could he hear or read lips?

5 (*East European accent; not much wind left in him*): What?

1: Oh, he's all right. I'm sorry I thought you were deaf; I didn't know you could—see I'm sorry; how are you? Is he in pain? Is he lying to be nice? Is he comfortable?

4: He's fine.

1: Tell me with uncle here do you have to change the bedpan? Does he have he use the bedpan? My mother—does he have a bedpan for god rest her soul—a lovely person she suffered everybody loved her—bedridden—my mother—for so long I'd change her bedpan almost daily when I was a little boy—a little girl—coming home from school—I'd stop by her room—on the way to my room I'd stop by her—she was sleeping or—awake with the TV on watching her programs I'd take her bedpan and dump it I hated it. Cancer, cancer; it was cancer! I hated washing out the doody and the pee from the pan in the sink or in the toilet I would do it. But always rinse—shit—out; what's the difference? I hated the scraping the doody's is such a mess it was sticking to the pan I'd have to scrape it. And spray with disinfectant of something spray. I loved her to death but I hated doing that. She—never mind: do you do that for your uncle?

4: No; I

1: Oh, forgive me; I've gotten personal.

2: Mother!!

1 (*suddenly vehement; impatient*): What?! (*Then honeyed.*) Darling?

2 (*stunned, then calmly*): Do you want to go freshen up? You know you don't have much time before I take you to the . . . bus to get to . . . "Dorothy," so maybe

1: Yes, that's a good idea. You'll excuse me?

4: Oh, sure.

1 (*to 5*): Have I made a good impression on you? I hope I have—because your daughter loves my son. I mean you—niece—here—whatever—loves my son—he tells me he loves her, and Danny's an honest one if there's one thing he wouldn't lie so tell me, I hope you like my Danny too—and give your blessing for Christ sake because these two I see should be together to have children. God wonders if I'll ever get—not that that's what I'm concerned with here—grandchildren? from my other boy, Harold—who knows what's the matter there—if it's his wife, Sylvia—I never liked her that Harold, who knows? He always was a strange boy; I don't know what he like—likes—like, I don't know maybe he's a . . . (*goes limp-wristed; to* 4:) Oh, but you I love! (*To* 2:) Where's the little girl's room, Danny? Can you show your mother? (*To* 5:) To carry on the name it's important. By the way, I'm sorry my husband couldn't be here he's got business, you—I know you understand. (*To* 4:) Oh, are you is she a doll?! (*To* 2:) I'll be right out, darling.

(2 *drags* 1 *off. Light is extinguished.*)

H A R O L D   I N   T H E   B A T H R O O M

From the dark the sound of a toilet being flushed. Then light illuminates CHARACTERS 1 *and* 2. 2 *knocks on a piece of wood.*

2 (*knocking*): Ma? Ma? It's almost time to go. (*Then whispering:*) Harold—are you all right in there, Harold?

1: Daniel—I'll be right out.

2: Just a few more minutes and I'll get you out of here.

1: Ok, that's great.

2: And listen . . .

1: What?

2: Listen, Harold, calm down out there.

1: Yea.

2: I mean, what's going on out there?

1: I don't know, I don't know. Every time I open my mouth it's like . . . it's

2: All right—okay—forget it. Just

1: Okay.

2: Yea. (*Pause.*) Why did you

1: What?

2: You

1: What?

2: You.

1: Who, me?

2: Yea, you.

1: What?

2: Why did you mention the—the hospital where—where who's this Dorothy?

1: Who?

2: Dorothy.

1: Dorothy?

2: Yea—you

1: I just made that up.

2: Yea, but you

1: What?

2: Harold, you made it sound like Mommy. Like Mommy, when

1: Like Mommy, yea. I don't know; I—I—I was thinking

2: That's where she took the pills.

1: The pills, that's right.

2: When Daddy—god, Harold, I can't forget how she screamed down the hall when they wheeled her away strapped in. You weren't there. Where were you? You were at home. Or on your honeymoon with Sylvia. Which was it? You didn't hear how she screamed out his name as we walked away down the hall. She screamed out his name, screamed out his name, screamed out his name Melvin, Melvin, Melvin, come back, they're going to kill me, they're killing me here, they're going to kill me.

1: I know.

2: I heard her call out his name not to leave me—don't leave me here, I'll kill myself Melvin, please, I'll kill myself, you son a bitch, you, you son of a bitch, she said. You

1: Daniel—

2: Poor Dad. (*Hold.*) We shouldn't talk about it, Harold.

1: Right.

2 (*pause*)**:** Right, and Harold, a few nice words to Uncle Saul, you know, if you could.

1: What?

2: Before you leave.

1: Okay.

2: Be a nice-like Mommy.

1: Okay.

2: I mean

1: What do you mean?

2: I mean just say a few nice things to him. Ask him how he enjoyed traveling, that you hope to see him at the wedding, about his business—he's in the junkyard business—in Chicago—he sells scrap metal. Scrap.

1: What? I didn't hear what you

2: Right. Okay, listen, I better get out there.

1: Wait. I

2: Just act nice a little. And then I'll drive you to your car.

1: What?

2: I'm going to go out and talk to them now, Harold, I'll be in the other room.

1: Okay. (*Pause. Then as if into a mirror.*) I just don't remember you being very nice. *What do you mean, darling?* I mean you were just *never speak to me like that, Harold.* You were never *Harold, don't you dare* to me you were—*Harold*—you were always so frightening *me with that kind of talk, darling. I don't l*ike the thought that I never felt at ease or peace with *you would say that to a sick woman like* Mommy, I *could die for all* your ranting or raving at *me, a sick woman* like this, right now —*you'd speak to me like this your own* Mommy, you were *Harold,* I could I please, could I *hope you burn in Hell for that kind of* Hell? What the hell are you always talking about *Hell, for Christ sake the* Mother, the Jews don't believe in *hell if they* don't give me what the *Jews—they— yes they* don't! They don't!—*I don't give a crap, Harold, what the goddamn Jews believe in they*—don't tell me then what the Jews *believe me Harold I can't take any more of* what?! What am I doing to you when—when I want an *answer me for Christ sake, Harold!* you won't give me a chance will *you wanna kill me is that what you're*—*is that what you're* just trying to see you more clearly for *once I wish I never gave birth to you —you disgraceful faggot! F*AGGOT!! (*Pause.*) What? What?

What do *you heard me.* I don't know what *you know what I'm talking about.* No, I don't know *bullshit. I'm tired of pretending your* Mother *you're* Mother *your marriage to* don't start in on *Sylvia didn't fool me one bit; so tell me how's your sex life with* Sylvia is satisfied with *no one could be satisfied with* you are just out of your—*out every night looking for*—what are you talking about? You're *a fag, a fag*—I don't—*Why don't you just go home at night after work instead of* stop! *stopping at that place—that park—that park, that you*—No! It's three times now *you're* all right, wait! *You're sleeping with men,* No! *aren't you?* No!! *Oh come on, Harold; you've been sleeping with*—All right! Don't!! Stop!!!

2 (*Seven knocks, in crescendo before speaking*): Ma? Hey, Ma.

1 (*as if into the mirror*): No. No more.

2: What? Harold? Are you. . . .

1 (*whispering in his own voice*): Okay, I'm coming out. I'll be right out.

2 (*whispering*): Harold. Harold.

(*Light is extinguished.*)

MELVIN ARRIVES

Light illuminates CHARACTERS 4 *and* 6.

4: Please come in, make yourself comfortable. What a wonderful surprise. Uncle Saul, this is Daniel's father.

5: What?

4: Isn't this nice? I'm so glad you were able to make it. Danny is going to be thrilled I'm sure to see you here. He told us you were away on business—I was so disappointed.

6: No, I was . . . yea—I was—yesterday—I had to . . . but, gee— no, if I had . . . sure, for cryin' out loud—I mean . . .

5: What?

4 (*to* 6): Oh, excuse me. (*To* 5:) Uncle Saul, are you tired? Do you need to rest? Do you want to take a nap? Are you hungry? Are your sure? Good. (*To* 6:) I'm sorry.

6: No, no, no. (*Pause.*) This is your uncle?

4: My great-great uncle? My father's father's mother's brother.

6: How do you like that?

4: Can I get you something to drink?

6: Oh sure, you got a—what do you got there?

4: Oh, just about everything.

6: Yea, how do you like that. You got a soda—maybe an orange or something—low cal?

4: Oh, sure. How's . . .

6: This is good.

4: Oh here, here's a diet.

6: Oh, that's good, that's good. I like that.

4: Danny should be right with us.

6: Oh, okay.

4: How did you find us, by the way?

6: I spoke with my son Harold's wife, Sylvia. She told me the boys had gone to meet with you and your family. Is Harold still here?

4: I've never met Harold, I'm looking forward to it.

6: Sylvia told me the boys had come up here together.

4: No, just Danny and his mother. She stepped into the bathroom; I'm sure she'll be right out—in a—oh here's Danny. (*As 2 enters.*) Danny is your mother all right?

2: Oh, she's fine—Dad?! Hi—hey, Dad, what are you? . . . get my message—to meet us here—is that how you found us? I'm so glad you could be here.

6: Yea—no—Sylvia—Sylvia. I—Where's Harold?

2: Who?

6: Harold.

2: Harold?

6: Your brother.

2: Oh, Harold, yea.

6: Yea—where is he?

2: What do you mean?

6: What do you mean what do I mean?

2: I don't know.

6: Sylvia said he came up here with you.

2: Who—Sylvia said that—Harold? . . . No, he just dropped me off at the—here—at the . . . hotel, then went back to

6: Sylvia didn't tell me that.

2: She didn't?

6: No.

2: Well, of course not, how could—she didn't know.

6: What do you mean?

2: What do I mean? I mean she didn't . . . know . . . it was . . . a surprise . . .

4: A what?

2: A surprise.

6: What's the surprise?

2: You mean you didn't—no, I guess Harold didn't have time to let you don't know about the surprise that Harold is planning a surprise—for Sylvia.

4: Sylvia is your sister-in-law.

2: Right, and Harold wanted to . . . well, I guess it's safe to say now about this Dad. Harold is surprising Sylvia with . . . with a trip to Las Vegas.

4: Las Vegas! Oh, that's so sweet.

2 (*to* 4)**:** Sure. (*To* 6:) What time did you call Sylvia?

4: That's great.

6: What?

2: What time did you speak to Sylvia?

6: Around nine, I don't know.

2: Okay, see Harold was going to pick up Sylvia after he dropped me off here, and surprise her with the trip.

4: I love that. And I really mean that, I love that.

2: So around ten he must have gotten back to their place—they're probably gone by now.

6: That's great. (*Pause.*) So who's in the bathroom?

2: I don't know, who?

4: Don't be silly, Danny, your mother is in the bathroom. Does she know?

6: That's impossible.

2 (*to* 4)**:** What?

4 (*to* 2)**:** About going to Las Vegas. What does he mean, that's impossible?

2: I don't know.

6: I mean it's impossible.

4: Is that what he means, Danny?

6: Your mother can't be in the bathroom.

2 (*to* 6)**:** That's right.

4 (*to* 2)**:** Why not?

6: Because.

4: Because?

2: Because . . .

6: Because she's . . . she's

2: Maxine, my mother is not in the bathroom.

4 (*troubled*): Why?

2: Because she's . . . she's

1 (*entering*): Because she's right here is why I— (*He sees* CHARACTER 6.) Da-Da-Da-Da-darling, Melvin, sweetheart; what are you . . . doing

4: Here she is. Here she is.

(MELVIN *faints.*)

We were getting worried about you—but look who showed up, your husband is here—oh, look at them, Danny, speechless, like they haven't seen each other for years—oh, look, there are tears in your mother's eyes—and your father's having a difficult time breathing—that's so sweet—and I really mean that—it's very sweet. Danny, I want us to feel that way when we've been married.

1: I've got to be going.

4: Nonsense, you stay right there. You're not going anywhere, I want to talk to you. This is a very special occasion—Danny, why don't you loosen your father's tie—two families getting together—and . . . well . . . Harold is not the only one around here who has surprises. You know, I was thinking that—well—that . . . that Danny, that you know, that I wanted us to do something special—like . . . I don't know, I couldn't think of anything—something, you know—nice—really special that we could all do together and then come back here for some nice coffee and cake or something—sit and talk.

And then I remembered I'm a subscriber to a very nice little small theater—The Iliad theater in West Hollywood, they do a lot of nice little small little plays—very intimate—that, you know, you wouldn't see in some of the big houses like the Shubert or the Ahmanson at the Music Center—or the Shrine Auditorium. You know, nice—in fact, my friend Fritzy, of Fritzy and Howard—you know them, Danny—she works at the day care center with me— she and Howie divorced about a year and a half ago—he was having an affair with—if you can believe it—his brother Donald's wife, Sonya—who I never liked—anyway—Fritzy and I—we know each other from when I was doing my nurse's training back in Chicago—which I never finished because I thought I was getting married to Jack—who Danny knows about—but Jack had a nervous breakdown—he could never get away from his mother, Ethel, who I always thought was very sweet, but evidently was driving or had driven Jack out of his mind—so when I came out west I recontacted Fritzy, she had married a really sweet, nice man, Peter, who I never met, he was Roman Catholic—he got killed in I forgotten how in some kind of horrible auto accident—anyway— his head was chopped off—ended up rolling down the La Cienega off-ramp, going east on the Santa Monica Freeway—it was terrible—I know it sounds funny—but it was—anyway, so when I got out here just after Peter was, you know, killed, Fritzy and I became subscribers to this nice little small theater in West Hollywood I was telling you about about a paragraph and a half ago—and they're doing—they often do really nice plays—sometimes I don't understand the plays they do—sometimes they do things that are just a little too way out—even for me—but you know you take your chances—you know, you get exposed to different kinds of things—it's nice—it's like taking your medicine—anyway, they are doing something now which is suppose to be—it sounds very interesting—Fritzy saw it—she didn't like it—but she said go see it—see for yourself—that actress we like—there's an actress who we love—she occasionally you'll see her on TV, or in a film—I spotted her once in a film with that—who's that actor I like—used to be so handsome—he acted on Broadway, I think, years ago, then had his own series on CBS or NBC—he played a private investigator on Wednesday or Thursday nights—divorced his wife, also an

actress, not very good, but very pretty—she was having an affair
with—if you can believe it—this guy's—this actor's accountant—
I know because my friend Jeannie that—Danny you know Jeannie—
Jeannie is a friend of mine—also from Chicago—nurse's training—
she just had a heart attack—she's young but she weighs about three
hundred pounds—anyway, Jeannie works for another accountant
—Phil something—he has a gorgeous office in Century City—just
went through a messy divorce himself—he was married to a woman
from the Philippines—in fact, one of his kids—Phil's kids, I
hear—I think his son Joey—is heavy into drugs—you know, they
have money—too much money, and there's not a lot of supervision
for these kids—my friend Fern—you know, with the brain
tumor—their kids—her and Seymour—Seymour's in the Peace
Corps—but she has money from her father, Milton, who was a big
macher in the jewelry business—their kids go to school in Beverly
Hills—they go to Beverly High and she tells me a lot of these kids
with money they get from their parents and cars—one of them, a
friend of Robbie's—Fern's oldest—his friend, Madeline—actually,
they're boyfriend and girlfriend—but they're not serious—there's
another girl, Valerie, I think he's more serious about—Valerie's
father is a producer—produces documentaries, and Robbie, you
know, who wants to be an actor, I think he sees this as a contact—
anyway, Madeline has an apartment on the grounds of her father's
estate in Beverly Hills, can you believe this—and there are some real
drug problems—Valerie, for instance, I think is heavily into pot—
anyway, this actress—I think her name is Misty something or
other—oh, you would love her—actually, we saw her do
Carousel—the musical—at that place in the valley—you remember,
Danny—she sings—what a voice some of these people have—I'm
telling you, you're going to love her—she works out of this theater,
The Iliad, and I guess in the play she plays three different roles—
she's suppose to be wonderful—Fritzy said she's worth the price of
admission—so I got us—that is I got—well I got four—tickets—
for the matinee, today—because I didn't—see—and I'm sorry—
I didn't know that you'd be showing up, so—but please, don't—

can't—can't you leave your friend Dorothy—who I would love to meet some time—leave her for today and join us please for the play—Uncle Saul, you see, is exhausted from all the excitement— I'm sure he'll want to rest here at the hotel, and then we should all—come on—all of us—go out to the theater and have a good time. Okay? Good.

(*Hold. Then light quickly out.*)

Light illuminates CHARACTER 1 *sitting on the couch, holding the Golden Apple. He takes off his clothing, becomes* ERIS. *His genitals are exposed.*

1: I am Eris, spirit of strife
and discord.

Some say I was conceived by Hera
when she brushed her slender figure
against a blackthorn; others
I am daughter of Hera and Zeus,
despised by all mortal
and immortal excepting my brother
Aries for who I always will
stir up occasion for war by spread
of rumor and jealousy.

Either way indignant have I climbed
the height of Mount Pelion,
the one divinity uninvited
to this the wedding feast of Peleus
and Thetis.

What god was it then
brought these two together
into matrimony? Zeus,
whose passion for Thetis was

discouraged by a prophecy that
any son born to Thetis would
be greater than his father.

Thus afraid his power
would be threatened did Zeus
arrange this marriage, inviting all
the gods except myself
to celebrate. But I have come
despite, determined to strike
division among the Olympians.

Silent I am
invisible. Here comes
the bride and groom.

PELEUS AND THETIS

CHARACTER 2 *and* CHARACTER 3, *left. Their genitals are not exposed.*

3: No—Peleus, it was Hera
chose you as my husband. She knew
Zeus would sleep with me, but I
rejected his advances. And he
insulted, vowed I would never marry
an immortal.

2: And I, advised that you
immortal would resent a marriage to me,

3: Hid yourself—I know it now—
behind a bush of myrtle berries
on the tiny island near the shores
of Thessaly.

2: For to that islet's shore would you
Thetis daily ride naked

on the back of a dolphin,
there to take a midday's sleep
in the recess of a secret cave.

3: You grabbed me as I slept
and dreamt; I quickly metamorphosed.

2: But I had been prepared you would resist
my embrace. And as you fiercely changed
first into fire, next into water
then into a leopard,

3: A lion.

2: What?

3: A lion, not

2: A lion, yes, and finally a serpent,
but I clung to you.

3: I changed into a slippery squid
and squirted you with sticky ink. You
were burned, drenched, scratched, bitten,
and covered with ink.

2: But I held onto you.

3: You would not let me go. And in the end
you lay upon me, and we were locked
into a passionate embrace.

2: Now we should take our place
at the banquet table beside
the deities.

(*Exit* 2 *and* 3 *right.* CHARACTER 1 *lobs the Golden Apple after them,
then exits left.*)

CHARACTER 5 *enters from right. He wears broken chains on his wrists. He is fully clothed.*

5: I am
Prometheus, some say son
of Iapethus, others
Eurymedon—my mother
I've heard was Clymene—but none
are sure; the future's clear
for me, the past
is somewhat clouded.

I once tricked Zeus—he told
me manage a dispute which
sacrificial portion should
be offered to the gods
and which reserved for humans.
The all-nutritious flesh
I wrapped up in the undesirable
stomach—the useless bones
concealed within the tempting
fat. The father Zeus
was easily deceived; he chose
the fat and left the meat
for the men.

He punished me, withholding fire
from my beloved mankind—but
I stole it from behind
his back and gave it them—and then—
spiteful bastard that he is—
he had me tortured—
chained onto Mt. Caucasus until

I threatened him with prophecy
of Thetis. Now unbound I'm free
and able once again to aid
the struggling homo.

(*Exit* 5 *left.*)

CHARACTER 6 *enters from right. Muscular body. His genitals are exposed.*

6: I am lord of all heaven,
Zeus. My father
was Kronos, my mother
Rhea—both children
of Terra and her son
Uranus.

There are those say Eurynome—
The Mother of Us All—
rose naked out of chaos dividing sea from sky dancing south
on the water breaking wind behind her;
she caught this fetid wind between her hands and rubbed
fashioning the serpent Ophion
who turning lustful penetrated her—and she
become a chicken laid an egg from which the universe sprang
including Terra
the earth—who as she slept bore Uranus
and he took the sky and reigned over her.

Then Terra's angry with Uranus because
he held the Cyclopes—
his rebellious sons—in the underworld
and she persuades her other sons attack Uranus.
And Titan Kronos led them lopping off his father's genitals
with a sickle;

himself ruling the sky until I
when I was born and grown to manhood waged
war with Kronos my father because
he would devour me.
I threw the goddam fucking bastard into the underworld,
and he never since troubled me.

That aside this wedding progressed
perfect until Eris in rage neglected
lobbed a golden apple inscribed
For the Fairest onto our dining table.
The fruit is claimed by Hera,
Athena, and Aphrodite demanding I
determined which of them receives it.

But I won't be embroiled
in their dispute; rather to Mount Ida
I sent the three goddesses; there
a handsome shepherd Paris
judges which of them is fairest.
Paris is unknown a son of Hecuba
and Priam king of Troy. Prior to his birth
a prophecy identified him as Troy's
destruction. He was exposed
in helpless infancy on
the mountainside but lived
and is grown a charming youth.

(*Exit 6 right.*)

PARIS

CHARACTER 2 *enters from left with a sheep and the Golden Apple. No
real sheep, please.*

2: It was this morning Hermes
the gods' messenger and son
of Zeus appeared to me and said
Athena, Hera, Aphrodite approach—
that I am to select the one
who's fairest.

(CHARACTER 2 *unfastens his garment, releasing a gigantic penis. He begins fucking the sheep from behind.*)

But how can I
a simple shepherd be
an arbiter of divine
beauty?

I think I will divide the golden fruit
three ways, rewarding each
an equal segment—that none
feel slighted; it would be terrible
to offend a goddess.

No, no, I cannot disobey the word of God—
he commands a choice be made;
to contradict would be a sin—
what can I do? If I choose one
I offend the others. If I don't
I encourage Zeus's wrath. Either way
I'm fucked.

(*The sheep bleats.*)

I see them, yes, three figures
female arm in arm walking from the sky
in our direction. Let's stop
for now.

(CHARACTER 2 *pulls himself out of the sheep—the sheep bleats loudly— and he tucks himself back in his clothes.*)

Sorry.

(*From off right, the voice of* CHARACTER 4.)

4 (*as* HERA): Paris—you know why
we come.

2: I do
divine Hera—though I think
I'm ill equipped to

4 (*as* ATHENA): We are confident you'll stand
and make the right selection.

2: As you say
wise Athena—still
I beg the two I cannot choose
not to be fierce with me; I
am human—thus fallible.

4 (*as* APHRODITE): We promise to abide by your decision.

2: Thanks, Aphrodite. I wonder
will it be enough
to judge you as you are, or can
you be naked?

4 (*as* HERA). What?!

4 (*as* ATHENA): Naked?!

4 (*as* APHRODITE): All of us?

4 (*as* ATHENA): Oh, for Christ sake.

2: Please—do as I ask.
I'll judge you each
one at a time. The others
kindly wait in silence by that tree.
Hera first.

(*Enter* CHARACTER 4 *as* HERA, *her genitals covered by a pretty apron.*)

4 (*as* HERA): Paris—here am I, Hera, wife
of Zeus—reduced to ruthless intrigue most
of my married life because of Zeus's
infidelities. Examine my magnificent figure
conscientiously.

2: I will.

4 (*as* HERA): Paris you should judge me fairest—
I can offer power and wealth to you beyond
your wildest dreams. I'll make you king
of oily Asia Minor, richest man a

2: No,
you shouldn't try to bribe me. I have seen enough. Enough.

(CHARACTER 4 *exits off right.*)

Athena—your turn.

(*Enter* CHARACTER 4 *as* ATHENA, *covering herself with her shield,
holding a long spear.*)

4 (*as* ATHENA): Okay, I know I am not much to look at.
Metis, my mother, was raped
by Zeus. An oracle declared
I'd be a girl, but if my mother had
a second child it be
a boy fated to depose Zeus as Kronos
was by Zeus, and Uranus was
by Kronos. So Zeus opened wide
his mouth and swallowed Metis—
and that was the end of my mother—by the way,

If I'm the chosen one I will
endow your mind with wisdom unsurpassed; you will
be always be victorious in battle;
in all affairs

2: No, do not offer like the other
insubstantial gifts—wealth
and wisdom power are nothing to me.
I am a shepherd on a mountainside;
I do not need these . . . whatever these . . .
Please, go away.

(CHARACTER 4 *exits off right.*)

And now I'll call the last contestant

(CHARACTER 4 *has entered as* APHRODITE, *wearing sunglasses and spike heels. She is uncovered.*)

4 (*as* APHRODITE): Hi. You saved the best for last
didn't you? I'm Aphrodite—
"foam born" from the scrotum of Uranus. (CHARACTER 4 *pronounces it "yer anus."*)
I want that apple. Now listen Paris
as we rode the winds from Pelion here to Ida
I couldn't help but notice your attachment
to these . . . animals; no, no,
I think it's sweet—really—but—
Paris—you don't want to waste your life
fucking the flock.
Do you?

(APHRODITE *pushes* PARIS *onto the couch.*)

2: Uhn . . .

4 (*as* APHRODITE): Most singles can tell you what they want in a
mate
but few can tell you what they need—too bad!
Because having a mate who can fulfill your needs
is the secret to a lifetime of love.

I happen to be an expert at identifying
personal needs. In fact,

helping successful singles like yourself
understand what they need in a mate
is my divine duty. Meeting someone is easy,
finding the right one—that's hard.

(*She locates his penis, grips it.*)

I do this through unique screening procedures—
there's nothing like it—anywhere;
it's the secret of my success.

2: Un huh.

4 (*as* APHRODITE; *pulls him up by his penis, they stand close together*): There
are no computers,
no embarrassing videos,
no awkward introductions to make you feel
uncomfortable. For instance.
Helen of Sparta.

2: Who?

4 (*as* APHRODITE): You've heard of Helen, haven't you?

2: No.

4 (*as* APHRODITE): She is the most
beautiful woman in the world
and passionate.

2: Really?

4 (*as* APHRODITE): Oh yes. Currently she is married
to Menelaus—Agamemnon's brother. But . . .
I would give her to you if you like.

2: But—you say she's married.

4 (*as* APHRODITE): Tough shit.
Paris, go to Helen with my son,
Eros, by your side;
once you've docked your tug in Sparta,
we'll see she falls for you.

2: You think

4 (*as* APHRODITE)**:** I think that once you've met
all you two will want to do
is fuck, fuck, fuck, fuck, fuck, fuck, fuck,
fuck, fuck. A lot.

(CHARACTER 2 *drops the Golden Apple into* 4*'s hand. Light is extinguished.*)

Light illuminates CHARACTER 5 *as* UNCLE SAUL *in his hotel room.* CHARACTER 1 *as* HAROLD *stands to the side, visible in shadow. Hold.* 5 *speaks.*

5: So when I'll go to the dentist they'll have the girl clean my teeth—what's her name? Lisa—something; she's a very nice girl—what is it? Lisa . . . Lynn! Lynn!—that's what the name—she's a colored girl—she says to me—she says—she tells me Mr. Goodman, you have to floss your teeth and I said what do you mean? And she says—she puts the floss—the thread in my mouth and she scrapes with it—she scrapes—and she says to me put the thread between the teeth to scrape with the microbes—you gotta scrape because you gonna have the microbes off the teeth—you gotta break up the colonies from the microbes that are on the teeth. And she looks at me and I said—I said all right I'm gonna do that. She's a very sweet girl—she takes with the toothbrush—she takes it— and she shows me—she asks me what do I brush my teeth? So I show with her what I do and she says that's no good. And she takes it—she takes the toothbrush—she takes—she takes it and she says—she takes it and she shows me what she wants I should be doing with it—the way she does it. And I said all right, I'm gonna do that. And then what does she takes the toothbrush and she turns it around with the rubber tip, and she puts the rubber tip in my mouth and she rubs it between the teeth and the gum and she says to me I want you should do this when you wash the teeth. So I said —what am I—I'm not gonna argue with her—I thought—I'll do it because . . . she knows.

So she scrapes and she rubs and she says to me I want you should stimulate the gum when you brush the teeth. And I said to her what am I gonna want to do this for? And she says to me no, you gotta stimulate the gum with the pressure because it's good for you. And I don't know what she means. And she says you gotta put the pressure with the gum because what's gonna happen is you gonna put on the pressure—and what's gonna happen is the blood supply—you gonna cut it off for a while, while you have on the pressure with the gum. And this is gonna be good for you because the blood—you see—she shows me—she takes with the finger—and she puts her finger in my mouth and she puts on the pressure with the gum, and it gets a little bit white and she says you see what happened? We cut off the blood supply—and I said all right, so what? And she says now look what happened when I take off the finger and I stop the pressure from the gum. And the gum gets red because she says the blood comes back—and I said that's good. And she says that's right that's good because the blood comes back is gonna flow into the gum strong and it's gonna be clean fresh blood. And I ask her is that good? And she says yes because the blood is full of nutrients and oxygen. She says the blood contains oxygen because when you breathe, the oxygen comes in with the lungs, it gets exchanged for the carbon dioxide—which you breathe out—and the oxygen gets in with the blood, and I ask her so what do I want with the oxygen? And she says you want to have the oxygen because the oxygen is gonna kill the microbes.

And this is what she tells me; she says to me

(*Without interruption of the text, 5 shuts eyes and his voice switches from the old man to a young woman.*)

Oxygen burns—it oxidizes. *Open wide. Thank you.* You see for over half its four point five billion year history—over half—the earth's *a little wider* atmosphere contains practically no oxygen. *Turn toward me.*

Thank you. There was life, of course, life was thriving on the earth from almost its inception—altering the planet's surface and atmosphere—maintaining itself against the permutations of the world.

The first three billion years of life on earth were microbial—

anaerobic bacterias extending themselves promiscuously, recombining genes. They reproduced by doubling their sizes replicating their single strand of DNA, then dividing. *You can close a little. Thanks.*

These nonnucleated cells—cells without a nucleus—invented the essential chemical reactions and metabolisms—not the least of which was photosynthesis—that's right; bacteria developed photosynthesis—not plants. There were no plants back then. No plants, no animals—animals!—we're an afterthought—and probably just for fertilizing plants. *Please rinse.*

So bacteria invented photosynthesis—which is the process of getting food from light and air . . . The process of getting food from light and air. Photo—synthesis.

Now you know that life *Turn towards me* needs hydrogen, because when added to carbon dioxide *Open. Good.* you can make organic foods—like sugar. Hydrogen gas was plentiful on the early earth—

but it's light—it floats—it floats right into space. Did you ever see a hydrogen balloon? What happened? (*Eyes open, as* SAUL—*as if mouth is stuffed with cotton:*) It Floats (*Eyes shut as* LYNN:) That's right, it floats—it floats away in space.

So hydrogen was getting scarce. But then bacteria tapped the most abundant source of hydrogen on earth . . . Water—dihydrogen oxide—H_2O.

The strong bonds between hydrogen and oxygen in water were previously unbreakable until a kind of blue-green bacteria developed a second photosynthetic reaction center utilizing higher energy light capable of splitting water molecules into their constituents of hydrogen and oxygen.

These frantic microbes grabbed the hydrogen, releasing oxygen into the atmosphere, setting off the most intense pollution crises the world has ever known. Bar none. *Please rinse.*

Oxygen is toxic—especially when combined with light. You get a cut—what do you do? *N—open wide. Whoops. Sorry. Did I hurt you? I'm sorry. Turn towards me. Turn towards me. Thank you.*

Oxygen grabs electrons, producing chemicals that wreak havoc on the basic elements of life. Remember I said—oxygen burns—it oxidizes; that's right—

it's toxic. When you get a cut—if it's not bad—leave it uncovered—let it breath; exposed to light and air, infecting anaerobic microbes die—they're killed—their tissues are exploded.

Well that's what happened on the earth—and hopefully in your mouth—as oxygen was released; it wiped out species left and right, exterminating the vast majority of living organisms on the earth—more than any plague or nuclear holocaust ever could.

Yet life ascended and survived—it rallied symbiotically—fusing once again with a sex so fluid—recombining genes, regenerating quickly, replicating DNA—transforming its compositions—duplicating—developing aerobic respiration.

This essay into symbiosis led to new cells—cells with nucleus—and later plants and animals. Bacteria cooperatively merged—collectively forming new life that could exploit the new combustible environment.

What if there was a devastating nuclear disaster—one that swept away all animals and plants?

Life would adjust—regenerating, mutating—reregulating the globe without us.

Exposed to toxins, microorganisms typically enhance their sex—reorganizing themselves—adjusting to catastrophe.

Should humans suicide with wars or waste, cancerous immunological diseases, whatever, life's longest living ancient microorganisms are more than capable of adjusting and expanding once again—networking through genetic transfer and mutation—symbiosis, cohabitation—altering the environment and themselves contingently as they've done before and will again, no matter.

This lucky life is too secure to be derailed by human beings. *Un uhn; don't close; stay open. Thank you.* We are temporary vessels—repositories of one hundred quadrillion prokaryotic bacterial cells and ten quadrillion eukaryotic animal cells—our presence is so far one thirtieth of a percent on the timeline of the planet.

And even if we don't expire in violence—though I think it's unavoidable—our time will come. And like the ninety-nine point ninety-nine percent of life forms that have lived on earth—either we'll evolve into another species or we'll be extinguished.

(*Eyes open, as* SAUL:) No thing is permanent—she said,
(*Eyes shut, as* LYNN:) or fixed; it's shifting endlessly. *Please rinse.*

(*Eyes open,* 5 *inhales quickly. He turns his head toward* 1, *exhaling a steady stream of breath. As he does, light dims on him and momentarily touches* 1, *then light is extinguished.*)

Light illuminates CHARACTER 1 *standing beside and intensely focused on* CHARACTER 5. *Hold.* CHARACTER 4 *enters with two boxes from the bakery.*

4 (*entering*): I'm sorry you had to wait at the—Oh, was—? What? was

1: The door was open.

4 (*pause*): Oh, I thought I locked it—I'm so glad—I felt terrible leaving you here—I had to run down to the desk to get—Uncle Saul—hi—we're back, we're back from the theater—hi—you were sleeping. Did you take a nap, or did you stay up? He's so sweet, isn't he—I'll tell you, growing up with Uncle Saul, it wasn't easy— he never talks—I had no one to talk with. Oh, he talks to himself, sure, or he'll talk in his sleep when he's dreaming because . . . Gee, I hope I dropped the key in Danny's car and didn't loose it at the theater or

2 (*calling to* CHARACTER 4 *as he enters*): Sweetheart?

4: Hi, we're

2 (*entering holding the hotel room key*): Sweetheart—you left the key in my

4: Oh, good—I was—yes—I was—you know, I had to leave your mother standing there by the door—it was in the car, wasn't it— see, I'm not such a dummy—for ten minutes while I—there was no one at the desk—and I—but who's ready for some cake? We have delicious cookies and there's a half-cake—I was going to get a whole cake, but then I thought—Danny, where's your father?

1: I'll have cake—and cookies.

4: Good, good for you.

2: He's moving his car.

4: Why, what's the matter?

2: Nothing, he didn't like where it was parked. There were some kids playing nearby. He was afraid they'd knock a ball or something through his windshield.

4 (*to* 1): You know, I got worried because your husband seemed upset during the play.

2: What do you mean?

4 (*to* 1): Well, you know, right near the end of the play when that character that—that what's his name, who couldn't get home for years and years and finally did and had to leave again—and wandered again—around again—and then finally got home but ended up getting killed by his son who he never knew—your father jumped up and ran out of the theater.

1: That's right.

2: I didn't notice.

4: Oh. (*Pause. Then whispering:*) Excuse me, I have to use the bathroom, I'll be right back. (*She exits.*)

2: Harold. (*No reply.*) Harold. (*No reply.*) Harold!

1: What?

2: What's going on?

1: What do you mean?

2: What do you mean what do I mean is what's going on?!—With you?—With Daddy?! He hasn't said a word about . . . about . . . you know, about . . .

1: Oh, yea. I told him I was a ghost.

2: Oh. What?

1: I convinced him I was a ghost.

2: A what?

1: A ghost.

2: A ghost?!!

1: A ghost.

2: A ghost. You convinced him you were a ghost.

1: Yes.

2: Of Mommy.

1: Oh yes.

2: And he believed you?

1: Oh yes.

2: I don't believe this.

1: I told him I was back from the grave for twenty-four hours to walk the earth.

2: And he believed this?!

1: He did.

2: I don't believe this. I don't believe this!

1: Un huh.

2: This is . . . this is unbelievable! This is totally unbelievable! What kind of person would be fooled by this?

1: I don't know.

2: Jesus Christ.

1: It's the best I could come up with.

2: Oh, brother. (*Slight pause.*) I mean, if I saw this on the stage I wouldn't believe it.

1: Well—

2: Nobody would.

1: You think so?

2: Come on, Harold, if you saw this on stage would you believe it?

1: Probably not.

2: You'd say I'm sorry—I don't believe it. (CHARACTER 4 *enters.*) I just don't believe it. I simply don't believe it!

4: Well, I didn't believe it either; that makes two of us. (*Hold.*) In fact, I never believed a word of it—not for a moment. (*Hold.*) You're talking about the play, aren't you?

2 (*relieved*)**:** Oh, yea.

4: It was so contrived, wasn't it?

2: It was.

4: And totally improbable—the things you're asked to believe. What kind of person would believe that?

2: Don't look at me.

4: Oh, and god, was it long.

2: It was.

4: It was too long, wasn't it?

2: Much too long.

4: Who ever heard of a seven-act play?

2: That's right.

4: I thought, I gotta get out of here.

1: That's just what I was thinking.

4: I didn't get it, did you? I mean, how did the Greek stuff fit into the rest of the play?

2: You got me.

4: And then the old man breaking out into that monologue about . . . what was *that* about? Too devicey. And that dream business—Fritzy was right; talk, talk, talk. But then, this is the problem with his work.

1: Oh really?

4: Oh yes. That incessant stream of words.

2: I hear that.

4: But—well, who knows? Maybe he'll get over it some day.

1: I sure hope so.

4: Yes. (*Pause.*) But the actress!!! Didn't you love that actress!!

2: She was good.

1: She was very good.

4: I think she's got it. (*Pause.*) So: Not really a good play, we think. But it was nice—we enjoyed ourselves—we're glad we went—we had a good time—we supported the arts—it got us out of the house—and now we're back! We're going to have some delicious cake—and we'll have a nice talk; who wants delicious cake?

1: I'll have . . .

4: Oh, right; you asked before. See; I remember. (*She holds up a silver cake platter.*) By the way, isn't this a beautiful platter? (CHARACTER 5 *begins moving toward the bathroom.*)

1 (*referring to the platter*)**:** Oh, look at that.

4: Oh, wait a minute—excuse me—Uncle Saul do you need to make a B.M.? Do you wanna make a B.M.? Okay, I'm gonna help you.

5 (*not turning toward her*): What?

4: Or do you want to do it on your own? I'm gonna let him take care of himself; he'll be all right. So, the platter—I got this the other day in an antique shop on Wilshire Boulevard, right near San Vincente.

1: Oh yea.

4: I wanted to have something nice, for to serve the cake today.

1: It's beautiful.

4: Do you love antiques? 'Cause I love antiques. I want to do the whole house in antiques.

1: Oh, really? What period?

4: Mmm, I don't know, country. (*Hold.*) Country style. You know, real warm and cozy, old-fashioned kind of. Anyway
Maxine continues talking but becomes inaudible. Her lips move, but there is no sound. Likewise, DANNY, when he speaks, no sound from him.
Harold is aware of the conversion—he notes that they go on like this.

2: Enter from right, the Whale.
(*Enter* CHARACTER 3 *as* THE WHALE.) Only Harold sees it. The other two continue as before. With Maxine doing the majority of the talking. The Whale's a massive sperm whale, white, a huge harpoon fixed in its flank; it beckons Harold follow

1: Where will you lead me.

2: Harold wonders? "Into some sulphurous, tormenting flames?" No matter; Harold must have sperm. Sperm! Sperm! Sperm! Rich, warm sperm. "Eat me. Eat me. Eat me, baby, drink me." Harold must have sperm, and so he follows.

(CHARACTER 1 *exits left following* THE WHALE.)

4: What a curious feeling, Maxine is thinking. "I bet it was that chili I ate at the theater." She exits quickly to the bathroom.

(CHARACTER 4 *exits right.* CHARACTER 2 *undresses to his underwear as* CHARACTER 6 *enters with a change of clothing for him.* CHARACTER 6 *exits, and returns several times with, ultimately, four tall stools and four music stands. He sets them in an evenly spaced line downstage center, the stands placed comfortably before the stools.* CHARACTER 5 *enters, in change of costume, and sits on the stool third from stage left.* 6 *sits on the far left stool. When* 2 *is changed he sits on the far right stool.* CHARACTER 1 *enters from right with four volumes and lights a cigarette. He gives a volume to each of the other male characters and sits on the remaining stool. Texts are opened, and off we go. Note: Men should all be dressed in variations of black, white, and gray for this section.*)

THE FERRY TALE

2: Enter from left, the Whale, with Harold in lascivious pursuit. The Whale sets itself on the floor of the stage and, flukes up, sounds, disappearing from sight. Harold swoons. He wakes to find himself, dressed in his business suit, standing center in a vast darkness.

1: Oh shit!
I'm in the cruising park. I swore
I wouldn't come here anymore.

2: At that, a female presence gathers out of shadow, perched on a tree limb, upstage right. It is Character 5; he is dressed in a simple blouse, plain skirt and sensible shoes—all circa nineteen twenty.

1: Have pity on me please
whoever you may be. It seems
you come for some time past
the present.

5: In life I was companion to
that woman who when asked "Why don't
you write the way you talk?" replied
"Why don't you read the way I write?"

1: You're Alice Toklas, then.

5: I'm Alice Toklas, yes; it's—hi,
it's nice to meet you.

1: Oh hi Miss Toklas, can
you—listen, can you help me?
I've gone astray from that straight road
and find myself within the dark wood
of this familiar park.

5: Familiar? Then you've made this round before.

1: It's three times that I've come here to
this place, this park, and circled like
the other men to look for sex.

First time I came nine months ago I met a man
who took me to his home. The second man
who took me home got very rough. The last time
just a week ago, I met a man
who after we had sex here in the park
asked me for money.

5: Each time you come sounds worse and worse. And worse,
the worse it gets the more you'll come. Allowed
you'd season here in hell.

1: Where will it end?

5: This dirt path has no end—it winds around itself
and suffocates the ones who run it. I know
a different route—a way within;
a lady there unwittingly would help you.
But you must use your wits and asked of her the past
before you can resurface as yourself.

I propose you come with me; I'll lead you into heaven.

2: At that, that Alice slow descends to Harold's level.

1: But if to heaven, shouldn't we ascend?

5: Oh no. Heaven is within
the earth—not up in the sky.
It's a returning;
the most moving on there is.

1: Miss Toklas, where is hell?

5: Hell? Bubeleh—
your life is hell. Why dream a hell
that's after life? Come on.

And like the poet led by Virgil—
though your dream aspires to less
than his Commedia—take note.
Once in we'll right
then left beside the freeway wait
until a ferry comes to take you to the dead.
Your mother's there—
from her you could procure some useful info.
There's the gate ahead.

2: And so they go in silence 'til they settle near the entrance, upstage
left.

1: Miss Toklas—please—that sign inscribed
ephemeral on the clouds above the gate—
it's writings' strange is unlike any I have seen before.
What does it say?

5: ABANDON HERE ALL HOPE
WHO ENTER OF DIRECT PARALLELS AND PRECISE CORRELATIONS.

WHAT YOU SEE IS AN AMORPHOUS WASH;
THE MYSTERY WON'T BE SATISFACTORILY RECONSTRUCTED.

MOST MYTHOLOGY AND SCIENCE IS
CORRUPT REPRESENTATION.

1: I puzzle over that.

5: That's the idea; let's move on in.

2: At that a trapdoor in the stage floor opens, trumpeting a cleansing gush of steam. Alice Toklas dives directly in; the geyser reverses, and she's sucked right down the tube. Harold, hesitant, places his left foot timid near the blowhole; instantly he's swallowed, too. Down, down, down they go in cyclone style until they reach the bottom and set out again. Light changes.

5: We've still a way to go;
to help us pass the time we walk
let's talk—sympose with me—
I'll be you Diotima.

1: What should we talk about?

5: That's up to you. But please
excuse me, Harold, if at times
referring to the past or to the future
I use the present tense;
in this your dream all time
will issue as an indistinguished moment.

2: And so it goes; they travel. Ideally, this Act takes years to play. The actors move about the stage in spiral fashion—two steps forward, one step back, two steps forward, one step back, thus narrating ever smaller circles.

Patient, that considerating Alice Toklas, guiding that, at times, reluctant and resistant Harold by the path of his own self-described direction. For even after certain truths are well established in this mind, some long discarded doubt's rekindled, plaguing his

1: But Alice what about Leviticus?
"Thou shall not lie with mankind as with womankind:
. . . abomination"—in the Torah.
I think of it, and I feel guilty.

5: Then Harold—kineahora—screw
your Levitical guilt to the shtiking place—
that's all it is, besides, that mitzvah, shtikdreck—
writ down by some alter kockers schmoozing in the desert three
thousand years ago.

1: Oy gott.

5: But good that you remind me of the Jews—there are illuminating
similarities and differences between the history of Jews and gays.

1: Oh yea?

5: Oh yes; as Doctor Boswell tells us
societies that do not tolerate religious diversity
are generally intolerant of those whose sexuality is nonconformant.

From early Christianity to concentration camps, he notes
both Jews and gays have been subjected to harassment simulta-
     neously—
portrayed as beasts bent on destroying the children of the majority
     and blamed—
get this—for causing wars, misfortunes—*plagues*, if you can believe
     it?
But Jews, don't you know, have Judaism—
ethics passed to child
from parent—wisdoms culled
from generations of oppression.

Gay people are not generally born into gay families and taught the
history of their kind or how they might conduct themselves amidst
the defamation and affliction of the majority.
    We suffer individually, alone, without support of our relations;
    in this sense, Harold, only gays are born into the home of the
oppressor.

So much of what our kind experienced however is deleted;
though worse than deletion's alteration—twisted truths:

the music of our history's been transposed into a key that's barely
     recognizable;
our lives, love, poetry, and art transvestited by sadistic, unjust incor-
     rectors.

This wasn't always true; there have been periods we lived, in peace
and prospered elevated in the state among our het'ro brothers and
     sisters.

But little testament or gospel of accomplishment's extant;
the record as I intimated is corrupted and infertilized—
thus rendered stale, flat, and unprofitable; the truth
has been molested by those justless buggers who
concurring with the justless whites white out the natural
     colors of history.

And since this falsifying does preserve the animosity and hatred,
It is an infamous crime against nature;
A deeper malignity than rape;
It casts aside millennia of moral teaching—
And its very mention's a disgrace to humanity—
A crime not fit to be mentioned—though it must be
     mentioned not forgotten.

1: But history aside,
I've often heard the urge to couple with one's gender's like—
it's like some conflict some
conflicting something like
the distant father and
the what is it—the overprotective mother who—

5: When you seek a counselor, Harold,
careful who you choose to help you navigate your ship;
many's the quack out there who'd drag you through the
unproven straights of Oedipus (CHARACTER 5 *pronounces it "eat a
puss"*).

It's one thing when this shit's excreted by incontinents —
the deprivated, uneducated Pubic Enemies rapping out the
    song of intolerance.

And even those unnat'ral fools who would
brownnose themselves into positions of authority in church or
    state —
I could forgive their trespass on my private parts.

But those who in the name of science and psychiatry oppress
and persecute in William Shockley fashion — honey
could I wish for hell to damn these generations of vipers, that cast
    their hypocritic shadows across the land.

There's that diseased,
satanic, psychiatric trinity.
Socarides, Hatterer, and Bergler.

The most malevolent is Socaridies — Charles Socaridies;
this ass maintains that gays have no reality awareness of their part-
    ners or their feelings —
the contact's "simply epidermal — mucous — anatomic."
"The homosexual act," he grinds, "is purely egocentric" and "any
    tender reciprocity is pretense."
He prates that all the "homosexuals" he treats are masochistic.

1: Is it true?

5: I wouldn't be surprised — clearly he's a sadist; who but a maso-
chist would choose him as a shrink.

His second's Lawrence Hatterer — he's tried to transform
    homos into het'ros.
He wrote a book entitled *Treatment for Men Troubled by Homosexual-
    ity* — ay, "troubled," there's the rub;
for no one is more "troubled" by homosexuality than he —
and no one more in need of clinical consultation.

He dedicates this crap to both his parents, who like a
    pervert he asserts first taught to him "the art of
    helping others."
No joke—he wrote that in his book. "The art of helping others."
The art of persecution is more like it.

Then finally we come to Edmund Bergler—grand diva of them all.
Another sexual alchemist. But totally camp.
Herr Bungler's chef d'ouevre is his epistle, *1000 Homosexuals*—
no doubt his own unconscious fantasy.
His other out-of-print masterpieces include *Fashion and the Uncon-
    scious* and *Laughter and the Sense of Humor.*
They're both potential Barbra Streisand vehicles.
Believe me, Harold, a mind like this comes only once every
    ten thousand years. He was a queer sadistic failure.

1: How would we classify these
unnecessary losses?

5: Circle Eight. Cantos twenty-nine and thirty—
they're Falsifiers—
for they engaged in fruitless Alchemy,
they Impersonated healers,
their findings were Counterfeit (based on prejudicial research),
and so they bore False Witness;
they all would waste eternity away in Hell—
slaving unsuccessfully to change each other into "homosexuals."

2: Light intensifies.

5: There are other lesser satellites orbiting this tainted sky. Too
    many to bother cataloging here.
But one who comes to mind is M. Scott Peck—
that roadless traveling salesman of love and traditional values—with
    an emphasis on the latter.

This speck, in citing instances of clients taking risks to foster per-
    sonal development

regurgitates that lurid theory of disease.

I quote you passage from the chapter "Love":

"The passively homosexual young man for the first time summons
   the initiative to ask a girl for a date."

Now why for Christ sake Harold would a gay man want to "date"
   a woman?

Or worse, as you should know, get stuck in het'ro matrimony.

I wrote old M. Scott, "Why?"

So from his Bliss Road homestead in Connecticut the letter came
   dribbled by his secretary.

Our little pecker meant no harm she said—and that—I quote verbatim—

"Homosexuals are welcome in churches across the land."

Clearly the doctor was not in.

1: And are there others I should know about
who've checked themselves in unenlightened limbo?

5: The list goes on forever, Harold;
for every fleshy Pound of anti-Semite blows
a killing Frost of antigay.

Even that Divine comedian threw us into hell;
he canto'd us as criminals of nature.
What a dump!

2: Their pace accelerates—the spiral tightens. Alice Toklas prophe-
cies to Harold of a Horrible Infecting Virus that will assault the
coming decades—and how at first infection's high among gay men.
At that, the stage is showered from the flys with reams of made-for-
TV movies that depict sweet little children and straight adults who
have contracted AIDS from blood transfusions. The actor's path is
thus made much more difficult; still they manage to kick their way
through all this garbage.

5: Among the many flushed away will be your nephew yet unborn—

oh yes
that theater-going-Maxine's son and Danny's—Kenny.

1: Wait

5: There's no more time
Don Juan—the ferry is approaching. When on board ask the driver
for his story; he'll refuse—you'll see—so tell him that you know he
wrote insulting words upon his dead wife's stone; he won't want that
repeated. What's writ I cannot say; but trick him; he is easily duped.
His dead wife's name was Faith—that's all you need to know.

Once landed on the other shore you'll find your mother—ask of
her the past. Each time she strains the mem'ry, pluck from out her
purse a cigarette. But do not let her see you do it; if she does then
all is lost.

Then when they're yours you wake yourself and wrap things up and
say good-bye.

1: Good-bye? What happens if I

5: Just

2: Too late. Character 5 vanishes in light then darkness. Smog
descends. From everywhere, the sound of heavy traffic. A sixty-nine
Mustang convertible pulls up from offstage left. Behind the wheel is
Character 6.

6: Hey!

1: What? Who?

6: You.

1: Me?

6: Yea.

1: Me?

6: Yea, you; you need a ride across?

1: I do.

6: Come on.

2: Okay, so Harold jumps inside the car. Light changes; daybreak; a fiery sun rises on a scrim, upstage center. Character 6 shifts into high gear, and the car goes zooming over the heads of the audience.

1: Now Ferryman my guide—
that guide that brought me to this freeway said
you'd have a story I should hear.

6: No way, no story.

1: Well
she said if you won't tell that I repeat what you
insensitively chiseled on your dead wife's grave.
A phrase that's read insulting to the memory—
insinuating that her life was waste. Her name
was Faith.

2: Character 6 shifts to a lower gear.

6: Okay. I'll tell you, sure.

I had a brother, Meyer;
"Meyer the Flyer" I would call him 'cause
he'd fly away and do just what I told him.

Meyer—he did things for me—
but when he'd done
I told him I did them for he.
And he, schlemiel, believed.
I sent him on a real hard journey once
to get me back our mother dead who died.
I heard that if she walked once more—
if only for a day—

I'd get some secret of eternal life from her—
I couldn't pass it up.

So Meyer dropped himself into the earth
and brought our mother's shadow into light.

My mother taught me nothing—
the story I had heard was false.
But Meyer clear it was to me gained something—
"What something?" I asked him, and he said
he "learned within"; but what, he didn't say.
And what he also didn't say—and this—
I don't know who it was who told to Meyer—
Meyer didn't say—
that if the guy who drives you 'cross in heaven asks
you to take the wheel a second of his car—
he didn't tell me to refuse this guy's request.
And so I made the journey Meyer made,
and took the wheel when I was asked;
the man jumped out—
and I've been saddled with the driving ever since.

1: That's int'resting.

6: You wanna take the wheel a sec.

1: No thanks.

2: The car sets ground again stage right.

6: Then here we are—and look
some lady's coming up the ramp.

2: As Harold deposits himself down right, Character 6 roars reck-
lessly off left. Enter from right Character 4 as Harold's most sincerely dead mother, Shirley—fully costumed for it, swinging a large
black bag. Her face is ashen; she supposes that her Sonny wants the
moon. Music. Harold swoons. He wakes to find himself beside his
mother in a small white space furnished only with a television set;

Harold flips on the tube; immediately his mother is engrossed in her program—for preference, "The Hollywood Squares." Harold asks Shirley three questions; and as she absent minded answers him, he manages each time to pluck from out her bag a cigarette. The television on through all this, drowning out the dial'gue from the stage. The questioning concluded, a contestant on the game show says "I'll take Paul Lynde to win." Then Peter Marshall asks Paul Lynde, "Paul—what does it mean if you are anally retentive?" Paul Lynde responds, "It means you're full of shit." Shirley smiles; at that, Harold bursts into fire, and flaming surges toward the surface. Curtain, Act 4.

(The actors close their texts as light is extinguished.)

Light illuminates MELVIN, *driving in his car.* THE WHALE *stands nearby.*

3: One more song for all that sprawl—the songless city—it's the city of the angels—Los Angeles.

One last song—the song of Melvin driving madly through L.A.—pertub'ed by the ghost he's seen—the grave has op'd—and up we go into the everlasting sunny eighty-five—the one unending season—Paradiso—it's the city of the angelahs. From Tower Road to Baring Cross, from Springvale Drive to August Street—oh what a fling through all that sprawl.

Let's find him now—let's find Melvinalah spun like a dreidelah through all that gross L.Aalah. He's run the road from Commerce all the way to L.A.X.

6: Get back.

3: He's coming out of Hillside now where Jolson's great erection to himself's cascading down past lesser lights like Mammy

6: Shirley's—

3: buried there, and Swanee Melvin

6: surely not—she's dead, but walking

3: driving

6: once again for one long day.

3: in all that sprawl—

6: L.A.

3: it's the city of the angels.

6: I gotta find a place to park.

3: So Melvin, sweetheart, why'd ya visit Shirley's grave out here at Hillside?

6: Why the hell I shlepp out here to Hillside—surely Shirley's dead, she's

3: Now at last the great grand theme—at last, the dithyrambic goal of evolution's not refinement, darling, it's expansion—all that's

6: Left.

3: On Centinella.

6: Shit. I should go right—why the hell'm I

3: What's he doing?

6: Left.

3: Onto La Brea.

6: No!

3: It's all purposelessness—the unplanned city inching east to Maywood, Vernon, South Gate, Lynwood, Downey, Rosemead. You wanna know the way this play works, listen up—this is the song of the smoggy road—this tells the whole, unstructured story.

6: Where'm I going?

3: Hell if we know, Melvin—all we know the meter's clipping along toward Glendale, Pasadena, Burbank.

6: Look at that, the mirror's filthy.

3: Yes, and as he grime wipes south he sees it's Inglewood and Hawthorne, El Segundo, Santa Ana, Torrance, Anaheim.

6: What a fucking city!

3: Chaos.

6: Right.

3: Oh Exposition Boulevard.

6: Oh shit.

3: The mishegoss. And that's the point—the point we'd make.

6: Goddamn.

3: He's east again—he leaves behind him Santa Monica, Culver City, and Beverly Hills, god love you.

6: I can't believe—I should'a stayed La Brea—their hotel is in Westwood on Wilshire—where'm I going?

3: That's the question, Melvin, baby, why ya' flying blind through all that sprawl?—Your author knows, but she's as lost as you— she takes poetic license plates were swerving out of Melvin's way he's—

6: Jesus!

3: Melvin—easy Melvin watch out Melvin honey watch the road— for Christ sake, Melvin, that's a red light

6: Stop!

3: He's freaked out now—he's driving like a crazy

6: Jesus.

3: Oh, but look at this; he's turned around—he's seen a vision of his dead wife—what's her name—who's excavated now—that saber-toothy spouse of his ris out the pit.

6: Get back.

3 (*coming downstage, sticking her head out of the Whale's mouth, addressing the audience directly*)**:** Come on now, let's be honest—our time is coming to an end—I'll speak with you as I've not spoke before. I've loost off limits and imagination's lines—we're on the open freeway

now—'cause Melvin doubled back to 405, left laning quick to
Westwood, I let him—what the hell—this comedy is cockamamy
from the moment go; I've tried—I've Troy'd—to masque up every
little hole—I fantasized a theme would be erected to transcend the
sticky glue of dramaturgy—but you've seen through all my disguises; you knew, for one, that Harold could not dream a dream of
hell the way he dreamed of hell, no way! This play's the song of
inconsistency—you're soaking in it—Madge–ination! (*In falsetto.*)
Ha, ha, ha, ha, ha.

6 AND 3: Harold'd never dream that shit;
How could he have thought of it?
No way nothing one small bit;
He don't got the brains for it.

6: Harold ain't read Gertrude Stein.

3: Dante, neither,

6: Shakespeare, nein,

3: But for play's sake that we pine,

3 AND 6: We'll pretend the plot works fine.

6: I gotta find a space—

3: This mavin author's looking for a path to wind around before she
winds things up—

6: a spot to park with no damn kids around.

3: a little local color.

6: Shirley, left.

3: And now no more poetic opportunity—'cause Melvy doubled
back on us—but wait—just wait—the showdown's coming up at
sundown: Melvin, Harold, Shirley—the father and the son, the holy
ghost. Oooh, what a resurrection set!

(*Exit* MELVIN *and* THE WHALE *in opposite directions.* WHALE *vamps a
vaudeville tune as it exits. Light is extinguished.*)

SHIRLEY TALKS BUSINESS TO SAUL

Light illuminates CHARACTERS 1 *and* 5 *in the hotel room.*

1 (*opening one of the bakery boxes*): So Saul, my son Danny tells me you're in the . . . What kind of business are you in?

5 (*sounds like "crap"*): Scrap.

1: What?

5 (*again*): Scrap.

1: Oh, crap. Well, how do you like that? (*As he speaks he takes from the box a rich chocolate cake. Looks like shit.*) We manufacture toilet paper and you sell crap; this is a marriage made in heaven. (*Pause.*) I'll bet there's good money in crap.

5: It's a living.

1 (*slicing himself a generous serving of cake and taking a seat on couch*): It's more than a living, Saul; it's a way of life. People don't have an appreciation. Listen, I lived twenty-three years of my life with Melvin; believe me, I know about waste. (*Stuffs a piece of cake in his mouth.*) We inherited the business from my father, Morry. It was a shit business. (*Stuffs a piece of cake in his mouth.*) My father pissed away all the profits at the track. Christ, what a family. They pushed me into my marriage. I didn't want to get married—to what to Melvin? I didn't want to get married to Melvin. But my mother was pushing, my father—my mother was pushing. Marriage? (*Stuffs a piece of cake in his mouth.*) I had my whole life before me, I was twenty-two years old. I was interested in music. But then I thought, what the hell am I gonna do with the rest of my life. So . . . I got married . . . I had children . . . and then I got sick. (*Stuffs a huge piece of cake in his mouth. Pause.*) Oh, the cake is good, isn't it? It's so light. It floats. It floats right into space.

(*Puts remainder of his serving of cake aside.*)

So where was I with the—oh yea; so when my father, Morry—may he rest in peace, that son of a bitch, finally kicked the can, we inherited his crappy business. But I'll tell you something, Saul, that Melvin, he made the business from nothing, from the bottom up, from scratch. And look at him now—he's scraped his way to the top; a big macher in toilet paper. (*He takes a cigarette from his shirt pocket—sets it on the tea cart.*) We don't manufacture for the home. Nothing fancy. The competition's tight and stiff. (*He takes a second cigarette from his shirt pocket—sets it on tea cart.*) For industry we do—gas stations, cafeterias, public schools (*He takes a third cigarette from his shirt pocket—picks up a lighter from the tea cart.*)—that's where you'll find our paper. Sometimes cheap hotels; wherever the business is looser.

(CHARACTER 1 *lights cigarette. Enter* CHARACTER 6.)

THE FAMILY HAS A DISCUSSION

1: So Melvin, there you are; you're gone for hours.

6: I was parking the car. Where's Danny?

1: He went with Maxine downstairs to the pharmacy.

6: What's a matter?

1: Something she ate—I don't know.

(*Hold.*)

6: So why'd you come back?

1: For Danny.

6: What do you mean?

1: What do you mean what do I mean? He needed me; he needed his mother's appearance.

6: Oh yea?

1: You heard Maxine, no mother, no marriage. Besides, I wanted to see the family just one more time.

6: One more time, and then that's it; you don't come back again?

1: Never.

6: You gonna see Harold?

1: I don't need to see Harold.

6: Just us?

1: Just you, just me.

(*Enter* CHARACTERS 4 *and* 2.)

4: Okay, we're back.

2: Hey Dad, you're back—you uh . . . find a safe spot?

6: I think so.

4: I'm sorry about all that commotion.

2: Don't be sorry.

4: It's terrible when you don't have control of yourself.

1: There's nothing worse.

4: I sure hope this medicine keeps me quiet.

1: I hope so too.

4: You know, I feel like I'm already becoming a part of the family—it's such a nice feeling. Don't you feel that way, Danny?

2: I feel—yea—good—yea.

4: I can't wait to meet your brother, Harold, and his wife.

2: Yea.

4: What's he like? I mean, just give me a hint—a little something—

2: Harold? Ummm . . . I don't know; he's uhh . . . I don't know; what's he like?

6: He's a lot like his mother.

4: He takes after you, that's so sweet. And when do they—I'm so nosy—but anyway, when do they get back from Las Vegas?

2: When do they get back? Unhh . . . I'm not sure; soon, I hope?

6: They better get back soon. I'll tell you, Harold's got a lot of nerve not telling me he's going away; he has a business to run. What do you think, a business runs itself?

1: Oh, listen to you—Simon Le Greed—Harold takes a vacation once every five years; he slips away for a weekend and Melvin's

6: Harold makes plenty of time for himself lately. He takes a course in the evening—some kind of facockta something.

1: Ethics—he's taking a course in basic ethics. Leave it to Melvin to refer to ethics as facockta.

6: Why? What does that mean?

1: It means you wouldn't know an ethic if it hit you over the head.

6: This is what I mean—Harold takes after his mother—a lot of talk that she doesn't know what she's talking about.

1: Right, but you know what you're talking about. You put Harold to work in that goddamn office of yours when he was fifteen years old.

6: Oh come on, Shirley.

1: And when it was time for college—business administration—accounting—Harold had no choice.

6: What are you talking about?

1: You think Harold wanted to study business—that he'd want to spend the rest of his life wrapped up in toilet paper?

6: Harold could have studied whatever he wanted.

1: Oh sure, but you wouldn't pay for it.

6: What?

1: Melvin—I'll never forget this—Melvin refused to pay for Harold's education unless he studied

1: —yes—what Melvin wanted him to study. He wouldn't pay unless Harold majored in business. "You want me to pay for college, you take what I want you to take. I'm not throwing away good money on—"	**6:** Shirley— get off it.

You see—Shirley likes to imagine. She likes to— She likes— |
| "—good money on—" | You know, you're talking ancient history, baby; these things happened a long time ago. |

6: Well, I was paying for it!

1: You see; and he still had Harold working at the plant on weekends in the office. Like a serf.

6: Come on Shirley—save it for your autobiography.

1 (*extinguishing his first cigarette*): It's the god's truth.

6: No, no.

1: And listen to him—"He better get back here." He begrudges him a lousy weekend in Vegas. I hope they stay a month, both of them—they should have some pleasure. God knows they don't enjoy their lives.

4: Oh really?

1: They're not happy people.

4: Oh, that's terrible.

6: What are you talking about?

1: Just what I said—Harold and Sylvia—they're not happy. They don't make each other happy.

4: Is one of them having an affair?

6: Shirley, don't start rumors.

1: It's not a rumor—what am I starting? (*Lighting the second cigarette.*) Danny knows.

2: What do I know?

6: Maxine, you want to know—they're very happy, Harold and Sylvia.

1: No they're not.

6: Oh, what do you know?

1: I know.

6: You see—you know what?—Shirley doesn't like Sylvia; she'd love it if

1: What do you mean I don't like Sylvia? I like Sylvia.

6: You! I could take you on a roller coaster ride with what Shirley thinks of Sylvia.

1: Oh, come on, Melvin.

6: No, you come on, Shirley—you know that

1: What do you know about Harold?

6: What do you mean what do I

1: You don't know anything about Harold—you never had

6: You see—this is what she's like.

1: It's true.

6: And what do you know

1: I know—   **6:** about Harold and
believe me, I know abo—   Sylvia? You don't—
If anyone, I know Harold.

6: You don't know about anything but yourself, Shirley—you're simple-minded and you're self-involved.

1: Oh, fuck you. (*To* 4:) Would you hand me a napkin, honey?

4: Oh, sure.

6: You hear that, fuck you? You see what she's like? Listen, Harold works in the business, he has a very nice life with his wife—who, to be honest with you—I didn't like at first—

1: That's right.

6: And neither did Shirley, for that matter. You thought she was dumb. She said "She's dumb." That's how Shirley talks about people. She calls them dumb. And then one night, very late, she rolls me over in bed—she's changed her mind—"We have to let Harold and Sylvia marry." You remember that?

1: Ah yes, I remember it well.

6: But then you changed your mind again. And you see, that's what she's like—she's moody. Two days later I'm telling her about I'm making arrangements—she's "What do you mean you're making arrangements? They're not getting married. What are you doing? I never said—" on and on—you see, Shirley has a very convenient memory. And then she's going to tell you about Harold, like she knows. He and Sylvia are very happy.

1: No, they're not happy.

6: You see, now she doesn't like Sylvia.

1: It has nothing to do with Sylvia—it's Harold. He's

4: And Harold runs the business?

6: I run the business.

2: Dad runs the business.

6: I run the business.

1: Oh, really?

6: Harold answers the phone—I run the business.

1 (*extinguishing the second cigarette*)**:** I didn't know that.

6: What are you—Harold—he's got ideas—he likes to talk, you know, he doesn't know what he's . . .

4: Well, I guess he's young. We're all young.

1: Like what?

6: What?

1: "What?" Like what?! Like what doesn't he know?

6. He doesn't know what he's talking about. He gets ideas from

2: Anyone want more cake?   **6:** some . . .
                                                            You know what he does?
1: I've had enough cake.

6: No—you know what he does?

1: No; tell us what he does, Melvin; in your own words—you tell us.

6: I'm gonna tell you, yea, you know what he does? He labels things, you know. He think he knows—he sees . . . he says such and such is sick—you know he uses these words like they have a meaning. This is what the Nazis did—they started to label.

1: What are you talking about?

6: No—Harold likes to label—he

1: We heard that already.

6: He's like you, Shirley—(CHARACTER 1 *lights the third cigarette.*) he gets an idea in his head, he says this one is sick—this one is such and such—this one is a fascist—you see, it's like McCarthy—someone starts calling someone else—and you have a witch hunt—you know—you have labels.

1: No. Melvin is angry because Harold called him a bigot; he said that

6: Yea—no—you see—you see—he's got a label. This is what happens; he gets—and it's very simplistic—and he gets this from Shirley.

1: But Melvin, I don't think you're a bigot. You're not a bigot. A bigot is someone who is prejudiced—who holds prejudice against a group of people. You're not like that, sweetheart. You're not a bigot.
You're a racist. You're a racist oppressor.

	6: No,
1: Yes you are.	no—you—
Oh, yes you are.	wait—

1: In 1966 we almost lost the business because Melvin—because a federal investigator discovered Melvin had twenty-four illegal Mexican boys working at his

6: Oh, come—I don't need this. I was giving these kids a break.

1: You were giving them a break! Give me a break, you bullshit artist. You never hired a black until nineteen sixty-nine—and only then because someone was going to drag you to a court over it. The only reason he hired these Mexican fellas is he found out he could pay them for—hey—hey, come on—

6: No, no, no, no . . .

1: Come on, what—what were you paying them? What? Less—less than half the minimum wage! Less than half. We almost lost the business. Luckily, Melvin found this Hollywood lawyer, Alan—whatever his name was—who arranged some kind of payoff.

6: All right, so I'm not going to stick around—you wanna

1: Oh, I could tell you a lot of interesting stories about my father—ababababababout Melvin.

6: You see—this is what happens; Shirley likes to get excited—

1: No, it's true.   **6:** She doesn't like

1: He gets it from his mother, Elsie, and his father—except his father lost his mind in 1958 and spent the last ten years of his life sitting around their apartment in his underpants with his testicles hanging out reading thirty-year-old newspapers. "The Stock Market Crashed." "We know Moishe, it happened in 1929—why don't you put some clothing on?"

6: You know, so Shirley didn't like my father, you know why? You know why?! Because he wasn't fancy like her family—you know; and my mother was very socially minded.

1: Oh, yea, Elsie—the good-will ambassador; she once sent five dollars to the March of Dimes, and bragged about it for the rest of her life.

6: All right, so I'm gonna go.

1: She was horrible—horribly prejudiced.

6: This is—excuse me this is why we had to put Shirley away—you see—because she has fantasies. My mother was frightened—she was traumatized because she was once beat up—she was mugged by a black man.

1: Oh, bullshit! Bullshit; are you full of shit!—you're so full of shit! Your mother wasn't mugged—some kid ran off with her purse at the airport—he never laid a hand on her.

6: And you don't think

1: Yea, and besides that was 1964—I first met the woman in 1952—from then until the day she died every other word out of her mouth was shvartzer. The shvartzers this, the shvartzers that, the shvartzers this, the shvartzers that.

    Just before she died, Melvin bought her an oil well in Pacific Palisades—one of those little oil wells that bobs up and down and up and down. She'd have herself wheeled out into the middle of the oil field every afternoon; she'd sit in front of the goddamn thing for hours, watching it bow to her. (*Using his arms to mimic the bowing of the oil well.*) "Yes, Elsie. Whatever you say, Elsie."

6: All right—and Shirley doesn't tell you how the woman suffered—

1: No, I'll give her that much at least—hers was not an easy life, believe me—between her meschuggener husband who drove her

6: You know, you'll find this interesting, Maxine, my grandfather— my mother's father was exterminated in

1: That's right. She lost her father, Tsimon, in the concentration camp.

6: That's right—and you know—you just sit here

1: I know, it was terrible.

6: You don't get over that kind of thing.

1: He sent his wife—your great-grandmother Miriam—to America with Elsie and her older brother, Jacob—who went on to a great career as a necrophiliac.

6: For Christ sake.

1: Meanwhile he stayed in Europe—

6: He stayed in Europe and made the sacrifice.

1: Oh, sacrifice, my ass; this was 1913—he ran off with a dress-maker from Strie in Austria where they came from. Her name was Reckel.

2: How do you know?

1: I know from your great-grandmother; I know from Miriam. She told me she heard that he and the dressmaker—Tsimon and the dressmaker—were at each other's throats from the day they met until

6: Miriam—yea—another one with a great imagination.

1: She told us. She once met a survivor from the concentration camp at some benefit in Philadelphia who had been in the same boxcar with them. He said, "What, Reckel and the boyfriend? Sure I remember them. They bickered all the way to Dachau." (*Hold.*) He would refer to them as "Heckel and Reckel." (*In his own voice.*) I gotta get out of this place. (*In Shirley's voice:*) Okay. Times up. Gotta go.

4 (*as* CHARACTER 1 *extinguishes the third cigarette*): Can I wrap up something for you?

1: No thank you, darling; I've had enough. So; I leave you. (*Putting out his arms to* CHARACTER 4.) Maxine, honey, welcome to the family.

4 (*embracing* CHARACTER 1): Oh, thank you.

1: Saul, it was a pleasure talking to you.

5: What?

1: Yeah.

5: Good.

1: Maxine . . . Danny . . . you'll be good to each other . . . ?

4: We will.

2: We will.

1 (*sotto voce*): Like hell you will. Melvin—drop dead.

6: Yea, you go straight to hell.

1: If I do, I'll save you a seat. No, better—you can sit on the floor.

6: You came back from the grave and tried to kill me.

1: Yea, well, good; we're even. Good-bye.

(*Exits. Hold. Other characters exit right as:*)

SYLVIA'S EPILOGUE

3 (*off left*): Haaaaaaaaarooooooooold. (*G to E*)
Haaaaaaaaarooooooooold. (*B flat to G*)
Haaaaaaaaarooooooooold. (*G sharp to D sharp*)

(*Hold. Enter* CHARACTER 3 *with a wooden park bench. She sets it center in front of couch. During the first two paragraphs of monologue she rolls off the tea cart, Saul's wheelchair, and finally pushes away that damned couch. She speaks to the audience as she changes the set.*)

3: Enter Character 3 as Sylvia. This is Sylvia's epilogue. Attempt is made in monologue below to convey all information within the context of dramatic action without trespassing into self-conscious or alienating unnaturalistic techniques; i.e., absurdism, surrealism, what have you.

The scene is a park located in the Eagle Rock district of Los Angeles. By day a children's playground, by night a scene of men engaged in sexual activity. Offstage right a troop of Boy Scouts are seated at picnic tables painting Easter eggs. No attempt, however, should be made in production to inform the audience of the significance of this setting. Clearly, the coincidence of Eagle Rock and Boy Scouts is telling—one immediately associates to Greek mythology—how Zeus, infatuated with the Trojan prince, Ganymede, swept down upon him from Olympus as an eagle and carried the handsome youth up into heaven. Int'resting, as well, the "rock" in Eagle Rock—no doubt a scrotal reference. The time, we note is Easter: one—a resurrection symbol as in the Dante *Comedy*—new life, new beginnings, etcetera; second, the Easter Bunny—significant in its association to the hare—an animal symbol associated with gay males in medieval Europe; and finally, recall the celebration of the Christian Easter falls near by the Jewish Passover—another new life, new beginning symbol, but also, and more importantly, I think, an example of liberation from slavery, the severance of bondage, and of course the commencement of wandering around in the desert for years and years. (*She sits on park bench.*) It is regretted that Yom Kippur could not be utilized—tying in atonement for sin, judgment of God, etcetera, but—you know, you stick in as much as you can. Take it away Sylvia.

(*To herself:*) Well, Harold it's been weeks—a month now since you disappeared. Your car was found parked, here, outside this park; I wonder what's become of you?

It's good you're gone, you know; I couldn't bear you any longer. I packed and split the day that you evaporated. No joke; not knowing you were gone I left. That's some coincidence.

You took with you a copy of our wedding picture—why was that? It would take one hell of a steady hand to snap our portrait Harold—you and I; and I don't mean an "I" in your cold shadow—or an "I" that makes a brief appearance when convenient—I mean an equal "I" a—a fleshed out "I" in equal light. Sharp the eye that would evoke with single-mindedness the constellation of attractions, yes, and disappointments that have made our little marriage, Harold—then plot them undistracted without tangent on a graph and show the evolution—the collapse. Thank god for that collapse.

Oh, look, the moon is up—full circle in the sky. (*To the audience:*) They say the moon was Nemesis—raped of course by Zeus, who else? She'd taken to flight from him as a goose, but he became a swan and triumphed over her. Of course, in its original form, "the love chase myth," the Great Goddess would hound the Sacred King through his seasonal changes of rabbit, fish, bird, and grain of wheat —then finally devour him. With the advent of the patriarchal system the chase reversed; the nymph fled the god.

(*To herself:*) It's getting dark. That troop of kids is taking off. I gotta go.

(*She rises from bench and exits. Light is extinguished.*)